STUDIES IN AMERICAN POPULAR
HISTORY AND CULTURE

Edited by
Jerome Nadelhaft
University of Maine

A ROUTLEDGE SERIES

Studies in American Popular History and Culture

Jerome Nadelhaft, *General Editor*

HOLLYWOOD AND ANTICOMMUNISM
HUAC and the Evolution of the Red Menace, 1935-1950

John Joseph Gladchuk

Routledge
New York & London

Routledge
Taylor & Francis Group
270 Madison Avenue
New York, NY 10016

Routledge
Taylor & Francis Group
2 Park Square
Milton Park, Abingdon
Oxon OX14 4RN

© 2007 by Taylor & Francis Group, LLC
Routledge is an imprint of Taylor & Francis Group, an Informa business

Printed in the United States of America on acid-free paper
10 9 8 7 6 5 4 3 2 1

International Standard Book Number-10: 0-415-95568-8 (Hardcover)
International Standard Book Number-13: 978-0-415-95568-3 (Hardcover)

Library of Congress Cataloging-in-Publication Data

Gladchuk, John Joseph.
    Hollywood and anticommunism : HUAC and the evolution of the red menace, 1935-1950 / by John Joseph Gladchuk.
        p. cm. -- (Studies in American popular history and culture)
    Includes bibliographical references and index.
    ISBN 0-415-95568-8 (alk. paper)
    1. Motion picture industry--California--Los Angeles--History. 2. Communism and motion pictures--United States. 3. United States. Congress. House. Committee on Un-American Activities.   I. Title.

PN1993.5.U65G554 2006
791.4309794'94--dc22   2006025544

Visit the Taylor & Francis Web site at
http://www.taylorandfrancis.com

and the Routledge Web site at
http://www.routledge-ny.com

Contents

Preface

Three and a half years ago I wrote an article in "defense" of a book that had a profound impact on me as a person and as a scholar. Daniel Goldhagen's *Hitler's Willing Executioners* proved utterly provocative and, to a degree, inspirational. Goldhagen's candid accounts of Nazi aggression motivated me to confront an issue that is unfortunately still very much a part of present day society. Although possessing a highly controversial thesis and the subject of much hostility within the academic community, Goldhagen's work forces the reader to confront the power of racism and impact that it can have on societies infected with it. Although racism is indeed present in one form or another in virtually every country in the world, it is saliently noticeable in the United States as it has played an integral role in the development of the nation. As seen in Goldhagen's work, it is one thing to have a society comprised of racists individuals. It is another, however, to govern such a society with an institution born of such pernicious insularity. The fusion of a racist population with a demagogic government creates an organ of repression capable of inconceivable physical and emotion destruction.

When looking at the House Committee on Un-American Activities, its history, its people, and the environment within which it operated, it is not too difficult to draw a faint parallel between its evolution and the development of the arm of repression that perpetrated near apocalypse in Nazi Germany throughout the 1930's and 1940's. This is not to say that the Committee was in any way privy to genocide, but its emergence, its function, and its environment are all reminiscent of the exact tyrannical "concoction" that it supposedly endeavored to eliminate. This work sets out to place the Committee in the context of the Red Scare environment as a means of demonstrating what is possible, even in the world's cradle of liberty, when an ultraconservative governmental institution is allowed to operate within the confines of an ultraconservative societal atmosphere. These two forces coalesced in Washington in 1947 as HUAC placed Hollywood on trial in arguably the most publicized episode in the Committee's career. This work attempts to demonstrate that it was the combination of the Committee and the incendiary environment nourishing it that allowed HUAC to condemn the Hollywood Ten and in turn, usher in the blacklist age. What is unique about the Hollywood hearings, however, is that given the event's publicity value, had the Ten been afforded an adequate forum within which to defend themselves they may have been able to expose the Committee as the undemocratic body that history has proven it to be. Success in such a quest would have been accompanied by ramifications that would have undoubtedly influenced the evolution and trajectory of the "anticommunist age." Derailing the Committee would have slowed the momentum of the un-American campaign, divesting the contentious atmosphere of critical anti-Red energy by calling into question the integrity, aims, and intentions of the ultraconservatives engineering the effort. The validity of the "Red Menace" moniker may have also faced scrutiny as a successful challenge would have been levied against the flawed Committee theory that "leftists" or "radicals" were incapable of patriotism. HUAC's ability to avoid such a predicament, however, allowed it to use Hollywood as a catalyst, a vehicle which arguably saved the Committee and in turn, perpetuate an investigation that would eventually morph into an era infamously known as McCarthyism.

Acknowledgments

Completing this work would not have been possible without the assistance of several individuals, organizations, and agencies. There are several individuals who warrant specific recognition as key contributors to this effort. This work would not have been possible if not for Clifford E. Trafzer. The guidance and direction he provided as I worked to complete this text proved invaluable. I must recognize Natalie Fousekis and the encouragement, support, and guidance that she bestowed in commencing and ultimately completing the first phase of this exercise. Arthur Hansen and his editing touch helped to instill a narrative quality previously lacking from this work. Cora Granata forced me to develop the resolve required to complete a work such as this and I thank her for that. I must acknowledge Rebecca Kugel and the encouragement that she provided throughout the course of this process. This project also received quite a lift from Dale Kent, someone who helped to sharpen my analytical skills and motivated me to strive for excellence as a scholar. Larry Burgess should also be recognized as his insights helped contribute to this book's narrative quality.

There is no way I could have finished this project without the help of Dan Bessie, who offered encouragement, advice, and support throughout the duration of this endeavor. His insight regarding the Hollywood episode proved invaluable and it helped me understand the magnitude of the blacklist in a way that I never imagined I could. I would like to recognize Helen Garvey and the time that she took out of her busy schedule to talk with me about the origins of the student movement. Her recollections regarding SDS were both revealing and profound.

I need to recognize the interlibrary loan office at the University of California, Riverside for countless hours of assistance. The materials I ascertained through the Rivera Library loan service helped to make this work possible. I would also like to recognize the Video Resource Center for making available films critical to this work's completion. Kristy French, the University Archivist and Records Manager at Long Beach State, was instrumental in helping me navigate the materials held in the Special Collections at LBSU. She opened up a wealth of information to me and I owe her a tremendous debt of gratitude. I would like to thank the University of California, Los Angeles and all of those employed in the Special Collections library. The film-related documents housed at UCLA, specifically the Maltz and Trumbo collections, were of supreme importance to this work. Other schools that opened up their resources to me include Loyola Marymount University, California State University, Fullerton, California State University, Northridge, the University of California at Davis, the University of California at Berkeley, the University of California at Santa Cruz, and the University of Southern California. I would like to recognize the Margaret Herrick Library at the Academy of Motion Picture Arts and Sciences for the opportunity that it provides scholars interested in the history of the film industry. I must to offer special thanks to Paul Jarrico, Michael Wilson, and Albert Maltz. Their words, works, and experiences provide this text with its character.

I would like to single out a few of the scholars whose works, in many ways, helped to establish the foundation of this piece. Victor Navasky, Kenneth O'Reilly, Robert K. Murray, Griffin Fariello, Paul Buhle, David Caute, David Wagner, August Raymond Ogden, Walter Goodman, Eric Bentley, Nancy Lynne Schwartz, Irving Howe, Lewis Coser, Ellen Schrecker, Todd Gitlin, David Lance Goins, Richard Cohen, Reginald Zelnik, Kai Bird and Martin J. Sherwin. I would like to thank Knox Mellon for his thoughts and reflections on his 1940's Hollywood experience. I need to recognize Dorothy Healy for providing access to her papers. I would also like to recognize the staff of the Government Publications office at the University of California Riverside. Through their assistance, I was provided access to papers critical to the completion of this work. I would also like to recognize my family, especially my Mom and Dad, for their support. My "other" family, my west coast family, should be singled out for all of their encouragement as well. This work would not have been possible without their contributions.

Last but certainly not least, I would like to thank my wife, Lisa. She is my inspiration and the sole reason why I am able to pursue my historical passion. This work is our project.

Chapter One

Introduction: HUAC, Hollywood and the Evolution of the Red Menace

Often referred to as "a golden era," the 1930's were a glorious time for the movie industry, an industry that stood as arguably the most recognizable in the world. Hollywood, for millions across the globe, symbolized a "dream factory," a mythological Eden where stars roamed pristine streets awash in Southern California's tender sun. It was the hallmark of the California "image," a place of both physical and mystical lore that not only produced "dreams," but in itself represented one. "There in the studio the dream re-awakened," commented Edmund Morris on young Ronald Reagan's arrival at Republic Productions studio in the spring of 1936, "it was a dream that had possessed him more than seven years before, of being 'carried into a new world' where things really mattered."[1] Hollywood was more than just the films it produced. As a place, it represented the heartbeat of a numinous universe where sun, sand, and eternal warmth lured curious souls in search of fame, fortune, and adventure in a certified land of enchantment. It was a city within a city, a "paradise," an urban jungle of "blue-trunked trees, tiled and whitewashed houses obscenely brilliant with bougainvillea," towering palms and majestic hills.[2]

Hollywood was also defined by its inhabitants, a truly eclectic mix of characters that all combined to imbue "movieland" with its magical essence. Its large "progressive" community, however, arguably stood as its most prominent and certainly its most maligned. Allegedly "infiltrated" by hard line Communists from the East, the Hollywood Communist Party, tinseltown's progressive organ, was in reality a rather benign organization composed of concerned citizens from a myriad of backgrounds. Contrary to the popularized image of the Communist Party in Hollywood (as portrayed by The House Committee on Un-American Activities (HUAC) in the 1947 "trials"), the film industry's "Red" community was more cultural than political in nature and posed little if any threat to the security and well being of the United States. Many associated with the Communist Party were attracted to its egalitarian precepts and did not understand the magnitude of Soviet totalitarianism. Marxism, on paper, offered relief from the horror of mass poverty and destitution in the wake of the Great Depression. The Communist Party was an outlet, a vehicle through which to vent frustration regarding capitalism and its shortcomings. Commitment to greater social and economic equality did not, however, equal un-Americanism. Many of these individuals, "parlor Reds," "Fellow Travelers," "pink" intellectuals, were fascinated with the concept of communism as a road to utopia but realized that democracy remained the only true "popular" political system. A greater extension of democracy, both socially and economically, is was what most were after.

Communism in the 1930's, in many ways, (although there certainly existed militant revolutionaries who harbored a thirst for violence) represented a fad for "New Dealers" with the Communist Party's more "moderate" branches, such as the Hollywood division, serving as "clubs" for "liberals" who wished to voice their concerns regarding America's social and economic shortcomings.[3] "The New Deal liberal in the 1930's," remarked historians Kai Bird and Martin J Sherwin, was "committed to supporting and working for racial equality, consumer protection, labor rights, and free speech."[4] Many curious with communism in the aftermath of the Depression legitimately feared a collapse of capitalism and experienced dread over the thought of a fascist alternative. Communism, to a degree, represented both a lesser evil as well as a bridge to a less exploitative world. Clarified by "Fellow Traveler" (though never a registered member of the Communist Party) and father of the atomic bomb Robert Oppenheimer during an executive session before the Joint Committee on Atomic energy in 1950, communism in the 1930's did not constitute a revolutionary conduit, but rather a vehicle through which concerned "populists" could encourage much needed reform. It represented, in many respects, a ray of hope for a seemingly fallen society. "[I] had naively thought," opined a somewhat remorseful Oppenheimer," [that] the Communists possessed some answers to the problems facing the country in the midst of the depression."[5] Despite his "red" reputation, Oppenheimer, like many attracted to the egalitarian tenets of communism in the 1930's, "loved America," asserted his longtime secretary Verna Hobson, "and this love was a deep as his love for science."[6]

One political position that all affiliated with the Party openly embraced in the 1930's revolved around "popular front" opposition to Nazism. "In a political age, Hollywood émigrés [primarily Eastern European Jews] found themselves in political situations," maintained Hollywood historian and biographer Ed Sikov, "while few were more than salon gauchistes, most had no qualms about working with Marxists to combat fascism [in the mid-1930's], as they had in Europe. But red baiting was abroad in the studios," continued Sikov, "and the refugees found themselves forced to choose between quietism and fellow traveling." [7] Positions assumed by several of its members regarding anti-Fascism and inequality in society did, however, constitute a threat to America's social and economic status quo and therefore drew the attention of the ultraconservative right. Energized by a contentious national climate defined by "Red Scare" paranoia, the House Committee on Un-American Activities assault on Hollywood, initiated by Texas Congressman Martin Dies in 1939, focused the eyes of the world on what John Rankin referred to as the "tarantula of Hollywood where loathsome paintings hung in the home of the seducer of white girls [Charlie Chaplin]."[8] Hollywood, according to a power thirsty and clearly delusional Rankin, represented the "the greatest hotbed of subversive activities in the United States, headquarters for one of the most dangerous plots ever instigated for the overthrow of the government."[9] In 1947 the Committee presided over the first of what would become several "official" Hollywood forays as the film industry emerged as a catalyst for the once endangered "red hunting" institution. Hollywood would eventually provide the Committee with the boost that ultimately propelled it into its banner year of 1948, a year that arguably paved the way for Wisconsin Senator Joseph McCarthy and his coast to coast un-American purge.[10] Lost amidst House Committee hoopla was the resistance effort put forth by those who refused, in the words of historian Victor Navasky, to "name names."[11]

Long before men such as Edward R. Murrow seized the American stage with his highly publicized attack on McCarthy, "The Hollywood Ten" put forth a resolute effort designed, in part, to expose the fallibility of the Committee.[12] Unfortunately for the Ten, however, anticommunist fever had the American public mesmerized in 1947 and cost the Ten the popular support necessary to successfully unveil the Committees' un-Americanism. Ultimately, the Ten were victims of not only the un-American Activities Committee's betrayal of the constitution, but of the asphyxiating social milieu commensurate with the "Red Scare" era. What could have been arguably a decisive blow to the entire un-American campaign became a bridge to prosperity for the Committee. The silencing of the Hollywood resistance correlated with the emergence of the House Committee on un-American Activities as America's leading line of defense in a "cold" war against domestic subversion as the "blacklist," the Committee's lasting Hollywood legacy, lingered in tinseltown as a dark reminder of the House Committee's pervasive potency. For the Ten, it was not "Good night and good luck," to quote the charismatic Murrow, but "good night and tough luck" as the Ten ironically became casualties of an epoch commonly referred to as "McCarthyism" without having ever brushed shoulders with the Senator. As evidenced by the Ten, the "McCarthy" era began well in advance of McCarthy.

The House Committee on Un-American Activities "success" in Hollywood, however, was not simply the product of its collective "genius." In fact, it could be argued that HUAC succeeded in Hollywood in spite of itself. Its ultraconservative composition and lack of solid leadership rendered it vulnerable to attack from many who deemed the organ an instrument of American totalitarianism. As demonstrated in its years under its "patriarch" Dies, the un-American Activities Committee's seeming unwillingness to conduct its operation in accordance with the constitution combined with the brazen manner with which it executed its agenda invited a rash of criticism from all corners of the political and social spectrum.[13] Attacks on the Committee's viability became more acute as the Second World War raged on and in fact, by the war's end, the Committee, with the loss of Dies, faced virtual extinction. With the subversion threat at home seemingly diminished and the congressional outcry against the Committee growing ever stronger, Congress contemplated shelving the much maligned investigative organ. As 1945 approached, the Committee found itself in a rather precarious position, short on both support and resources. "Toward the close of that year," wrote William F. Buckley, "only a few people still believed in the mission of HUAC." Fortunately for the Committee, "John Rankin," observed Buckley, "was one of them."[14]

As southern as a southern democrat could be, Mississippi's John Rankin emerged in late 1944 as arguably the Committee's last hope. Void of momentum and lacking its charismatic front man in Dies, the Committee teetered on the verge of obscurity and faced, what appeared to be, complete dissolution. Rankin, however, despite his many shortcomings, was astute enough to observe that fear over the so-called Red menace had resurfaced in postwar America. As a result, the return of the "red" phenomenon once again created a "market" for a Red hunting enterprise. "Unless it is held that there is no such thing as un-American activity," maintained South Dakota's Karl Mundt, "American's should be able to agree on what it is and [a] Committee could then expose it."[15] Although the Dies Committee was no more, its powerful pre-war investigation coupled with over twenty years of Red Scare paranoia dating back to the Palmer raids of 1920 rendered the Committee somewhat viable in the immediate postwar period. In fact, as early as 1944 fear over the Soviet Union and its post war aims on both Europe and Asia had begun to manifest itself in the form of anticommunist articles and editorials featured in major publications throughout America. "The greatest threat to mankind and civilization is the spread of the totalitarian philosophy," wrote Russian immigrant, actress, screenwriter, and infamous "Friendly" witness Ayn Rand in *Reader's Digest's* January 1944 edition, "Totalitarianism is collectivism, the subjugation of the individual to the group. Collectivism is the ancient principle of savagery. A savage's whole existence is ruled by the leaders of his tribe. Civilization is the process of setting men free from men. Collectivism," Rand concluded, "is not the New Order of Tomorrow. But there is a New Order of tomorrow, it belongs to the individual man."[16] Regarding communist movement abroad, *Reader's Digest* noted in March of 1944 that "While Americans are heatedly arguing 'what shall we do with Europe,' a revolution has already started. Russia's presence in the victorious coalition assures powerful support for those who prefer to follow the road leading to an authoritarian state and a controlled economy. Europeans," cautioned the magazine, "today stand at a crossroads."[17] There is little doubt that the reading public had once again begun to contemplate the scope of the "red menace" and the impact that it could have both at home and abroad. A "second coming" of the "Red Scare" appeared imminent.[18]

With the atmosphere ripening, Rankin began his campaign to revive in full the investigation of subversive activity in America. Cognizant of the environment overseas and attune to growing concern over Reds within, the Mississippian remained convinced that communism would soon emerge as a palpable internal threat. Such a development would ultimately force the nation to rally behind a bid to flush Bolshevism from America's shores. A revived un-American Activities Committee would provide Rankin, along with fellow conservatives in Congress, with a "patriotic" opportunity certain to bolster their political careers. Also intriguing Rankin was the prospect of a full fledged Hollywood investigation, a mission begun by Dies but never truly brought to fruition. If Rankin could somehow convince Congress that a revival of the Committee was indeed necessary, an initial investigation of the film industry was certain to provide the House Committee with the legitimizing publicity required to ascertain permanent status. What better place to demonstrate the necessary nature of such a body than Hollywood, the world's entertainment epicenter? "It was a match made in heaven," recalled Eric Bently, clearly chosen, in the words of screenwriter Arthur Miller, "because they [HUAC] were cheap publicity hounds."[19] Rankin's thirst for fame spurred him as he tirelessly urged his fellow congressmen to recognize the communist threat and restore the un-American organization. His interminable politicking combined with a ripening climate finally paid of in January of 1945 with the reinstatement of the Committee.

Rankin had, according to Committee historian Robert K. Carr, engineered one of the most "remarkable procedural coups in modern history."[20] The investigation of subversive activity was once again on and Hollywood, with its star power, global allure, and large progressive population, provided the perfect target for the zealous band of conservatives who viewed the "Committee" as a vehicle to social and political prosperity.

No longer "forced" to investigate "fascism" (in the form of the German-American Bund), an endeavor that Dies and several of his committeemen had been less than excited about in the 1930's and early 1940's, the "Rankin" committee (as it was often called although Edward J. Hart (R-N.J) was named initial chair) was able to channel a tremendous amount of energy and enthusiasm into the postwar scourge of communistic un-Americanism.[21] Communism had always been the un-American Activities Committee's "menace of choice" and with Stalin on the move abroad coupled with a rise in communistic fear at home, the prospect of a large scale investigation of the Red Menace looked promising. After conducting a preliminary investigation of the American Communist Party and its most influential characters (men such as William Z. Foster, Earl Browder, and Gerhart Eisler), the Committee made an abrupt turn west and began to concentrate its energies on a thorough inquiry into the extent of the Communist Party's influence on the American movie making business. "To kick off its postwar campaign HUAC needed a headline grabber and what better than filmland," noted historian Griffin Fariello, "through the efforts of a titanic publicity machine and the production of more than six thousand films a year, Hollywood in its golden age was the focus of the nation's fantasies. Hollywood was news," Fariello asserted, "and the purge of its Communists captured the nation's attention."[22]

The 1947 Hollywood hearings stand as arguably the most significant in the history of the "un-American" Committee. Although never able to produce a legitimate example of Communist agitprop in film, the House Committee, under the "guidance" of New Jersey's J. Parnell Thomas, effectively confirmed the existence of a large "Red" presence in Hollywood, a "fact" that alarmed Americans across the country and served to further legitimize both the Committee and its mission. "In the past ten-years the Hollywood-Los Angeles area has become the mouthpiece, heart and pocketbook of the American Communist Party," wrote Oliver Carson in the *American Mercury* in February of 1948.[23] Due in part to the Thomas Committee, however, "the deep red which has covered so much of Hollywood for the past few years is rapidly fading to light pink. The Lush era of easy money, vast crowds and big names is over for Communists in Hollywood."[24] The "blacklist," which evolved in the wake of the hearings, proved to be one of the most crippling developments of the entire McCarthy age. Very few escaped its perniciousness unscathed as both "Friendly" and "Unfriendly" witnesses experienced its potency in one way or another. As Dalton Trumbo once phrased, in light of the full scope of the investigation, all were "victims" as the un-American Activities Committee prosecuted its hysteria-fueled campaign, shattering the film community and its progressive ethos in the process.[25] What remained in the wake of the investigation was an agency driven by fear, arguably a governmental puppet which operated on eggshells in the hope of remaining afloat in the aftermath of the ugliest episode in its history. Producers, writers, and actors all pandered to conservatives in government as the movies themselves became products of the contentious climate within which they were made. For those on the blacklist, a career on the black-market was all one could expect as expulsion from the industry cost writers, directors, and actors alike the opportunity to live and work in the magical environment that had had labored so hard to sustain.

As Trumbo noted in his infamous 1970 Laurel Award speech to the Screenwriters Guild, when looking back on the blacklist, do not bother looking for heroes or villains. There were none. All involved, in essence, were victims (although not "equally") in one way or another.[26] Those looking for a culprit in the "blacklist" saga have to look no further than HUAC. Individual players in Hollywood were drawn into the blacklist controversy by the Committee as it can easily be said that no one, either Friendly or Unfriendly, would have chosen the fate that they received. Those who resisted should be recognized for the courage that they displayed in combating what they accurately recognized to be a certifiable arm of oppression in the Committee. As for those who informed, although vilified by many, including former "Ten" members" Alvah Bessie and Albert Maltz, the stigma of "stool pigeon" simply does not apply. The sixty-plus men and women who favorably testified in Hollywood undoubtedly acted in opposition to their will and they have paid, via the permanent tarnishing of their reputations, accordingly. They were victims, as Trumbo claimed, of the "system," the combination of the HUAC machine and the "Red Scare" environment which powered it. Thomas and the Committee used Hollywood and decimated its collective chemistry in the process. The industry, as a result, has never been the same.

What is truly iniquitous regarding the HUAC-Hollywood clash is the manner in which House Committee fabricated a "threat" to serve its own aims. The years before the arrival of the Committee constituted arguably Hollywood's best years. Millions turned to the screen to live vicariously through the actors and actresses who symbolized the fulfillment of a dream.

Hollywood provided America with its primary source of entertainment in the 1930's and its star had never shone any brighter. Needless to say, it was an opportune time to attack. The Committee, however, required motive. Dies had returned from Hollywood in 1939 and given the industry a clean bill of health concerning revolutionary activity. Rankin, Thomas, Nixon, and Mundt, however, chose to view things differently. To the members of the Thomas Committee, Hollywood, as Rankin so eloquently articulated, represented a "hotbed of subversion" and warranted an investigation of unparalleled magnitude and scope. The question, however, remained: if absent of a revolutionary threat, what existed in Hollywood worth targeting? The Committee found its answer with the Hollywood Communist Party, an organization that may not have endangered the physical security of the United States, but one that stood in clear opposition to the inequitable social and economic "status quo," a conservative pillar which the Committee undoubtedly sought to maintain.

Although the evolution of the Hollywood Communist Party was certainly a development worth following, as Communism remains clearly incompatible with democracy, the nature of the party, its orientation, its ideology, was in no way comparable to what was being nurtured in Soviet Russia. Most of those that joined the Party in the 1930's and early 1940's did so for altruistic reasons, not because they harbored a thirst for revolution.[27] The Communist Party had long been a leading advocate of civil rights and its anti-fascist position lured many liberals, including many Jews, to its ranks. In general, most of these men and women were progressives who sought change in the social and economic configuration of America, not the political. "Many who joined the American Communist Party during the depression did so out of genuine, naïve idealism," wrote historian Ron Rosebaum, "It was a time when the capitalists nations were kowtowing to Hitler, and when the major political parties in America tolerated a vicious, racist system in the American South that was morally indistinguishable from apartheid."[28] Certainly there existed members of the Hollywood Communist Party who were more doctrinaire than others, but the majority belonging to or affiliated with the Hollywood Party were "moderate" communists, "parlor reds," "communists with a small c," who sought companionship in an organization dedicated to combating America's social and economic ills."[29] "By 1935, it was not at all unusual for Americans who were concerned with economic injustice-including many New Deal liberals-to identify with the Communist movement," clarified historians Kai Bird and Martin J. Sherwin, "many laborers, as well as writers, journalists and teachers, supported the most radical features of Franklin Roosevelt's New Deal. And even if most intellectuals," Bird and Sherwin maintained, "didn't actually join the Communist Party, their hearts lay with a populist movement that promised a just world steeped in a culture of egalitarianism."[30] The House Committee's inability to differentiate between such moderate, or non-revolutionary "idealists" and "cold hearted," hard line Stalinists resulted in the creation of its blanket labeling strategy, a line of attack which lumped all "progressives" under one subversive label. "Officials who ran most of the machinery of McCarthyism," details Ellen Schrecker, "overlooked such distinctions, adopting a worst-case scenario that implicated all suspected Communists in everything bad the party had ever done."[31] This blanket stratagem cost many undeserving liberals their careers as the Committee indiscriminately pillaged the Hollywood left, treating all affiliated with communism in the industry as enemies of the state. With the "help" of an asphyxiating social environment, the un-American Activities Committee engendered the blacklist and in turn, jumpstarted its "career."

Reticent Reds builds on this contention as Hollywood as a "catalyst" serves as a major theme. It is clear that the Committee viewed the film industry as a means to and end and this assertion is discussed at length. Its prey, "cultural" communists or "moderates," their attraction to communism and the role that several of these individuals played in resisting the un-American campaign are also of primary importance. This work's primary function, however, is to place the Hollywood episode in the context of the "red scare era" in an effort to demonstrate how the Committee manipulated individuals in order to cripple an enterprise. The House Committee on Un-American Activities purge touched the entire industry as Hollywood endured a traumatic transition from "golden age" to blacklist era. Unfortunately for movie-land, there existed only a handful of individuals clever enough to see through the Committee's patriotic façade into the heart of a most un-American organization. The men who constituted the original resistance, the "Hollywood Ten," represent a focal point as they possessed a unique opportunity to derail the Committee before it could truly get on track. Their collective failure in this endeavor, however, allowed the Un-American Activities Committee to use Hollywood as the star studded cornerstone upon which it constructed its post-war anticommunist edifice.

Primarily, this work views the Hollywood episode as an integral piece of the larger "Red Scare" puzzle. HUAC was not successful in Hollywood because of its shared political acumen. It was successful because the atmosphere surrounding the investigation had become ripe for such a venture. Beginning with the Palmer Raids of the 1920's, Americans had harbored a fear of "Reds" that grew during the Dies campaigns of the 1930's, and 1940's, lived through the war years, and reemerged with tremendous vigor during the early stages of the Cold War. Primarily a media sensation, the

"Red Menace" had been introduced to living rooms across the nation through articles, editorials, cartoons, and films throughout the 1920's, 1930's, and 1940's, eventually evolving into a phobia by 1950 that arguably fueled the development of "McCarthyism."

Critical to the health and vigor of the media's "menace" phenomenon, the HUAC-Hollywood clash took on a great degree of importance as it came at a time when the majority of common Americans were still unwilling to completely condemn the Soviet Union (given its integral role in the Second World War). Congress itself, as seen in debate on the house floor between Rankin and men like Iowa's William C. Ramsayer, who suggested that "Committee members might use their positions for their own advantage," remained undecided regarding a revived un-American query.[32] It was a time, observed historian Walter Goodman, when members of Congress were ready and willing to "let their creature [HUAC] drift away from them into oblivion."[33]

For J. Parnell Thomas of New Jersey and John Rankin of Mississippi, the two men credited for "revitalizing" the Committee in those precarious times, Hollywood served as a beacon. The film industry would no doubt create such a national stir that it would be impossible not to recognize the necessity of such an investigative body. Success in Hollywood would also translate into amplified fears over the "red menace" and undoubtedly restore the contentious social climate that nourished the Dies Committee in the 1930's. Rankin and Thomas viewed Hollywood as instrumental in the effort to galvanize support for a renewed anticommunist effort. Exposure of the "Red Menace" in filmland would serve as an essential contributor to the resurfacing of an intensified anticommunist climate, the critical variable, as demonstrated by Palmer in the 1920's and the Dies Committee in the 1930's, in the "red hunting" equation.[34]

It is in this light that the Hollywood episode emerged as critically important within the scope of the anticommunist crusade. Had those that resisted the Committee successfully exposed it as an organ of un-Americanism, impressionable Americans, waiting to render their verdict on Communism in the aftermath of the United States-Soviet alliance, would undoubtedly have been less willing to accept the Committee's villainous condemnation of Communist progressivism in America. Exposing the Committee as unconstitutional would have also convinced many (more) of its fallibility, stripping the Thomas Committee of the popular support which arguably sustained it. Most of those targeted by the Committee had once been affiliated with the Communist Party but, by 1947, had severed official ties with the organization. The Un-American Activities Committee, however, did not paint the picture this way. The Committee carried on as if all paraded before it were confirmed Stalinists, a falsity that was predominantly accepted due to the tenor of the time. In the case of the Hollywood investigation, by denying members of the "Hollywood Ten" the opportunity to challenge credibility of the Committee and its accusations, HUAC successfully maintained the myth that the Committee constituted the front line of defense in a battle against militant American Bolshevism.[35] The Committee achieved this "accomplishment" without having even produced a single thread of communist propaganda in film. The blacklist was the result, a plague that would haunt the industry for the better part of a decade. It was a genuine coup that proved integral to the extension of the un-American crusade and ultimately, to the evolution and expansion of McCarthyism.

The efforts of the Ten and those that joined them in resisting the Committee did not, however, go in vain. Their progressive, resilient legacy, manifest in the film *Salt of the Earth* written and produced by former Ten member Herbert Biberman and fellow blacklistees Paul Jarrico and Michael Wilson, survived the HUAC-Hollywood rampage to inspire a new generation of determined "radicals." Although many, such as Todd Gitlin, have argued that the student movement in the west was primarily a product of the Civil Rights movement in the South, it is clear that there were other motivating factors which contributed the rise of the student left in the late 1950's.[36] Opposition to House Committee on Un-American Activities was certainly one of those as many leftists at the University of California at Berkeley in the late 1950's were children, or acquainted with children, whose parents had been directly affected by the HUAC purge. SLATE, the 1950's left-wing organization that arguably erected the "anti-establishment" framework essential to the emergence of the more heralded Free Speech Movement (FSM) of the early 1960's, provided a "soapbox" for many "red diaper babies" opposed to ultraconservatism.[37] Moderately radical in orientation, SLATE (a name attributed to a "slate" of progressive candidates running for Berkeley student government in 1957) in the end operated in the name of civic and economic equality well in advance of both the Free Speech Movement and its Midwestern sister organization, Students for a Democratic Society (SDS). "SLATE," as acknowledged by historian W.J. Rorabaugh, "was the first post-McCarthy era organization to reject anticommunism [as it] established a working model for later Berkeley umbrella groups."[38] This organization, operating in a climate hostile to its aims, looked to expose the Committee and its legacy as ultimately responsible for the transgressions of the 1950's.

From the Hollywood campaign to the loyalty oaths, the House Committee on Un-American activities drove the repressive, ultraconservative vehicle that ran its wheels over the lives and lifestyles of progressives throughout the west.[39] SLATE, and eventually, the Free Speech Movement, operated in response to this suppressive conservativism. Manifest in the Ten and embodied by radicals on campuses across the nation, the determined spirit of resistance, resistance to the peril of tyranny and unconstitutionality, to oppression and discrimination, to exploitation and manipulation, is what ultimately defined the quest to dissolve the Un-American Activities Committee in Hollywood and, in turn, the "radical" movement of the 1960's. In this sense, the legacy of the Ten did live on and in some ways, is still very much alive today.

This study is not a comprehensive analysis of the Hollywood hearings, as Victor Navasky completed in *Naming Names*. It is not a study of labor issues and the role that organized labor played in the evolution of Communism as a leading force in the film industry. Gerald Horne in *Class Struggle in Hollywood* does a wonderful job of that.[40] It is not a comprehensive study of the Committee for Walter Goodman, William F. Buckley Jr. and Robert K. Carr, to name a few, have already completed such works. And it is not a thorough analysis of the Communist Party in America, for Irving Howe and Lewis Coser, among others, can claim that particular accomplishment.[41] This study, *Hollywood and Anticommunism,* places the House Committee on Un-American Activities Committee investigation of Hollywood within the context of the "Red Scare" age and analyzes the impact that the purge of the Hollywood left had on the scope and tenor of the anticommunist era. The HUAC-Hollywood clash was a byproduct of the environment within which it took place. Understanding the atmosphere which surrounded the "trials" is integral to understanding both the course of the hearings and their overall impact.

The Hollywood trials were not an overnight sensation. They were the result of years of media-charged anticommunist buildup, beginning with Palmer in the 1910's and 1920's, stretching through Dies in the 1930's, and culminating with Thomas, Rankin, and post war fever in the late 1940's. Committee efficiency is not what allowed it to successfully "paint" the movie industry red. It was in fact the sensational environment which surrounded the trials, the result of anticommunist articles, editorials, cartoons, and movies, which empowered the Committee and paved the way for the development of the blacklist. This study details the public evolution of the "Red Menace" and demonstrates how influential anticommunist hysteria actually was within the scope of the Hollywood investigations. It also forces the reader to contemplate the impact that the Hollywood hearings could have had on both the continued evolution of "red menace" hysteria and its purveyor, the House Committee on Un-American Activities. Occurring at a pivotal time in HUAC history, had the Committee been exposed as unconstitutional in 1947 Washington, the entire course of the anticommunist campaign would have undoubtedly been altered. With the Un-American Activities Committee derailed, Congress would have been divested of its un-American organ and the nation of its primary source of anticommunist aggression. The impact that such a development would have had on the coming age of McCarthyism is difficult to overlook. In this regard, Hollywood assumes a more significant position within the course of anticommunist history as a central force in the drama that would become McCarthyism.

Chapter Two

Land of the Free, Home of the Hysterical: American Communism and the Cultivation of "Red" Hysteria

Spurred by rapid industrialization, the "modernization" of America hit full stride at the dawn of the twentieth century. Cities sprouted as throngs of eager workers flocked to emerging urban epicenters in search of the American dream. It was during this time that the potential of American capitalism seemed limitless. With booming growth energized by cheap labor, free market trade, and few operating restrictions, the nation's business elite capitalized on the propitious economic climate and built corporate empires the likes of which the world had never seen. Juxtaposed to this incredible wealth, however, toiled the means of such prodigious production. Ironically, despite the essential nature of its role as the key cog in the industrial machine, the economic standing and general well being of the working class was often ignored. Paid pennies for work that generated billions, urban workers struggled to compete for a semblance of quality in their lives, a reprieve from the depravity ubiquitous in the tenements and ghettoes that millions called home.

The American Socialist Party, founded in 1902, provided the disenfranchised with an outlet through which to voice their concerns regarding America's economic hierarchy. This party, however, proved to be one which relied more on words than action, a fact that frustrated many lingering in the depths of civilization. The emergence of the American Communist Party, on the heels of the 1917 Bolshevik revolution in Russia, provided those eager for change with a ray of hope. Calling for worker solidarity and insisting on greater economic equality, the Communist Party of the United States of America (CPUSA) became the vanguard of the worker's movement in early 1920's America. Needless to say, this development greatly alarmed America's political and economic right. Fearful of the American Communist Party's potential to proliferate "radical" activity in a climate wrought by runaway inflation and widespread worker unrest, the government looked to "stamp out economic liberalism wherever it existed."[1] Escalating governmental fear culminated in the birth of the first American Red Scare. This event, marked by the image of the "Red Menace" and defined by a public assault of the American Left, permanently branded those affiliated with "radicalism" un-American and contributed to the establishment of the repressive social tenor that governed over 50 years of American "Red hunting."

On November 7, 1917, a group of armed Russian socialist revolutionaries under the leadership of the famed Marxist intellectual Vladimir (Uylanov) Lenin seized the Winter Palace in Petrograd and began what would become nearly 70 years of Communist reign in Russia. The Bolsheviks, or the majority membership of the Russian Social Democratic Labor Party, had spent nearly twenty-years, operating most of the time in seclusion outside of Russia, building the proletariat-peasant alliance needed to procure victory over the Romanov regime. Lenin, the principle engineer of the struggle, had come from a family of radicals and viewed the revolution as not only an opportunity to bring the people to power in Russia, but to avenge the death of his revolutionary brother, Alexander, executed on order from the Russian Tsar on May 8, 1887. His thirst for revenge combined with his burning desire to usurp the Russian monarchy and create a "new Russia, a European Russia, a Westernized Russia" drove him and his fellow revolutionaries as they successfully executed the world's first large scale socialist uprising.[2] The Bolshevik victory ignited socialist passions around the globe. In the United States, American leftists were overjoyed at hearing the news from Russia. Lenin's victory, many hoped, would spark change throughout the world. "The formation of the first socialist government thrilled and inspired American radicals," notes historian Philip S. Foner, "now, at long last, the champions of socialism could point to one example of success."[3]

The joy emanating from the United States following Lenin's coup was somewhat tempered, however, by the controversy plaguing the Socialist Party over its isolationist position on the Great War. Success overseas, according to the government, depended upon support at home. The Socialist contention that the affair was an exercise in imperialism infuriated officials on Capitol Hill and a good majority of the general public. The media onslaught against the left during this time only compounded matters for American socialists. Articles produced by leading publications such as *The New York Times* vilified the anti-war socialists as enemies of the state. As recognized by Foner, during this period "horror stories of every kind filled the columns of American newspapers."[4]

Questions surrounding subversive activity, attempts to paralyze the war abroad via clandestine activity at home, and immigrant loyalty circulated widely during the war years. Talk of sedition prompted Americans to look within in an attempt to determine the extent of traitorous activity. "He who is not with us is against us," declared a fiery Theodore Roosevelt in reference to "subversive" activity, "our bitter experience should teach us for a generation to crush under our heel any movement that smacks in the slightest of playing the German game."[5] Such comments produced anti-socialist sentiment that lingered well into the post-war years and made it difficult for leftists to express their full appreciation for Lenin's accomplishment. In fact, the Bolshevik victory actually heightened general fear of domestic duplicity. As an organized socialist movement had come to fruition in Russia, a nation lacking the ideal capitalistic conditions required for a pure socialist uprising (according to Marx), who was to say that a similar event could not transpire in America, the world's capitalistic epicenter? The specter of global revolution prompted President Woodrow Wilson to intensify the government's surveillance of the Left. The attention allocated to a perceived socialist threat led to an increase in the number of anti-socialist articles produced by the press, articles that contributed to the creation of an electric climate dominated by growing hysteria. The contentious atmosphere set the stage for a more thorough "examination" of subversive activity in the coming years.

In addition to amplified external pressure, the Bolshevik revolution also precipitated strife within the American Socialist Party. Extreme party leftists desired a more aggressive political and social agenda in the wake of Lenin's conquest. For these individuals, Lenin's coup signaled a time for a shift in party direction. No longer should the party to be one strong on words but short on deeds. Left wing party members believed firmly in revolution and saw the United Sates as fertile ground for a socialist uprising. Opposing these individuals were more pragmatic socialists, enamored with the idea of a purely democratic state (politically and economically), but not so with the idea of an armed revolution. Contributing to the left's militancy was its large contingent of Eastern European immigrants who "felt a direct kinship with the Russian Bolsheviks and with a European revolutionary tradition from which the Americans were by definition debarred."[6] Brewing tension within the party eventually culminated in a September 1, 1919 Chicago convention. At this assembly, the party's divided left wing announced the formation of the American Communist Party and the Communist Labor Party, two organizations more ideologically aligned with Lenin's Russia. The split cost the Socialist Party nearly seventy-five percent of its membership. Where the party once stood at nearly one-hundred thousand strong, by 1921 it had an active membership of just under twenty-five thousand.[7]

The fall of the Socialist Party and the Rise of the American Communist "movement" (in its two forms, the Communist Party and the Communist Labor Party) coincided with rising fear among Americans regarding "subversive" or seditious activity within. "Nativism" had begun to pervade America in 1919 and with it came a vehement brand of nationalism that had many Americans anxious to crush any and all perceived threats to the "status quo." These so-called "Super-patriots," according to Stanley Coben, possessed strong conservative values, traits that evolved out of a growing sense of xenophobia. Coben noted that most of these Americans, who numbered "in the millions," suffered from an ultra-patriotic "syndrome" fueled by a false belief that conspiracy lurked around every corner. "Psychological experiments show that a great many Americans-at least several million-are always ready to participate in a "red scare," affirmed Coben, "These people," writes Coben, "possessed hostile attitudes towards "certain minority groups, especially radicals and recent immigrants" and were defined by their "fanatical patriotism, and [their] belief that internal enemies seriously threaten national security." [8]

The Allied victory overseas only contributed to this growing sense of American introversion which blinded individuals to the diverse qualities that singled America out among other nations. "Intolerance of those days took many forms," historian Frederick Lewis Allen recognized, "the emotions of group loyalty and of hatred perverted a release in the persecution of not only radicals, but also of other elements which to the dominant American group-white Protestants-seemed alien or "un-American."[9] A nation built on immigration and known throughout the globe as a bastion of liberty, the proliferation of "nativism" in the aftermath of the Great War engendered a conservative myopia that arguably characterized the country's collective psyche for the next fifty years.[10] "Any disturbance in the status quo threatens the precarious psychic equilibrium of this individual," Coben asserted, this person "seeks an island of institutional safety and security. The nation is the island he selects. . . . It has the definitiveness he needs."[11] This "mentality" would manifest itself in the form of those who emerged as leaders of America's twentieth-century crusade against the Left.

Such growing domestic fear complicated matters for America's two Communist organs, forcing the two organizations to operate clandestinely. This reality cost the two leftist bands valuable recruiting opportunities and resulted in depleted enrollments. Despite the inflated numbers that Communists put forth regarding membership in 1919 (upwards of 70,000), in truth the party's enrollment lists were short and their budgets small. Whatever threat the Communist Party posed to the nation was minimal at most. Although the American CP had benefited from the Socialist Party's demise, it remained a fledgling organization in 1919, divided on ideological and cultural lines. The Socialists, on the other hand, were reeling. Lost was the progressive momentum that afforded Eugene V. Debs a presidential run and had attracted such influential Americans as Jack London and Upton Sinclair. "Thousands of members, true revolutionaries, as any who remain in the party, are dropped out," noted New York socialist Benjamin Gitlow, former party members "are discouraged and disheartened because of the schism."[12] The disorganized state of the American left did not, however, lessen the government's desire to liquidate American socialism.

The escalation of communist fear at home correlated directly with communistic success abroad. As the "Red Army" continued to rout the American assisted counterrevolutionary "White" forces in Russia, American officials became increasingly worried about the prospect of a global socialist uprising. Ironically, Wilson had actually opposed foreign intervention in the Russian Civil War when pressed on the matter by Great Britain and France in the summer of 1918. He feared that meddling in Russian affairs would strike the Russians as an American attempt to establish a rival, American-friendly government within the nation. This was not the message that he wished to convey to the fiery Lenin. "The participation of these two governments will give enterprise the character of interference with domestic affairs of Russia," proclaimed a determined Wilson, "and create the impression that the underlying purpose is to set up a pro-Allied government in Siberia, if not in Russia."[13] Ultimately, however, Wilson submitted to his distaste of Bolshevik atheism and begrudgingly agreed to contribute American troops and supplies to the Allied coalition in Siberia. "Whatever may be said concerning America's neutrality in Siberia in 1918," observed historian Arthur S. Link, "the state department actively assisted the [White Army], particularly after Wilson's illness."[14]

It became clear to the Soviets, based on the strong allied presence in Russia during the Civil War, that establishing a line of trade with the United States following the conflict would be difficult. Nevertheless, Lenin attempted to foster congenial relations with the Wilson administration.[15] His overtures, however, fell on deaf ears as fear of communism, notably its economic and atheistic qualities, began to take hold in Washington. In the eyes of American officials, Bolshevism was anathema to democracy and accommodating Lenin would certainly be globally construed as an informal acceptance of the Bolshevik regime. As a result, American insularity arguably prevented the evolution of an alliance that could possibly have ameliorated tensions between the two nations and contributed to a lasting union. "Bolshevism represented not only a threat to America's interest in a stable global order, but also a menace to American domestic unity," writes Historian David S. Fogelsong, "[Bolshevism] posed a challenge to their "Puritan" values and men of Calvinistic temperament [Wilson] could not be content to coexist with an evil force obstructing the reformation of the world."[16] There is no doubt that Wilson's support of an underground network in Russia designed to harass Lenin and eventually undermine his regime chilled relations between the two nations. Furnishing the clandestine anti-Bolshevik network in Russia with the tools required to reverse the nation's socialist course alienated the Russians and set the tone for the coming years. According to Fogelsong, although there had been no official declaration of war, "Wilson fought a long undeclared war against Bolshevism."[17] Had Wilson's administration been more open minded, communication between the two countries may have been less static. With tensions assuaged, the road to "cold war" may have been less direct. Of course, it could also be argued that Lenin's call for global revolution certainly did not ingratiate Wilson. Speculation aside, however, the two countries remained as divided ideologically as they were physically and would remain so until the communist collapse of the late 1980's.

With the campaign against Bolshevism in full gear overseas, the prosecution of a similar policy in the states began to intensify as news of the formation of the American Communist Party began to spread throughout Washington. The Communist left, however, did not provide much of a target as the two-headed organization remained in a in a state of disarray following the break with the Socialists. Although many in Washington perceived the Communist Party to be a tightly knit organization, in reality the party was loosely constructed and lacked organizational fabric. "It [was] assumed that the Communist movement actually was rigid, highly centralized, and disciplined," commented Irving Howe, "but the truth is otherwise. Looseness was characteristic of the early Communist movement at all levels."[18]

Muckraker John Reed, the former Harvard cheerleader and disciple of the famed bohemian journalist Lincoln Steffens, surfaced as a leading voice at this critical time for the Communist left and led a drive to establish the Communist Labor Party as America's leading leftist organ. A child of privilege who would go on to be one of the first from the state of Oregon to attend Harvard, Reed was the quintessential progressive, an intellectual who felt as though the party required cohesion if it planned on acquiring legitimacy. With the numbers as small as they were, Reed was convinced that division among the far left would lead to eventual dissolution. His career as a journalist, which began under the direction of Max Eastman while writing for the *Masses,* had given him an incredible sense for contemporary issues and garnered him respect among his peers. Reed's greatest allure, however, emanated from his experience as an eye witness to the Bolshevik revolution in 1917.

Funded by Eastman, Reed celebrated an opportunity to cover the revolution abroad as a reporter for the *Masses* and quickly became entranced with the intricacies of the uprising. Reed admired Lenin and his quest to overcome tyranny and longed to contribute in any way that he could to the advancement of the cause. Although he had been born into affluence, Reed identified with the poverty stricken peasantry of Russia and believed strongly that the Bolsheviks represented the needs and desires of the common Russian.[19] "[John Reed] went to Russia purely as a journalist, but he was not a pure journalist," writes Draper, "he could not resist identifying himself with the underdogs, especially if they followed strong, ruthless leaders."[20] As Draper acknowledges, "the Bolsheviks overwhelmed him," inspiring him to return home and attempt to address glaring inadequacies in American society.[21] This intention would manifest itself in his efforts to nourish Bolshevism in the United States via the establishment of the American Communist Labor Party. His experience combined with his leadership skills served him invaluably as he guided the nascent American organization. "My idea is to make socialists," proclaimed an energetic Reed as he pondered a socialist America. Enamored with a mystical image of Lenin inconsistent with the true character of the brutal leader, Reed's idealism prompted him to fabricate an image of Bolshevism that mystified leftists for years to come.

Reed, however, proved polemical and made unification between the American Communist Party and the Communist Labor Party arduous. His revolutionary zeal was infectious and many in the Labor Party bought into the idea of a workers revolution, something that irked many of the more moderate party affiliates who, in Reed's eyes, were simply "Jeffersonian democrats."[22] The Communist Labor Party was also more "American," "more humane, friendly, accessible to American radicals" than the Communist Party.[23] This allowed it to communicate with the socialists on a more collegial level than their migrant counterparts in the CP. The prodigious foreign influence within the Communist left, however, made it difficult to infuse either band with a native personality. "Left wingers like Reed," note historian Irving Howe, "who favored [a relationship] with the Socialist Party found themselves overwhelmed."[24] The Russian Federation, among others, dominated the movement numbers wise and hindered Reed's (and others) efforts to contour the party in a manner conducive to building a strong native base. "The most striking characteristic of [early] Communist Party membership was that it was overwhelmingly composed of recently arrived immigrants," commented historian Nathan Glazer, "probably one in ten members was a native American."[25] This split between the large foreign language contingent and the English speaking band within the party created constant friction within the "extreme left" and prevented the formation of a unified communistic body.

Things began to change, however, once many Eastern Europeans returned home to Russian following the Russian Civil War. With an exodus of foreigners came an opportunity for Americans such as Reed and veteran socialist Charles Emil Ruthenberg to assume party control. This development also facilitated communication between party factions and paved the way for the establishment of a unified communist coalition among Americans. One thing that all far leftists agreed on was that for the American Party to succeed, it had to be American in orientation. Natives needed to take the party reigns and convince their liberal brethren that socialistic change was both necessary and achievable. The long time socialist Ruthenberg, somewhat removed from inner party dealings during the embryonic years, surfaced to put an American face on what still remained a largely foreign organization.

A native of Cleveland, Ohio, Ruthenberg "came to socialism as a substitute for the ministry."[26] He had been drawn to the cloth as a young man but came to the conclusion in his mid-30s that the bible could not answer his questions regarding contemporary political and societal construction. As a result, he turned to Karl Marx, shied away from religion, and became an outspoken member of the extreme left. Ruthenberg brought a strong leftist resume to the CP. He had made a name for himself as an anti-war proponent and was known as an effective organizer. He stemmed from a white collar background and had spent years in managerial roles. His leadership skills surfaced during the bloody 1919 May Day "celebration" in New York where he served as the preeminent speaker on the socialist platform.[27] Despite the violence that surrounded him, Ruthenberg continued to preach to the raucous crowd. His persistence earned him an iron bed in jail for a night but his performance was well documented by fellow leftists. "When he came to New York the following month [to attend the National Left Wing Conference], he stood out as both a successful organizer and eminent martyr" observed Theodore Draper.[28] For a floundering movement desperately seeking a charismatic front man, Ruthenberg's emergence couldn't have come at a better time.

Respect gained over his short tenure as a Socialist front man earned Ruthenberg a prominent spot within the early Communist Party ruling pantheon. In 1919, he was named National Secretary of the Communist Party. His immediate goal was to unify American Communists under one party label. Recognized by Draper, "successive splits had paralyzed the

Communist Party but Ruthenberg demanded unity within the CP."[29] This task, however, proved difficult given the movement's large foreign language contingent and the diverse range of labor oriented far left factions which, in many cases, longed for legitimate party affiliation but remained in limbo based on the CP's instability. In fact, in a move that ran counter to his predilection for unity, Ruthenberg spearheaded the secession of a small English-speaking band from the main party body in order to try and galvanize the movement's dwindling "native" American sect. His action, designed to procure a greater voice for the minority group, alarmed the foreign language speakers (namely the Russian Federation) and precipitated the formation a "new United Communist Party in 1920" followed by the creation, a year later, of the Communist Party of America.[30]

A unified party, however, certainly did not signify stability. The party, forced to operate mainly underground given burgeoning anti-Red pressure emanating from Washington, faced its greatest test to date with the first installment of the "Red Scare" which began in early 1920.[31] With the economy down, anti-labor sentiment up, and the antiwar socialistic stance fresh in their minds, conservatives on Capitol Hill called for a vested governmental effort to flush out American Reds. Whatever leadership the party might have had during this period vanished as the purge reduced the movement from close to seventy-thousand to six. Acknowledged by Irving Howe, within the course of the government crusade against the left (1919–1924), party "heads" "failed completely to hold firm the loyalty of the vast majority of rank and file members."[32] Via a mass propaganda campaign combined with the use of draconian tactics, the government ran roughshod through the upstart CP and left the party near extinction. The raid, however, was not an overnight sensation. Social unrest brought on by economic instability, burgeoning xenophobia, and an atmosphere marked by "boring" post-war placidity nurtured a contentious climate poised to explode.

Contrary to popular belief, the American mood in the aftermath of the allied victory in the "Great War" was less than jovial. The American people were tired after two years of suffering with constant anxiety. The war was the most grotesque the world had ever seen and certainly took its toll on the American public. The first global conflict fought with "modern" machinery, World War I cost thousands their lives and millions more the opportunity to live life as they once did. Death and destruction reigned supreme as one returning from abroad noted that there was "something horribly fascinating about such appalling devastation. [The war] had deaths hand written all over it."[33]

It was a war that refused to discriminate between citizens and soldiers as machine guns, tanks, gas, and for the first time, planes ushered in an apocalyptic epoch that touched, in one way or another, all corners of the globe. "Total War," as recognized by Frenchmen Louis Mairet, created a scene "wet with death, muddy death, dripping with blood, death in the slaughterhouse. The bodies lie frozen in the earth which gradually sucks them in."[34] Such horror left people longing to escape both the physical and psychological anguish associated with the conflict. In America, such suffering translated into "spiritual fatigue," which, as observed by historian Robert K. Murray, resulted in a "lack of moral stamina, of faith in the principles of democracy, of wisdom, and of effective leadership."[35] Such a condition placed the nation, according to Murray, on "the brink of nervous exhaustion."[36] In such as state, fears are amplified and paranoia is easily nourished. In essence, the climate was ripe for a nation-wide panic attack.

Adding to the incendiary post-war domestic atmosphere was an economy suffering from a peacetime letdown and a manufacturing industry desperately seeking to liquidate unionized labor. Although the Wilson administration had been relatively labor friendly during the war (a relationship based on necessity), following the engagement support for America's means of production began to waver. Within hours of the 1918 armistice, war-time contacts were abolished and plants integral to allied success overseas closed. Industries reliant on the war took a major hit and those employed in war-time capacities bore the brunt of America's economic war to peace conversion. This development demoralized a good portion of the workforce and contributed to a contentious social milieu. "Statistics do not record the psychological torment and confusion experienced by those who were suddenly left jobless," writes Murray, "forced to readjust to their own and their families lives."[37] Inflation hit hard as well. Living costs soared as the dollar weakened causing considerable angst among those struggling to make ends meet. Such conditions forced working men and women to unite.

The result was an increase in union activity at a time when tension between employers and employees were at peak levels. Employers began to view labor leaders as "radical agitators who intended to transform the economic system along collectivist lines."[38] Wilson and his administration were obviously cognizant of the gains made by organized labor during the war as the government relied on the industrial sector's support to wage an effective campaign abroad. These gains, however, worried Wilson. Leaders in the industrial sector stood as potential political rivals and the rise in union activity threatened the government's ability to control America's manufacturing machine. Looking to defuse his potential competition, Wilson, recognized Murray, "fought with every means at his disposal to undermine organized labor and stamp out economic liberalism wherever it existed."[39]

The American Socialist Party had played an integral role in the formation of labor unions throughout the early 1900's. The party of the "common man," the Socialists had fought long and hard in trying to procure a voice for the American laborer. Although it was not directly affiliated with the American Federation of Labor (AFL) or the Industrial Workers of the World (IWW or the "Wobblies"), the Socialist Party (which often competed with these groups for members) mirrored these organizations in many ways. Racism, economic inequality, and chauvinism were all party targets as it set its sights on the status quo and furnished the "progressive era" with the liberal fuel required to ignite change. "Socialism deals with what is, not what ought to be," wrote Jack London in summarizing his attraction to the party, "the material with which it deals with is the 'clay of the common road,' the warm human, fallible and frail, and yet, withal, shot through with flashes on something finer and Godlike, with here and there the sweetness of service and unselfishness, demanding the right-nothing more, nothing less than the right."[40] Driven by such passion, Socialists pioneered a campaign against unregulated capitalism which saw union activity grow by leaps and bounds. Strikes became commonplace as united workers laid siege to hostile workplaces. Worker success, however, quickly drew the ire of conservative Americans weary of the power commanded by unionized laborers. This fear only intensified with the finalization of the Bolshevik victory in Russia, a true "proletarian" revolution and one certain, in the minds of many Americans, to spark unrest among the working population of the United States. "It was generally agreed that if domestic radicalism would succeed at all it would succeed first with the laboring man," noted Murray.[41]

For the nation's largest labor organization, however, "radicalism" was anything but an integral part of its platform. The American Federation of Labor (AFL) prided itself on being an American institution, relatively conservative in both its composition and its politics. Its firm position behind the American war effort also stood in stark contrast to socialist pacifism. For many in the American Federation of Labor, socialism, as recognized by John Reed, was "a system worked out in foreign countries, not born of his own particular needs and opposed to democracy and fair play."[42] As a result, for socialists such as Reed, the AFL and the Industrial Workers of the World (although decidedly more "aggressive" than the AFL) were too "practical" in their ideology to be considered truly socialist in orientation. The revolutionary spirit, according to many upstart communists, was absent from these organizations as their main thrust revolved exclusively around the acquisition or worker's rights within the scope of the industrial workplace. The American Federation of Labor, according to Murray, threw its support behind strikes designed "solely to demand for higher wages, shorter hours, and collective bargaining."[43]

The thought of a general uprising and the completion of a full scale socialist revolution was not something most American Federation of Labor and IWW members were willing to seriously consider. Revolutionary socialism, as seen through the Bolshevik revolution, was a more extreme brand of liberalism that provided an outlet for "radicals" like Reed to exercise their zealous impulses. "Revolutionary socialism," pronounced Reed, "must make socialists out of workers, and make them quick. Comrades who call themselves 'members of the left wing' must make the workers want more-make them want the revolution."[44] Such pointed language alienated many members of the American Federation of Labor and heaped negative attention upon the infantile American Communist Party. With American Communist Party leaders such as Reed promoting revolution, the government grew ever more suspicious of the radical left.

It did not take long for conservative economic and political forces to attribute the increase in post-war strike activity to a rise in Bolshevik activity within the United States. The turbulent state of the post-war economic climate had attracted new members to the Communist Party and its growth correlated with a rise in Washington fear. Although the American Federation of Labor and its leader Samuel Gompers had resisted any call for revolution, large scale strikes in Seattle, Washington, Lawrence, Massachusetts, and Butte, Montana, signaled a rise in left wing "militant" activity. The Seattle strike, "the first American general strike to shut down an entire city," proved especially alarming to Washington officials.[45] "The Seattle strike was particularly significant," observed Murray, "for the first time, public attention was focused sharply and solely on the issue of domestic radicalism to the virtual exclusion of all other factors."[46] Commenting on the wave of strikes while speaking at the First Congress of the Communist international in March of 1919, American Socialist Labor Party front man Boris Reinstein proclaimed that the "Russian revolution has exerted an enormous influence upon the proletarian masses in America."[47] Such vigor terrified conservatives across the nation, many of whom now believed that revolution was indeed imminent.

Washington state Representative Albert Johnson, appalled at the prominence of widespread "Bolshevik activity," declared in the wake of the Seattle strike that "from Russia they [the agitators] came and to Russian they should be made to go."[48] Lenin's banter from abroad further inflamed the situation. "It is inconceivable for the Soviet Republic to exist alongside the imperialist states for any length of time," voiced Lenin in the spring of 1919, "one or the other must triumph in the end."[49] With Seattle serving as a revolutionary "microcosm," the Wilson administration, operating primarily in his absence due to the president's failing health, sought to initiate a comprehensive "red purge" before American Bolsheviks could manufacture anymore labor frustration. The press facilitated this goal by serving as a conduit to intensifying hysteria.

There is no arguing the fact that the American media played an integral role in the materialization of the "Red Scare." The generation of paranoia via provocative headlines and sensationalized stories worked in the favor of the conservative right throughout the course of the domestic war against the radical left. The manner in which the media covered the Seattle strike of 1919 is consistent with this contention. Countless articles were produced by newspapers stretching from coast to coast which heralded the action as a communist conspiracy and a prelude to revolution. Lost amidst the hype was the participant, the common laborer who sought what any hard working man or woman would want: a living wage. Due to the conspiratorial intensity of the articles covering the event, however, Seattle became a so-called bastion of bolshevism, a radical epicenter that placed the nation on panic alert.

The Los Angeles Times, a leading news source on the west coast, figured prominently in the cultivation of Seattle-related hysteria. The paper printed a series of articles detailing "Red" activity in Seattle. Most of the articles centered on Communist influence within the Industrial Workers of the World and the role that "radicalism" played within the evolution of the walkout. An event which saw over 30,000 men abandon their dockside jobs, shipyard workers stood strong as a solid body in the face of "the growing militancy of all northwestern employers."[50] The worker's plight, however, took a back seat to the spectacle that was the "revolutionary" atmosphere conjured up by the "the I.W.W. and other Reds."[51] The media heaped attention on the "communist" component of the strike as a means of generating the mystery and excitement that they knew would sell papers. It was a tactic that would hold true throughout the duration of America's "Red Scare" era (1919 through the Cold War).

On February 8, 1919, in the heat of the walkout, the *Times* ran a most disturbing headline certain to capture the attention of the general public. "Reds Directing General Strike" chimed the headline, which continued to indict the CP with "Trouble Believed Bolshevik, Movement to Test Chance For Revolution"[52] In a piece which lauded the tenacity of Seattle mayor Ule Hanson, a man who would resign his post following the affair to become a lecturer on the peril of Bolshevism, "Reds Directing General Strike" was clearly designed with publicity in mind. With the headline providing a shock factor, the text read like an anticommunist exposition with provocative language certain heighten anxiety. "It is recognized here that the general strike at Tacoma is a real Bolshevik movement," contended the *Times,* "it is freely asserted by administrative officials that there will be no temporizing with radicals. Mayor Hanson announced that guards have the orders to shoot to kill at the first sign of rioting."[53] Ignoring the striker's wage and working hour related intentions, the sensationalized expose endeavored to convince the reading public of a Soviet conspiracy, the strike being one of the many preliminary steps in the march towards full scale revolution. "Men with the spirit of the Russian Bolsheviki are in the saddle in Tacoma," proclaimed the piece, "Seattle has been chosen as a testing ground for radical ideas. This is Bolshevism. The city has been chosen with the shipyard strike as a pretext for staging the revolution. The city is ready for an emergency and its officers have instructions to shoot to kill when rioting starts."[54] With anxiety running high, such apocalyptic language only fanned the flames of hysteria and contributed to a growing, yet unwarranted American fear of Bolshevik inspired revolution. This, however, was the design. Fear over Bolshevism deflected attention away from the matter at hand and on to the fabricated conspiracy. Workers were being exploited yet now, amazingly enough, they constituted the enemy. The "red" charge served as a timely elixir to capitalism's labor related woes. It also, as the *Times* deduced rather quickly, sold papers.

"The Red Issue at Seattle" rang The *Los Angeles Times* headline on February 12, 1919. In an article furnished with a caption imbued with glaring "shock value," the *Times* insinuated that the strike symbolized Communist agitators at their seditious best. Seattle represented, according to the *Times,* the first stop on a "Red" tour of the west coast destined to culminate in complete communist domination of organized labor. Through labor, argued the newspaper, the American Communist Party would build its popular base and in time, accrue enough momentum to bring democracy to its knees. Red hegemony was seemingly inevitable, according to the *Times,* which posited that the "Bolsheviks" behind the Seattle strike had attempted to "turn the state of Washington into 'Little Russia' and are planning raids on industrial districts of other cities."[55] A preposterous claim with little substantive support, such language undoubtedly struck fear into the hearts of impressionable readers. Without offering any proof of direct Communist participation in the event, the article outlandishly encouraged Americans to rally around the "defense" of the nation.

The strike, however, was not the work of the Communist Party, but rather the product of concerned workers. Although there were communists who participated in the action, the "radical" element made up a very small percentage of the striking body. Recognized by Robert K. Murray, the strike force consisted primarily of rank and filers who "wanted nothing more revolutionary than to force a victory for the shipyard."[56] Eager to fuel hysteria, however, the *Times* insisted that the strike was much more than an act of worker solidarity, it was "a brazen attempt to overthrow the government itself," an event staged to "overthrow American institutions."[57]

Hailing "strike breaker" mayor Hansen, who claimed that the strike "signaled revolution by scoundrels who want to take possession of our government," the article implored the government to "arrest and punish all leaders of the conspiracy. No skim milk policy should be adopted. It is the government's responsibility to punish. The whitewash brush must be used."[58] Sad words which clearly constituted the promotion of all out war on the heartbeat of American industry. Again, fright associated with Red Menace hysteria transcended the plight of the American worker. Was it a campaign for communism or compassion in Seattle? If communism equaled an eight hour day, perhaps a little bit of both. The *Times*, however, made the case "clear" for its readership. Organized labor had been infiltrated and Seattle represented a microcosm for what awaited urban centers across America.

Articles on Bolshevik malevolence and Red conspiracy in Seattle continued to appear in the *Times* and other major publications throughout the course of the confrontation. With each new piece, paranoia surrounding "The Red Menace" intensified. "Reds Directing Seattle Strike-To Test Chance For Revolution" announced on *The Rocky Mountain News* on February 8, "Citizens Of Seattle Oppose The Revolution" pitched the *Times* on February 9, and "The Seattle Strike Is Marxian" proclaimed *The Washington Post* on February 10.[59] Although the strike was unofficially defused on February 11, the contentious tone had been set and, to the demise of the left, the press had found a headline that sold. By representing the American Red as a menace and embellishing the threat that the fledgling CP posed to the nation, news agencies had discovered a powerful marketing tool. "For the remainder of the scare period, the general press suffered a temporary lapse of accuracy," acknowledged Murray, "and it certainly did not fill its vaunted function in a democratic society of telling the truth." Print what sells became the motto of the American media as the CP began a run as a media "darling" that lasted over five decades. Communism, in the ultimate of ironies, had become commoditized.

The general impact of "Seattle" did not evaporate, however, with the negotiated settlement of February 11. The seeds of hysteria had been planted and press continued to feed off Seattle's enchanting energy. On August 17, 1919, "Los Angeles Invaded" appeared in the *Los Angeles Times* insinuating that the city had been infiltrated "by a new gang of radical agitators of the Soviet type."[60] A piece obviously inspired by Seattle, the article contended that communist agitators, "set on starting something" and "having learned from Seattle," had invaded Los Angeles' labor community intent on inspiring unrest among the city's blue collar workforce. "The world is passing through a cycle of violence," suggested the *Times,* and any temporizing with the forces of anarchy, whether intellectual or physical, is perilous."[61] Thanks in part to the paranoia generated by Seattle, Americans now perceived the "Red Menace" to be not simply a labor problem, but a societal one. As seen in the *Times* piece, Bolshevism now posed a threat to the nation's psychological as well as physical sphere. Seattle had succeeded in bringing the Red threat to the national fore. The Seattle strike, confirms Murray, "set in motion a pattern of response which would be the standard for the rest of the scare period."[62] No longer was Bolshevist plague a localized issue, communism had become a nationwide pandemic and required immediate federal attention.

If the Seattle strike was not enough to spark the government to committed action, the June 2, 1919 bombing of Attorney General A. Mitchell Palmer's Washington D.C. home certainly did the trick. Tied to the infamous May Day bombings, the attack on the Palmer residence captured the nation's attention and cost the Left one of its most powerful sympathizers (Palmer). Carried out by a rouge member of the radical group the "Anarchist Fighters," the attack, poorly conceived and pathetically executed, served as a lightening rod both in D.C. and throughout the nation. Clearly, the extreme component of American radicalism had reared its ugly head and there was ostensibly no limit to how far the radicals were wiling to go in their thrust for political and social upheaval. Intensifying the situation even further was a note left by the bomber, placed beside the Palmer's front door and saturated with splenetic vitriol. "There will have to be bloodshed; there will have to be murder," read the note, "we will not dodge, we will destroy, we are ready to do anything and everything to suppress the capitalist class. . . . .signed, the Anarchist Fighters."[63] The government, along with the press, viewed the bombing as a clear sign that Communist Party had begun to gel in the United States. The battle lines had been drawn and the Reds would soon feel the "consequences" of their ill timed bravado.

"Palmer Family Safe, Red Literature Found" graced the front page of *The New York Times* on June 3, 1919.[64] An article seemingly designed to assuage fears concerning the attorney general and his family, the piece quickly identified the American Communist Party as a potential perpetrator and wasted little time vilifying the fledgling organization. "That the attempt was made by an anarchist or Bolsheviki was evident from the fact that anarchist literature was scattered around the street."[65] According to the piece, the attack was "part of an organized outburst, doubtless planned by the same groups of radicals that engineered the outrages perpetrated in April and May."[66] What the article failed to mention was that the escapade very well could have been a response to Palmer's refusal to offer clemency to Socialist Party front man Eugene V. Debs, a Sedition Act violator who had petitioned the attorney general for clemency while locked away in Atlanta. Palmer, who would have nothing of it, proclaimed in April of 1918 that "Debs had violated the law of the land" therefore "[I do] not feel compelled to make any recommendation in his case."[67] Mention of this may have provided a degree of context to the catastrophe by establishing motive. Failing to include this information allowed the *Times* to insinuate that the attack was part of a larger leftist revolutionary plan.

The last two thirds of the article are consumed with excerpts from the anarchist material found at the site. In what could be construed as an attempt on behalf of the *Times* to inflame fear, the inclusion of the literary clips provided a window into what appears to be an extremely militant organization. "The powers that be make no secret of their will to stop here in America the worldwide revolution," read one of the pamphlets, "the powers that be must recognize that they will have to accept the fight that they provoked."[68] "There will be bloodshed," proclaimed a second handout, "there will have to be murder, we will kill because it is necessary."[69] Further talk of labor and class struggle seem to link the attack to the young Communist Party. The *Times* position is clear: radials stood as the root of the problem and radicalism originated with the American Communist Party.

Party heads, however, refuted any and all claims that they had instigated the action. In fact, John Reed issued a statement to the effect that the attack had been "staged" as a means of further incriminating the party publicly. Reed harshly denounced the attack and made it clear that the American Communist Labor Party was not a terrorist organization. The bombs were planted, according to Reed, by "some reactionary" who wished to stimulate the "ruling class" to action against the American labor movement.[70] Based on the division within the party and the underground nature of its operations, there is no way that Reed could speak for the party at large. It is certainly conceivable that the bombing was carried out by a communist or a party sympathizer. Nevertheless, it is also quite plausible that the party had nothing to do with the attack and remained primarily concerned with labor issues. Such an act would certainly not have benefited the CP and CLP's efforts to attract a larger percentage of the native born working class to its ranks. As decreed by Lenin, the party was to be "an American one," and should be "aligned as closely as possible with the organizations of the American workers."[71] The Palmer bombing arguably exposed the party as

a foreign organ, an image that coincided with its largely foreign membership. With Ruthenberg doing his vested best to shade the party in Red,
white, and blue, the attack on the Palmer home served as a major setback
and served as a prelude to perhaps the darkest epoch in American progressive history. Certainly neither Ruthenberg nor Reed would have condoned
such an attack given the precarious state of the party and its ongoing effort
to Americanize. Regardless, Palmer and the government viewed the action
as a CP mandate and set out, with help from the press, to vanquish the
extreme left from the American social and political scene.

Known throughout scholarly circles as "Palmer's reign of terror," the
first comprehensive federal assault on America's communist left began on
the heels 1919's intensified radical activity. In addition to increased strike
activity and the Palmer bombing, race riots in Washington D.C., the investigation of New York's "radical" community by senator Clayton R. Lusk,
and the anti-Red media barrage convinced the government that the "Red
Menace" warranted a federal campaign.[72] As recognized by Eugene Lyons,
it was at this time that "Attorney General Mitchell A. Palmer, the American
Legion, certain sections of the press, and superpatriot alarmists shared the
Moscow delusion that revolution was around the corner."[73] Lyons position
is corroborated by Robert K. Murray who noted that the extreme left did
not represent a revolutionary threat in 1919. "Up to that point, American
radicals had not constituted a real menace," wrote Murray, "and, when
viewed rationally, even during the war period itself they did not represent any serious chink in the democratic armor."[74] Nevertheless, with the
nation void of patriotic fervor in the absence of war, the emergence of the
"demonic" CP proved timely for a government longing to nurture nationalism.

The Espionage Act of 1917 and the Sedition Act of the following year
had already begun to sink their teeth into the American Left by the time
Palmer commanded center stage. Perhaps the most notable casualties of
the two anti-sedition initiatives were socialists tried for conduct unbecom-
ing during or immediately following the First World War. Victor L Berger,
one of the Socialist Party's founding fathers, Charles T. Schneck, the party's
general secretary, and Debs, socialist presidential candidate in 1912, were
all Sedition Act victims.

The trials that befell these men permanently stained their careers.
Conservative officials, such as Justice Oliver Holmes Jr., who, according to Murray, established "the clear and present danger principle" during the Schneck case, linked these men to un-American activity and in the
process, attached a traitorous stigma that became the hallmark of their
careers.[75] The fate that these men received, however, was not consistent

with the course of their careers or the views that they espoused. Regardless of their antiwar positions, they were not revolutionaries and were basically "opposed to violence and force."[76] Also worthy of note was Debs' religious foundation. An anomaly among radicals, "Debs was a devout Christian," asserts Murray, "one of the few radicals who could mention God's name on a public platform and get away with it."[77]

The IWW or the "Wobblies" and their engineer, William "Big Bill" Haywood, had also been a cause for concern among the conservative right. The more militant of America's two major labor organizations (and significantly smaller), the "Wobblies" had spearheaded action against the nation's capitalist system since its founding in 1905 and had been instrumental in such major strikes as Seattle. The Marxist Haywood, along with co-founders Debs and Daniel De Leon, formed a leftist coalition committed to the eventual expulsion of capitalism in favor of a worker friendly socialist state. "The working class and the employing class have nothing in common," states the IWW constitution, "between these two classes a struggle must go on until the workers of the world organize a class and abolish the wage system."[78] During the Great War, the IWW took a militant stand against American involvement garnering the organization ample federal attention. Its contention that the war was an imperial struggle struck a cord with the conservative right which in turn employed the media to wage an attack. "Newspapers labeled the organization 'America's cancer sore,'" Murray observed, "and characterized the Wobbly as 'a sort of half wild animal.'"[79] The propaganda campaign splintered the organization. Dozens of its leaders were arrested and hundreds more deported, "ostracized," or, in some instances, murdered.[80]

The "Lusk Committee" raids of spring and summer, 1919, a prelude to the Palmer affair, only amplified the intensity of burgeoning American anti-communism. Formed in March and headed by precocious first-year New York Senator Lusk, the "Lusk Committee" spearheaded the first comprehensive, inner city purge of New York's "radical" community. Short on experience but chocked full of "natavistic" energy, Lusk viewed the establishment of the conservative organ as an opportunity to rid New York of its large population of "alien enemies."[81] For Lusk, the communist left represented an atheistic body which harbored intentions inimical to the growth and prosperity of American democracy. It was an organization built upon Marxist pillars and stabilized by a socialistic ideological foundation contrary to all things American. "The scheme of Karl Marx-or German-Jewish origin-is the basis for the materialism inherent in present day socialism, for its antagonism to religion, to ethics," stated a Lusk Committee report, "and to all idealism based on principles, on sentiments and intellectual concepts that do not relate to purely material life and wealth interests."[82]

Lusk held a series of hearings within the course of his investigation designed to expose both the potency and intent of the radical movement. He also conducted raids, such as his assault on the Rand School and his invasion of the Russian Bureau on June 12, an incident where "police and private detectives employed by the Lusk Committee arrested everybody in sight." [83] Such militancy was clearly designed to physically intimidate and psychologically deflate the "movement." Extremist activity, such as the recent "red" related bombings, made Lusk's task much easier as he enjoyed widespread political and popular support. Although isolated in nature and not definitively linked to the CP, the bombings raised fear throughout the city and ostensibly justified Lusk's intense operation. As a result, Lusk, and later, Palmer, enjoyed liberal "access" to New York radicals and prosecuted their respective campaigns with reckless abandon. Senator King of Utah synthesized the vigor of the Lusk crusade proclaiming "It is time that these disturbers of our peace [radicals] and enemies of our country be driven from this land whose hospitality they have so grievously abused." [84]

Lusk did not confine his operations to the big city. In the fall of 1919 his "agents" moved north into New York's upstate region, targeting cities such as Buffalo and Utica. Teachers, labor organizers, and political leftists were all pinpointed by Lusk. *The New York Times* noted, in an article printed less than a month prior to the January Palmer Raids, that a Buffalo teacher "was taken to police headquarters tonight by a policewoman. Charges had been made to the school board that she held membership in the Communist Party." [85] The article continued to reveal that "Lusk Committee agencies were driving hard against radicals in Rochester and Utica." The Utica raids "were aimed at several branches of the Communist Party" and yielded nine arrests. Those arrested, stated the article, were to be examined by Archibald E. Stevenson, "consul to the Lusk Committee." [86] In the end, as recognized by Jaffe, the Lusk committee had successfully "shaken up" the communist left leaving its adherents susceptible to the more thorough Palmer assault. [87] Additionally, the Lusk raids provided neophyte anticommunists such as J. Edgar Hoover, serving at the time as the Bureau of Investigation's chief intelligence officer, with an opportunity to gain invaluable experience in the "business" of "red hunting." Perhaps most importantly, the committee "trampled over the constitutional rights of many individuals" on its way to creating the incendiary environment that made the Palmer infused "red scare" of 1920 possible. [88] With the press zealously grooming the "menace" metaphor, a "climate of dread took hold of the United States" which ripened the conditions for Palmer. [89]

Needless to say, Palmer's attack came at a most propitious time. Lusk, along with the Overman Committee, had assisted in moving the "menace" to the forefront and his "success," combined with a growing distrust of organized labor and a rise in anti-immigrant sentiment, ripened conditions for the attorney general. [90] Ironically, Palmer had actually been somewhat of a "friend" to the disenfranchised throughout his political career. The 1919 bombings, however, drastically changed him. A man who had often sheltered immigrant communities from social and political hostility, Palmer, in the aftermath of the attempt on his life, now viewed ghettoes as hot beds of anarchist activity. "Those who cannot or will not live the life of Americans under our institutions," stated Palmer in June of 1919, "should go back to the countries from which they came." [91] Knowing that the Communist Party was comprised mainly of aliens, Palmer realized that a purge of the immigrant communities would not only fetter out potential anarchists, it would also contribute directly to the undermining of American Communism. Playing on communist fears would allow Palmer to exercise his anti-immigrant animosity while simultaneously garnering favor with the ever-fearful American populace. With Lenin in power abroad and two branches of his party now functioning within, Americans had grown incredibly weary of Communism and eagerly awaited a government-led purge. Palmer, a man with presidential aspirations, sought to capitalize on this "opportunity" by orchestrating a drive to eliminate the extreme left, an endeavor that would certainly provide a boost to his political career.

Palmer's anti-radical acrimony, however, was not without substance. Not only did he barely avoid death allegedly at the hands of a radical organization, the extreme left was on the move in early 1919, engaged in a recruiting campaign that relied on heavy doses of propaganda. The Communist Party, the more militant branch of American Bolshevism, possessed a membership of close to sixty-thousand at the time of the Palmer raids, with most of those individuals of foreign origin. This "Left wing" base of the CP became increasingly hostile to the more moderate, primarily native Communist Labor Party and began to advocate a Soviet line grounded in the call for immediate proletarian revolt. Although somewhat mitigated by Ruthenberg's attempts to Americanize the band, the CP took an uncompromising line and remained determined to breed revolution. This call reached well beyond the confines of the two communist organizations. As acknowledged by Murray, many who were not officially affiliated with the party had begun to "listen" to the revolutionary message. It is impossible to determine exactly how many of these radical "sympathizers" existed, but Murray suggests the number approached one million. "Through their official organs, the *Voice of Labor* (CLP) and the *Communist* (CP), the two organizations established contact with many people who were not members of either party." In addition, writes Murray, "thousands of persons were reached through a large variety of Communist publications. According to the Justice Department records, there were 471 radical newspapers in the country in late 1919 advocating the violent overthrow of capitalism." [92]

Yet in spite of such gaudy numbers, the Bolshevik threat in America in 1919 was minimal at best. The Communist Party was so prodigiously plagued by disorganization that the thought of revolution was nothing more than a pipe dream. In fact, the Communist Labor Party, the "native" arm of the CP, never espoused militant activity. The CLP believed in supplanting capitalism with socialism through democratic channels. Although outspoken party figureheads such as John Reed clearly identified with the Russian revolution, the organization, along with other targeted groups such as the Union of Russian Workers, was "actually quite peaceful in nature."[93] Nevertheless, Palmer, building on the momentum generated by the Lusk raids of November 1919, engineered a crusade that culminated in thousands of arrests and hundreds of unjustified deportations.

Little did the nation know at the time, but Palmer's attack, which netted nearly 5,000 arrests, served as an ominous sign of what lied ahead concerning the political and social future of the United States. Somewhat lost amidst the hype generated by the raids was the emergence of J. Edgar Hoover. The young, polished director of the Justice Department's Bureau of Investigation, Hoover provided Palmer with intelligence integral to the success of the raids. Perhaps more importantly for history's sake, Hoover had received his fist taste of "Red hunting" while working for the Lusk Committee in New York and was eager to assist Palmer. Hoover had long distrusted the socialist left and took particular issue with the party's recruitment of "Negroes." When the CP targeted America's black community as a possible membership base, Hoover condemned the strategy positing that the party viewed black oppression as a lightening rod for racial revolution. Reflecting on the "Negro situation," Hoover commented in a November report to Congress that there existed "a well-concerted movement among a certain class of Negro leaders [who] constitute a determined and persistent source of radical opposition to the government and established law an order."[94] According to Hoover, these African American radicals (who remained anonymous) had openly advocated "Bolsheviki or Soviet doctrines "and had been "openly assertive of their own equality, even superiority."[95]

Showing his socially myopic hand early, Hoover's diatribe against the Red-Black alliance spoke to his infamously crooked character. Chomping at the bit to root out Reds and equally eager to preserve the racial status quo, Hoover jumped at the chance to assist Palmer. Hoover's participation provided a glimpse of what would eventually become the "Director's" foremost passion. Although the 1920 episode did not satisfy his desire to liquidate the Left, he would certainly get his chance the following decade while facilitating the Dies Committee's 1930's "investigation" of subversive activity.

With Hoover, former director William Flynn, and the Wilson administration behind him, Palmer brought the red scare into living rooms across the nation and frightened Americans into believing that the revolutionary threat was indeed legitimate. "The Palmer raids widened the scope of the Red Scare from a purely local and state phenomenon to a massive undertaking carried out by the government itself," wrote Jaffe.[96] Palmer, according to Theodore Draper, inspired an "epidemic of prosecutions. Thousands were rounded up in raids on homes and meetings. Little distinction was made," noted Draper, "between anarchists, syndicalists, Communists, socialists, and pacifists."[97] Backed by prodigious political and popular support, Palmer fed off of growing anti-Red sentiment and captured headlines across the country as he crippled the infant American Communist Party.

Undoubtedly, Palmer's effort would not have achieved the level of success that it did had it not been for the media. News agencies from coast to coast contributed to the emergence of the contentious atmosphere that facilitated his endeavor. A series of anticommunist articles run by America's leading news agencies in the months preceding the purge contributed to the establishment of the asphyxiating social tenor that fueled the raids. The public creation of the "Red Menace" by news agencies such as The *New York* and *Los Angeles Times* vilified the American Left and represented all those affiliated with American Bolshevism as insurrectionary pawns. This blanket strategy unfairly cast an un-American shadow over the entire progressive Left and opened the door to bigotry, discrimination, and ultimately, persecution. Although the incitement of proletarian revolution remained the modus operandi of the inchoate CP, in reality, "schoolboys playing cops and robbers [was] far closer to reality," noted Lyons.[98] The press, however, realized early on that Bolshevism in the headlines correlated with strong sales so the effort to keep communism in the news was exuded in earnest.

Printed on January 28, 1919 in the *Los Angeles Times,* "Bolshevism's Champion" issued a stern warning to Americans claiming that "Bolshevism is right here, right now, an American Menace."[99] Absent of a byline, the article succinctly outlined the Bolshevik threat while demonizing Russia in the process. According to the piece, Russia stood as a lawless breeding ground for heathens, a nation without moral standards, ethical guidelines, and religious underpinnings. The Bolsheviks "urge the repetition here of Russian conditions," proclaimed the *Times,* "where one takes what one wants, whether it is the contents of a store, another man's overcoat or his wife, or his life; and one with impunity may shoot anyone wearing a white collar."[100] Paranoid about the "Seattle strike," the *Times* looked to connect the episode to a growing Bolshevik presence on the west coast, noting that the act in Seattle simply foreshadowed what awaited California's port cities of Los Angeles and San Francisco. "The strike in Seattle is not an isolated act, but a symptom of international unrest, fomented everywhere by international Reds and the crowd of Russian murderers."[101] The article concluded by underscoring the "legitimacy" of the threat and the barbaric nature of global Bolshevism. Per the *Times,* Communism had arrived in America and unless addressed, its insidious ministers would undoubtedly succeed in provoking revolution. "International Bolshevism is now plotting to overthrow of the Government of the United States," asserted the *Times,* "The menace is real, the movement is being spread in this country by agitators, [we need to] make America safe for patriotic men and women."[102]

A "warning" regarding the coming raids appeared in the *New York Times* on June 19, 1919 in a piece titled "Flynn Prepares Big Haul Of Reds: Reign Of Terror Planned."[103] Blunt in its condemnation of American radicals, the article revealed that William J. Flynn, active Chief of the Bureau of Investigations, had become convinced that the June 2 bombings were perpetrated by an organized group of "terrorists" linked to the Communist Party. The article disclosed that Flynn and his bureau had begun to work closely with local police agencies throughout North America in an effort to flush out red insurgents. Flynn, according to the *Times,* patiently awaited the $2,000,000 requested by Palmer to "carry out its plans," plans designed to stop "this movement described as a revolution" which aimed to "use up and destroy the Government in one fell swoop."[104] Also featured in the article was the Attorney General himself who insisted that action would be taken against the extreme left and that Americans could expect major changes in radical circles from coast to coast. "We can and we will get a great deal of information," announced Palmer, "which will serve to prevent the perpetration of such crimes [such as the June 1919 bombing of his home] and I am as much interested in [that] as I am in the punishment of the perpetrators."[105] Punishment would certainly be forthcoming and in fact, in New York, it had already come.

"Unpreparedness In The War Against Radicalism" ran on November 23, 1919 in the *New York Times* alerting readers to the threat posed by "radical war," war "launched through the spread of seditious propaganda against the country's institutions."[106] Predicting a Bolshevik uprising, reporters Harris and Ewing insist that America lay unprepared for the revolution at hand. "The relaxed alertness of our citizens," states Harris and Ewing, made the nation susceptible to "immaculate and redeeming anarchy."[107] All American Bolsheviks, according to the article, must be "rounded up and deported" and all cases of Bolshevik propaganda should "be prosecuted by the Attorney General for their role in precipitating "insurrection against the authority of the United States."[108] The article closes by positing that "an emergency situation exists" and that the amount of attention allocated to the "Bolshevik crisis" by the federal government needs to be aggrandized in the interest of "meeting the drive of the radicals."[109]

Coverage of the famous "Soviet Ark" sailing in December of 1919 served as the final portend of the coming Palmer crusade. As the *New York Times* reported, on December 21, 1919, 300 of the most "influential" communists and socialists in America, including Emma Goldman and Alexander Berkman, set sail for Russia on the "Mississippi," a run down vessel formerly used in the Spanish-American war.[110] Shipping this load of "Reds" East helped to thin the expanding radical population of Ellis Island, serving in late 1919 and 1920 as a detainment camp for reds hunted down by Lusk and Palmer. It was also a means of ridding the United States of some of the country's most feared "anarchists," such as Goldman and Berkman, who had participated in promoting revolution for years prior to their respective "apprehensions." Palmer proved unsatisfied, however, with the paltry number of seditionists on board and promised that Americans would soon be "treated to a second, third, and fourth Soviet Ark sailing down the beautiful harbor in the future."[111] Strong words which signified his strong commitment to his cause.

Palmer's determined language reflected a burgeoning sense of confidence within the Attorney General. With the media as his ally, by March of 1920, Palmer had successfully arrested over 4,000 of the nation's most prominent radicals and stood poised to extend his campaign into the innermost realm of America's extreme left. "This is the government of the people," a resolute Palmer proclaimed in February 1920, "We can give those Reds assurance that it is powerful enough to protect itself from any threat of overthrow."[112] Palmer's steadfastness manifested itself in his words as he assured the American people that the raid of the left would continue until the anarchist threat had been completely vanquished. "There will be no abatement in the Government's effort to handle these people properly," Palmer announced, "It must be made a crime to threaten destruction. When [a radical] goes beyond the lips and teaches the overthrow of all political governments there must be a law to fit his case."[113]

Free speech, according to the Attorney General, did not apply to those preaching anarchy. As far as Palmer was concerned, those advocating violent usurpation of American democracy were not deserving of First

Amendment privileges. "The right of free speech is not the right of unbridled speech without responsibility," stated Palmer, "There is a deadline when a man promises, implies, or threatens the use of violence to overthrow the government of his country."[114] In the spring of 1920, Palmer called for the "enactment of a federal statute" in order to provide the government with the power to detain any citizen charged with fostering physical revolution. Such a law would silence the "Red radicals, the greatest menace to our country."[115] Criminalizing seditious language would also facilitate Palmer's quest to jettison the alien element in American society. Deportation was Palmer's greatest weapon for it allowed the Attorney General to "circumvent the normal legal procedures."[116] With his campaign shrouded in a cloud of brutality and with the left hammering away at the undemocratic character of his investigation, Palmer sought the most efficient means of exercising his agenda. Deportation provided Palmer with a trump card that he used to wreak havoc on presumed radicals from coast to coast.

Boston, New York, Chicago, Los Angeles, and Detroit all felt the wrath of Palmer's crusade. It was a nationwide campaign that dealt the left a blow that it arguably never fully recovered from. Although there had been many individual battles in the war against extremism, it was Palmer's effort that perhaps served as the most decisive. For Palmer, his efforts successfully "halted the advance of radicalism in the United States" and initiated what William Flynn described as "the beginning of the end of organized revolutionaries in this country."[117] The "Red Scare," as far as Palmer and a majority of Americans were concerned, had been realized yet subdued by a determined coalition of "patriots." As for the left, any and all dreams of creating what many believed to be a more equitable, "better society" had been all but dashed. For the country at large, the memory of the event became a permanent part of the nation's identity as the first battle in what eventually would become a "Cold War" against internal bolshevism had been waged.

The "Palmer Raids" had a dramatic effect on the on both communist and socialist bands of the American Left. The Socialists had already been fragmented by the communist split and lacked numbers, resources, and leadership. Its leading figure, Eugene Debs, had been sentenced to 10 years in prison for violation of the Espionage Act and waited out the Red Scare in an Atlanta penitentiary. Other prominent socialists, like Earl Browder, William Z. Foster (both of whom would serve as CP heads), and James Cannon shifted allegiance to the Communist Party. Needless to say, the scare of 1920 placed a preverbal nail in the socialist coffin and left the party struggling to stay afloat. The scare had a similar effect on the Communist Party, which had morphed into a monolith in the immediate aftermath of the raids. Boasting a total membership of close to seventy-thousand prior to the purge of 1919–1920, the unified party hovered around ten-thousand in the immediate aftermath.

What remained of the Communist Party following the Palmer raids was a loose organization comprised of mainly foreign speakers plagued by a lack of direction. In the absence of both numbers and stable leadership, the party faced complete liquidation. The party's reliance on second hand information from communist publications (such as the *Novy Mir*) was symptomatic of a lack of assistance from abroad. Lenin had his own nation to build and American Communists, although important, were not the priority in 1920. Additionally, all thoughts of revolution were abrogated as a quest for stabilization began in earnest. In fact, according to Lyons, any thought of revolution, especially in the aftermath of the scare, was pure "lunacy" on the party's behalf, "lunacy that marked the inception of American Bolshevism and that was to remain a constant in a career wherein nearly everything else was variable."[118] Nevertheless, despite its endangered state, Communism was consistently featured in the media as a revolutionary force. Its revolutionary message propagated, its leaders demonized, and its affiliates castigated. News of the American Communist Party filled newspapers throughout the scare period, news that contributed to the cultivation of a deep seeded hatred of the organization and its platforms among the American populace. For a nation in need of peacetime nationalism, the Red Scare proved just the ticket. For a government looking to expand its influence over the American populace, Reds were not simply a menace, but a means.

Perhaps equal in importance to the loss of party population was the fact that the raids forced the Communist Party underground. Having fought its illegal status throughout the raids, party heads, including Ruthenberg, accepted a subterranean existence in the face of growing opposition. This development would plague the party throughout the course of the next five decades as its refusal to conduct itself openly rendered it vulnerable to "subversive" accusations. "There was no other choice but to go underground," observed Irving Howe, "the justice department harassed them, kept them off balance, frightened away potential members, prosecuted leaders, and kept a close check on those who remained."[119] Also hindering the party was its loss of many moderate communists, or communists with a "small c" that maintained the political and social equilibrium of the party. Hard liners now dominated the party ranks which only increased the factionalized state of the CP and contributed to growing strife among remaining members. Among the departing moderates were many of the prized native recruits who had provided the Communist Party with an American flavor.

Left predominantly "foreign," the party would struggle to Americanize and in turn, deflect looming questions regarding its identity.

The 1920's proved to be a mixed bag for the flagging American Communist Party. In the American mainstream, a thriving manufacturing sector propelled a robust national economy. High style ruled the day, skyscrapers the air, and automobiles the streets as America glistened in a decade that has come to be known as the "roaring twenties." Not all, however, enjoyed the fruits of the economic upswing. There existed a societal substrata where everyday workers continued to flounder in unsanitary, low wage positions. A technological infusion in the workplace created a more efficient means of production but it also eliminated many menial positions occupied by members of America's economic underworld. America's affluence was uneven," writes historian James G. Ryan, "depressed industries abounded. Workers in brewing, textiles, coal, and needle trades faced desperation."[120] The growth of elitism and the carefree attitude employers had towards their employees combined with a rise in the poverty level among the immigrant and uneducated classes of society created a recruiting pool for the Communist Party.

Operating underground, however, made it difficult for the Communist Party to lure new members to its ranks. Social changes in America also hindered the party's effort to grow. The rise of the Ku Klux Klan in the Midwest and South symbolized a growth in conservative xenophobia. With the "Red Scare" prominent in the minds of many, an organization dedicated to Western European Aryanism and the preservation of a solidly Anglo-America attracted many. Vehemently anti-immigrant, especially the Eastern European variety, the Klan provided an outlet for many looking to preserve the protestant status quo while keeping America free of radical contamination. A rise in anti-Semitism also began to pervade America in the early 1920's which factored into the emergence of ultra-conservatism. With radicalism seen as a primarily an Eastern European product, many began to attribute a growth in subversive activity to an increase in the number of Jews arriving on American shores. Car mogul Henry Ford's open abhorrence of Jews only intensified growing anti-Semitic animosity. The country's innovative leader in automobile manufacturing held tremendous popular clout making his anti-Semitic attitude all the more influential. "Prejudice became as pervasive as the air," recognized Frederick Lewis Allen, "It was in such an atmosphere that the Ku Klux Klan blossomed into power."[121]

The AFL's persistent anti-Bolshevik policy, maintained by its outspoken leader Samuel Gompers, also compounded matters for the Communist Party. The American Federation of Labor's commitment to a workplace free of "radical" activity combined with its generally conservative leadership base provided the organization with ample incentive to harass the Communist Party. Bolshevism, according to Gompers, "is as great an attempt to disrupt the trade unions as it is to overturn the government of the United States."[122] Gomper's attitude infected the labor milieu with a strong case of anti-Communism which effectively contributed the growing woes of the Communist Party. With Lenin calling, in 1920, for the underground American Communist Party to infiltrate the labor sphere, the American Federation of Labor's strong anti-Communist position rendered such an endeavor monumentally arduous. Gompers looked to groom "American workers" with "unflinching support of democracy" and guaranteed that the "menace" would be defeated because of the "Americanism of the American Federation of Labor."[123] Suffice to say, Gomper's stand severely handicapped CP recruiting efforts.

Changes in modes of behavior also contributed to amplified conservativism. Accompanying the twenties was a degree of "joie de vivre" unseen before in American history. The proliferation of the automobile meant a newfound freedom that Americans exercised with zealous flair. Smoking became en vogue among Americans of all ages and genders as tobacco giants promoted their product as a symbol of style and sophistication. Women began to test the limits of what had been previously considered proper or acceptable. Skirts inched their way up the leg, "flapper" style came into fashion, and the use of cosmetics all pointed to the emergence of "the modern woman" (a development that many correlated with a rise in promiscuity). "None of the Victorian mothers-and most of the mothers were Victorian-had any idea how casually their daughters were accustomed to being kissed" revealed F. Scott Fitzgerald in his eye-opening work *This Side of Paradise* (1920).[124] Such developments, including a rise in mob-type activity stemming from prohibition, caused shudder down the national spine," wrote Allen, "It was incredible. It was abominable."[125] With the country becoming ever more socially liberal, conservatives looked to discern the catalyst for such change. Many pointed to the American Left, specifically the Communist Party, which heightened surveillance of the organization and forced it even further into the abyss.

All the while, the Communist Party continued to flounder in relative obscurity. Despite ample recruiting pools, the party had begun to dissolve. On April 7, 1923, the CP all but disappeared as the legal "Workers Party" became in all but name the official organ of Bolshevism in the United States. Ruthenberg had proven unable to unify the Communist left and despite the emergence of would be leaders William Z. Foster and Earl Browder, the party remained on shaky footing and required a change in direction. New Soviet Premier Joseph Stalin's tightening of the communist screws in Russia also greatly impacted the course of the American Party. Stalin, who had accepted the Soviet reigns following Lenin's 1924 death, abandoned his "mentor's" part-capitalist New Economic Policy and centered in on an authoritarian social policy and a command economy. "The process of Stalinization within the American Party began considerably earlier than some historians suggest," observed Howe, "by 1923 it was already in full swing and by 1925, had reached a climax."[126]

Stalin's reforms, which alienated many instrumental in the October Revolution, namely his central rival Leon Trotsky, created a tight oligarchy in Russia. The state became an all powerful organ controlled by Stalin and selected veteran Bolsheviks in conjunction with a newly emerged agricultural elite. Isolated due to Lenin's failed prediction of a global worker revolution, Stalin looked to go it alone as a "communist" monolith, "socialism in one state," a decision, grounded in a departure from Marxism, that required immediate political and economic reform. Concomitant to reform was the initiation of a "great purge" of all those whom he deemed a threat to his agenda. Millions of Russians, including many former "vanguard" Bolsheviks, would suffer as Stalin filled the Gulags with political prisoners, making space when needed via execution. It was a brutal policy but one he certainly justified by turning to Lenin. The father of Russian Bolshevism had, after all, advocated the use of unmitigated force in order to maintain Bolshevik power. Stalin, however, proved even more extreme than his predecessor and his Machiavellian tendencies signaled not only a betrayal of Marx, but arguably caused more grief for Soviet Russia than gain.

Stalin's emergence in Soviet Russia created a stir within American communist circles. His actions arguably "awoke" the American Party from its post-raid slumber prompting members of the party's extreme wings to vie for controlling supremacy. Operating under the aegis of the Workers Party, the Communist Party, by 1925, had split into two rival factions and remained bitterly divided along ideological lines. Ruthenburg headed the more intellectual band of the party with the help of Jay Lovestone, a committed Marxist and adept leader known for his cerebral prowess. William Z. Foster, a product of Philadelphia poverty and labor leader extraordinaire surfaced as the head of the labor-oriented division. Yet in spite of the split, one thing remained a constant: the attempt on behalf of both factions to win the favor of the Soviet Union. "Perhaps because few American Communists could help regarding themselves as poor cousins at the outer edge of the Comintern feast," wrote Howe, "almost every American faction fawned and maneuvered for Russian favor." [127] The dispute was finally settled in 1925 during the party's Fourth Convention in Chicago.

The incendiary atmosphere of the 1925 Chicago convention reflected the inner party strife that defined the Communist Party throughout the 1920's. Looking for recognition and a more visible position within the American Left, the party sought respectability and longed for the opportunity to be recognized as America's primary socialist conduit. The first step in this process revolved around receiving word from Russia as to which faction, Ruthenberg's or Foster's, had earned the right to govern the Workers Communist Party. Although both groups had been jockeying for Soviet favor, Ruthenberg had been more faithful to the original Soviet plan than Foster. Lenin had called for an "American" party and that is what Ruthenberg had set out to accomplish. Foster remained more closely aligned with the party's strong foreign delegation which endeared him to the labor community but cost him the intellectual support that Ruthenberg enjoyed.

In the end, the Soviet's rewarded Ruthenberg's "loyalty to the decisions of the Communist international" by declaring him the undisputed leader of the Worker's Party.[128] Foster, who had held the position of party chair, had his position eradicated in order to make way for the new "post general secretary" of the party, Ruthenberg. Shortly after accepting the reigns of the Communist Party, Ruthenberg announced the birth of a new constitution, one that positioned the American Communist Party at the forefront of the Communist movement in the United States. The Communist Party and the Worker's Party were one, officially affiliated with the Comintern. The American CP now equaled "The American Section of the Communist International," a victorious Ruthenberg proclaimed.[129] Amazingly, Ruthenberg's confident proclamation did not equal an end to party factionalism. The feud continued for close to four more years with Foster eventually surfacing, following the 1927 death of Ruthenberg, as the face of the rejuvenated, post-depression American Communist Party.

Although the party continued to struggle under the weight of internal dispute, the decision to move the central office from Chicago to New York in 1927 provided the party with a degree of stability. New York was America's radical epicenter and it only made sense to conduct operations out of the big apple. The move, however, did not temper friction within the party. The polemical Foster quickly found himself up against Jay Lovestone in a battle for party control. Lovestone, a representative of Ruthenberg's intellectual contingent, advocated a more moderate line with an American emphasis while Foster remained immutably dedicated to Stalin. The pivotal moment in this dispute came in 1928 with Stalin's announcement of the "Third Period Communism," a post-1925 "period" where, according to the premier, capitalism would fall and the workers of the world would take the initiative in precipitating global unrest. The "report" also called for a unified effort to combat "social fascism" and signaled the initiation of the infamous five-year plan, a mad drive to modernize completed at the expense of the working Russian. With the American Party still struggling to "Americanize," Stalin's sectarian shift in direction dealt a blow to the WCP.

This development also marked the begging of the end for Lovestone, who found himself in trouble after publicly arguing that "communist statements abut the decadence of capitalism and the imminence of world revolution did not apply to the United States."[130] Many interpreted such an "arrogant" statement as a sign that Lovestone thought himself "the equal of Stalin."[131] His challenge placed the party secretary in a precarious position and he initiated a purge of center-line Trotskyists as a diversionary tactic. Meanwhile, Foster's clan pounced on the opportunity to reaffirm their Stalinist stance and gained immediate Soviet favor in the process. Foster capitalized on Lovestone's "imperiousness" to once again catapult himself to the forefront of the organization. Within months, Lovestone had lost his following and was forced, in desperation, to start a separate party which he named the Communist Party of the United States (CPUSA). This group, however, never got off the ground. This ultimately jettisoned Lovestone from the American communist movement and opened the door for Foster. In 1929, the Worker's Communist Party officially became the American CP under Foster as things began to look up for the organization for the first time since the aftermath of the Bolshevik revolution.

A sign that matters were improving for the American Communist Party came with the 1928 presidential election. The Communist ticket of Foster and Benjamin Gitlow earned over 48,000 votes in the 34 states where the party appeared on the ballot.[132] Although the numbers were miniscule, the vote count illustrated the growing "popularity" of the Communist Party. Finally somewhat stabilized, the party had begun to make inroads, gains that would increase exponentially with the coming of the New Deal. One of the areas where the CP had made significant headway was in the arts. There existed a strong "radical" contingent within New York's theatre milieu and the party viewed the entertainment sector as a potential recruiting base. Many involved with the creation and production of plays in New York had ties to the city's large Eastern European immigrant community, of which several million were of Jewish descent. As Jews comprised a good majority of the Communist Party, it was only natural that many progressive Jewish playwrights, producers, and actors gravitated towards the CP.

Young Jewish intellectuals such as Elia Kazan and Albert Maltz joined a growing leftist movement in New York City that sympathized with the Communist cause. "Many writers welcomed the notion that by writing under Marxist cultural doctrine they were producing a superior product," observed historian Kenneth Lloyd Billingsly, "whatever the quality of dramaturgy, plays written from this vision found an eager audience in the 1930's."[133] For many of these "parlor reds," however, communism was an instrument for cultural and economic change in a democratic, not a revolutionary sense. Change was needed and the CP, or in the case of young adults like Kazan and Maltz in the early 1930's, the The Young Communist Party (YCP) offered a vehicle for that. "What so strongly drove them leftward was their sense that American society was adrift," recognized Howe in commenting on the allure that the Young Communist Party had for the country's young intellectuals, "that no large moral purpose animated the world of business and of work, that the *idea* of social crackup had become the common possession of millions of people who did not think of themselves as radicals."[134] As Eugene Lyons has pointed out, for many in the artistic and educational or intellectual communities, "it was enough to "accept" communism or to "approach" the Marxian ideology, or to simply join up with a John Reed Club, Theatre of Action, The Red Dancers (all "front" groups), or some other Proletcult catchall."[135]

The crash of 1929 provided another boost to the Communist Party. Although one of the darkest days in American history, "black Tuesday" came with a silver lining for the Communist Party. Stalin's "prediction" of the fall of capitalism had come to fruition and millions of Americans roamed the streets penniless as a result. Needless to say, people became increasingly curious about the Communist Party and enrollment numbers began to grow. Boosting numbers were thousands of "pinks," communists with a "small c" or moderate communist who became attracted to the party based on its "ground up" vision and commitment to the working men and women of America. Many of these individuals, whether intellectual "parlor reds" such as Kazan and Maltz or blue collar "moderate reds" frustrated with the lack of quality in their lives, were not nearly as interested in militancy as they were in finding respite from the abominable conditions of the early 1930's. "In city after city," commented Howe, "party led committees organized demonstrations and marches upon city halls to demand adequate relief and to urge passage of unemployment legislation. From the Communist point of view, these demonstrations came at exactly the right time."[136] Although recruiting the unemployed eventually proved to be difficult, the Communist Party did tap this potential membership base, albeit slowly. Intellectuals came at a greater rate as the fear of fascism abroad, on the move in Germany in 1930, attracted individuals to the American Party's call for an effort against "social fascism" (an ambiguous term but one grounded in the theory that the ills of social democracy paved the way for the emergence of the dreaded ideology). Observed by historian William E. Leuchtenburg, "Impressed by the zeal of the Communists, convinced that the Soviet Union was a bullwork against Hitler, finding in the cause a kind of personal salvation, some intellectuals joined the party or parroted the party line."[137] Many of these curious intellectuals would soon be labeled "Fellow Travelers," a label attached to individuals sympathetic to the party's social cause but uninterested or unwilling to formally join the Communist Party.

Despite the "gains," however, the party remained rather insignificant within the scope of American politics in the early 1930's. "What is really impressive," notes Leuchtenburg, "is how little allegiance the communists won at a time when conditions could not have been more propitious."[138] It would not be until the mid 1930's, with Earl Browder spearheading a program "de-emphasizing revolutionary dogma" and purported to represent "twentieth-century Americanism" that the party would begin to see its influence spread.[139] With the shift, many "New Dealers" would latch on to the party and augment its numbers significantly. In the meantime, Foster continued to advocate a sectarian line which limited its appeal. It also made the party vulnerable to attack from the right as a second campaign against the radical left loomed just around the corner. Nevertheless, it had come along way from its "schism" years of the 1920's and had seemingly recovered from the nation's first "red scare."

Large cities continued to serve as radical centers as the party stretched its appeal from New York to Los Angeles. In fact, a growing interest in the communist platform could be seen within the sights and sounds of Hollywood. The "west coast center of progressivism" served as home to many who had been introduced to "radicalism" while schooling in New York.[140] With the transition from theatre to cinema in full swing in the early 1930's, several of New York's most talented and progressive artists, such as Kazan and Maltz, had ventured to tinsel town to try their hand at film. The progressive base created a window of opportunity for the Communist Party, an opportunity that the party was certain not to pass up.

In general, the evolution of the Communist Party from its early days as an organ of bolshevism to its emergence as a vehicle for the acceleration of the New Deal could be summarized as rocky at best. Its lack of solid leadership and its constant infighting would slow party growth throughout the course of its existence. Its ultimate Achilles heal, however, would always be the threat that the party posed to the status quo. Conservative America, as seen through the 1919–1920 "red scare," saw the party as an organ of sedition and remained dedicated to its downfall for over fifty years. With the help of a media machine designed to vilify progressivism, the right painted a picture of the extreme left that was not always consistent with the ideals and views harbored by many so called American "radicals." As the party grew, hundreds of differing sects evolved, many operating independently from the central band in New York and possessing agendas that would barely be considered progressive by modern standards. The Hollywood Party was one of these "satellite" organizations replete with cultural, not revolutionary progressives. The government, however, lumped the communist left under one prodigiously subversive label and prosecuted a nationwide campaign that left thousands stigmatized as un-American stranded in a nation that no longer resembled home. As illustrated by its disorganized state, its minute and primarily culturally progressive membership, and its lack of direction, the American Communist Party never posed a legitimate threat to the nation's security. Yet to Martin Dies and the anti-Communist coalition of the 1930's, the party constituted the vanguard of second American Revolution, a revolution "painted red" without the white and blue.

Chapter Three
Painting Them Red: Periodicals and the Proliferation of American Anti-Communism 1935–1950

In the mid-1930s Martin Dies, a conservative, New Deal bashing congress-man from Texas established a congressional committee designed in part to determine the scope and influence of the Communist Party of the United Sates. Coined the Dies Committee, this band of xenophobic congressman embarked on a campaign to identify the presence of "subversive" activity within the United States and targeted both right wing extremists and left wing progressives. In the late 1930s, Dies directed his attention west and pinpointed the film industry as an epicenter of "red" activity. His initial investigation of Hollywood, eventually continued by his protégé and suc-cessor J. Parnell Thomas (under the moniker the House Committee on Un-American Activities or HUAC), marked the unofficial beginning of arguably the greatest domestic purge in American history.

The success of the Dies Committee, and eventually the Thomas Committee, created a window of opportunity for demagogues such as Joseph McCar-thy who capitalized on the contentious climate and rose to fame. Preaching the imminent downfall of the nation, McCarthy cultivated an atmosphere defined by fear and paranoia by advancing the theory that a "red" revolu-tion had been commenced within. Why the majority of the nation so will-ingly accepted such a premise stands as the subject of this chapter. With the cooperation of some of America's most circulated magazines, the "red scare" was successfully propagated allowing the Un-American Activities Committee and eventually Senator McCarthy to paralyze the nation and ruin the careers of so many unsuspecting Americans. A thorough analysis of the anti-Communist commentary contained in popular American news-papers and magazines from 1935 to 1950 demonstrates that the repressive social tenor established in the pre and immediate post war years "painted" many targeted individuals "red" and prevented them from avoiding the stigma of traitor.

Prior to the evolution of popular magazines as the key propaganda medium in the anti-Communist movement, several of America's most influential congressmen launched a campaign to establish an official anti-"subversive" federal organ. Tabbed the "father of the Committee" by Un-American Activities Committee historian Walter Goodman, Samuel Dickstein, a Jewish member of the House of Representatives from 1923–1944, embarked on a mission in the early 1930's to form a special congressional committee specifically designed to investigate "seditious" or "subversive" activity within America. Unlike many of his more famous successors, Dickstein saw fascism, not communism, as the most glaring threat to American democracy in the 1930's.

A native New Yorker, Dickstein had grown weary of the anti-Semitic German Teutonic Association's growing presence in and around his principally immigrant district of New York City. It was only natural for Dickstein, a Jew serving a largely Jewish district, to perceive an increase in home grown anti-Semitism as an ominous development. "Nazi's were on the march in Europe," writes historian Walter Goodman in reference to the growing presence of American fascism, "and at home, Nazi sympathizers were openly rallying, goose stepping, and reviling Jews." [1] As the taunting and the tension between Jews and, by 1934, members of the renamed German-American Bund, intensified, Dickstein took it upon himself to call federal attention to the matter. Dickstein hoped to bring the Bund before Congress and address the potentially explosive situation before his neighborhood became an American-version of late 1930's Berlin. With the formation of the Committee of Rules in 1930, Dickstein's advance on un-Americanism officially commenced.

Ironically, Dickstein's lead in the assault against un-Americanism was actually overshadowed by a blue blooded congressman from his own state. Hamilton Fish III, a New York Republican, had made a name for himself in Washington as an enemy of immigration. With the depression in full swing in 1930, the "threat" that immigration posed to unemployed Americans served as a rallying point for Fish. A man who would later be linked to German Bundists, Fish suggested that the United States "deport every single alien Communist" as a mean of opening up jobs for those out of work.[2] Although eventually presented by Representative Bertrand Snell of New York on May 12, 1930, House Resolution 220, which called for an investigation of Communist agitprop, was the work of Fish. "It is not the purpose of this resolution to interfere with any group except Communists in the United States," proclaimed Fish, "and we propose to deport all alien Communists."[3] Despite the fact that Fish's resolution was defeated 210 to 18 in the House, his outspokenness earned him a position at the head of the

Rules Committee, providing him with the congressional authority necessary to wage an effective purge of the American Communist Party.[4]

With his fiery rhetoric and aristocratic flair, Fish effectively channeled growing anti-American anxiety on Capitol Hill into a drive designed primarily to target his choice adversary, communism, while simultaneously diverting attention away from the potential threat posed by the Teutonic Fellowship or the German Bund. Although the Bund would remain a priority for the Committee, it took a back seat to American communism which Fish and others successfully labeled the preeminent threat to American security. Fish stood determined, according to Goodman, "to send all the Reds back to where they came from."[5] The Fish Committee, however, proved to be relatively ineffective. Despite having interrogated a number of "high ranking" Communist officials, including Communist Party of the United States of America head William Z. Foster, the Committee was unable produce any evidence warranting immediate action. Fish recommended that the use of mail be denied to Communists and that a special division within the Bureau of Investigation be established to investigate seditious activity. Yet despite his anticommunist zeal, Fish remained, as observed by historian Kenneth O'Reilly, ultimately unconvincing. Although they may have appealed to those infected with burgeoning xenophobia, "none of the Fish Committee proposals were enacted" confirmed O'Reilly. [6]

Fish's initial attempt to thwart communism may have ended in failure, but he succeeded in creating a buzz around Washington regarding "subversion" and the threat that groups such as the Communist Party of the United States of America posed to the security of the nation. "The Committee considered that the surest way of combating communism in the United States," observes historian August Raymond Ogden, "was to give the fullest possible publicity to the fundamental principles and aims of the Communists."[7] As a result, the Fish Committee was not a total loss. Not only did its establishment mark Congress' first battle in a long war with domestic Communism, it sewed the seeds for a more thorough congressional investigation of "subversive" activity by sparking interest upon Capitol Hill. Fish also introduced the infamous blanket labeling strategy which included a cache of erroneous stereotypes that Congress would use and expand over the next thirty years. In fact, it was Fish's "definition" of Communism, one that claimed Communists favored "the abolition of all religion, the destruction of private property, absolute racial equality, the use of strikes to spark riots, the destruction of democratic government, world revolution to establish proletariat dictatorships, and the use of hatred to achieve these ends," that was picked up and used by both the Dies and the Thomas Committees in the succeeding years. This definition also served a convenient purpose for magazines looking to profit off of anticommunist hysteria.[8] The more menacing the better as far as several of America's most popular periodicals were concerned.

Dickstein, the original visionary, became somewhat lost in the hysteria conjured up by Fish. Left without much of an alternative, he came out in support of Fish and allied himself with a young, brash Texan named Martin Dies who had emerged, in 1932, as the most outspoken proponent of Fish and his anti-Communist platform. A product of East Texas, Dies traced his roots back to the Confederacy and typified the old southern style.[9] Dies, according to journalist and author Ted Morgan, "was as Southern as Spanish moss."[10] With his slicked back blond hair and deep drawl, Dies readily displayed an "Aryan" arrogance and firmly believed in the subjugation of the black-American. A man who wore his racist attitude on his sleeve, Dies had once proclaimed that "[white] supremacy in the South is secure and unshakable as the eternal hills."[11]

Dies hailed from a political family. In 1909, Texas elected his father to the U.S. House of Representatives where he served his state for over twenty years. A strict segregationalist, Martin Dies Sr. kept company with fellow Dixiecrats while in Washington and developed strong political and social ties, most of which were grounded in a "hatred of the eastern establishment."[12] Martin Jr. often attributed a portion of his "success" to the political inroads carved by his father while a congressmen in Washington D.C.. "The presence of many of his loyal friends in this hall evokes the memory of his life," announced the younger Dies during his first speech in the House in 1931, "my father was a true son of East Texas who served his people during one of the greatest crises that ever faced the nation."[13] A relationship of particular importance involved fellow Texan John Nance Garner, the only democratic Representative in the house "at the begging of the congressional careers of both father and son."[14] Garner, who began his career a year after Martin Sr. in 1903, served for thirty years as a congressman before becoming Franklin D. Roosevelt's vice president in 1932 (his reward for clinching Texas, and the election, for the president). It was Garner's position as Speaker of the House in 1931, however, a title that he held prior to ascending to the Vice Presidency, that benefited the newly minted congressmen Martin Dies Jr. Dies' relationship to Garner provided him with immediate political capital, clout that he used to position himself on numerous congressional committees. One of those committees happened to be the Rules Committee, formerly the Fish Committee, now, by 1932, back under the guidance of Samuel Dickstein.

Dickstein perceived Dies to be a potential ally in his effort to combat subversion. Dies, who carried himself like a veteran on Capitol Hill despite his inexperience, did not disappoint. One of his first acts as a congressman was to introduce an anti-sedition bill. Warning of the dangers that communism presented, Dies proclaimed in a 1932 speech that "an industrial and financial feudalism has arisen in the United States that threatens to nullify the ideas of the founders of this republic."[15] It was Dickstein, however, not Dies, that actively promoted the bill despite its anticommunist, not fascist, orientation. Anything that might eventually be used to target the Bund interested Dickstein and his enthusiasm for Dies' bill points to his desire to gain congressional backing in his attack of fascism.

Although the Dies bill stalled in Congress, the fury of attention allocated to "subversion" in the early 1930s brought with it a burgeoning concern over anti-Americanism that permeated Washington and created quite a story for popular news agencies. By the mid-1930's, such heightened anxiety over the specter of "subversion" accelerated Washington's effort to mount an offensive against "Stalin's agents who can be depended upon to follow his instructions at little or no hazard to themselves."[16] In 1934, Congress finally placated Dickstein and approved the creation of a committee intended to investigate "Nazi activities and other forms of subversive propaganda."[17] For Dickstein, this was the license he had long sought to investigate the ever-expanding German Bund organization. It did not come off without a hitch, however. For starters, Dickstein was not named chair of the Committee. Notwithstanding his efforts to create such an investigative body, he was passed over in favor of Massachusetts Congressmen John McCormack, a decision that Dickstein attributed to anti-Semitism.[18] Secondly, despite the fact that it was unanimously sanctioned by Congress, there were a few representatives who contended that it was unjustly designed to harass German Americans. One of the outspoken congressmen was none other than Hamilton Fish, who claimed, according to Goodman, "that the whole thing was a scheme by Jews to offend German-Americans like those in his state [New York] who admired the Fuhrer (Adolph Hitler)."[19] Fish, however, eventually came to support the establishment of the committee, realizing that sanctioning the investigation of "other forms of subversive propaganda" placed a spotlight directly on American Communism.

Clearly, when weighing the "dangers" posed by fascism and communism to American security in the mid 1930's, the former stood as a more salient, potentially destructive threat. By 1933, in place of the Teutonic Association emerged "The Friends of the New Germany," a more militant, fanatical version of the TA committed to promoting the ideals embodied by the Third Reich. Renamed the German-American Bund in 1934, the fascist society became one of the most pervasive organizations in the United States.

Under the direction of ex-ford mechanic Fritz Kuhn, the Bund actively promoted its agenda nationwide and grew in strength and popularity as the 30's marched on.

An educated man and brother of a Nazi Supreme Court Judge, Kuhn rose from his job at Ford to the pinnacle of the most subversive organization in America by 1936. Kuhn, who greatly admired Henry Ford, cultivated his racist intuitions while employed at Ford's Detroit factory. Observed by historian Charles Higham, Kuhn's "anti-Semitic, anti-Communistic position found its perfect place in the Ford empire."[20] Once named "American Fuhrer" at a 1936 ceremony in Buffalo, Kuhn began to establish Bund offices throughout the country to be used as propaganda plants and recruiting factories. An organization "bent upon wholesale subversion, subordination, and the collapse of the U.S. democratic system from within," the Bund, under the leadership of Kuhn, surfaced as the foremost "menace" to American democracy by 1938.[21] With its massive propagation of the Swastika, devotion to racial purity, and establishment of youth camps, the Bund appealed to a wide range of German-Americans, many of whom were too young to comprehend the totalitarian nature of Nazi fascism. "The uniform, the marching, the emphasis on physical fitness, and the opportunity to meet nubile girls," writes Higham, "encouraged membership and inflated the budding male ego."[22] Not restricted solely to Germans, the Bund reached out and recruited "anyone who was of Aryan stock free of Black or Jewish blood" augmenting their numbers to levels that far exceeded those of the CPUSA.[23] According to Higham, by 1938, there were roughly 100,000 Bund members and sympathizers, a figure that raised the eyebrows of concerned citizens and congressmen alike.

It had always been the objective of Dickstein to target Nazi sympathizers within the U.S., With the formation of the 1934 McCormack-Dickstein committee, he thought he had been presented with that chance. Dickstein learned rather quickly, however, that a lack of enthusiasm for tracking Nazi's prevailed among many members of Congress. Ironically, Dickstein found himself routinely on the defensive, forced to confront anti-Semitic flavored charges that he had it out for German Americans. At the final Committee meeting staged in New York in 1935, Dickstein, according to Goodman, felt the wrath of a large congregation of German Americans who "packed the committee room" and reigned disorder down on the proceedings with "Nazi salutes and chants of Heil Hitler!"[24]

The "subversive" organization of choice for most in Congress was communism. By the end of the decade, Martin Dies has supplanted both Dickstein and Fish as the engineer of the un-American crusade and it was his predilection to concentrate on communism rather than Fascism. Dies' choice of direction proved historical as it dictated the path that un-American activities committees would take for the next thirty years. It also set the stage for the emergence of vehement anti-communism and established the repressive tenor that facilitated the rise of demagogues such a J. Parnell Thomas, John Rankin, and eventually Joseph McCarthy, to power. With his ascension to the helm of a committee designed to investigate "subversive and un-American propaganda" in May of 1938 Dies, as acknowledged by Ogden, "embarked on a legislative career opposed to subversive influences which was ultimately to win him nationwide fame and the chairmanship of the most important committee [The House Committee on Un-American Activities] ever created to investigate such activities."[25]

Before declaring all out war on communism, however, Dies gestured to appease the dwindling anti-fascist contingent in Congress. At the "trial" of Fritz Kuhn before his Committee in 1939, it was clear to all those who witnessed the hearing that the chair of the Committee was less than enthusiastic about executing the proceedings. "Dies seemed not to see a significant difference between communism and Nazism," writes Higham, "socialism and national socialism."[26] The fact that Dies actually put forth the effort and energy to bring the Bund to trial actually came as a surprise, especially to those on the Left who had begun to feel Dies' wrath as early as 1932. "Dies often charged ahead blindly when probing the Left," notes O'Reilly, "but they [he and FBI Director J. Edgar Hoover] were considerably more circumspect when probing the other end of the political spectrum."[27] Dies himself made it a point to publicly state that his Committee was not intended "to target any one race, especially German-Americans."[28] He instead directed his furor at American Communists, asserting that "Communism is nothing more nor less than organized treason, and we not only tolerate, but legalize an organization made up of thousands of traitorous minded people."[29] Dies uninspired "investigation" of Nazism was simply a front, his means of throwing a proverbial bone to anti-Fascists such as Dickstein. In reality, as O'Reilly confirms, "many native Fascists and other anti-Semites supported Dies despite its occasional forays into their affairs."[30] Not surprisingly, Dickstein was kept off of the Dies Committee. Apparently his zealous anti-Fascism, although well justified, prevented him, in the eyes of Congress, from being impartial. Allowed to operate in the absence dedicated anti-Fascists such as Dickstein, the Dies Committee "ignored American Nazism and became the sounding board for charges against Communist infiltration."[31] Unfortunately for progressive Americans, Dies' attitude towards "subversion" would be the prevailing one throughout the course of the un-American purge (1932–1965).[32]

Dies' apathy toward fascism and fervor for communism would come to both symbolize the un-American campaign and define the men charged with leading it. His book, *The Trojan Horse in America,* ghost written by his chief investigator, J.B. Matthews, a former Communist turned "patriot," is dominated by discussion of communism and its evils. Although it touches on the fascist threat to America, it is primarily devoted to demonizing American Communists and successfully blurs the line between the two ideologies. A comparison that is completely unjustified, especially given the humanitarian nature of many who belonged to the CPUSA, Dies routinely refers to communism and fascism in the same breath, speaking as if one mirrored the other. "Communism and Nazism are possessed by the same demon of hate," observed Dies, "which sets class against race."[33]

Evident in an article published in the *Saturday Evening Post* on April 25, 1935, it was the Eastern European, the "alien," the curse of America's once great "white, homogenous" civilization that Dies feared most. Dies noted that up until the mid-nineteenth century, America, drawing immigrants from England, Scotland, Germany, and Italy, was still "racially unified."[34] During the late nineteenth century, however, as the nation grew more industrial, "cheap paupers" from "Southern and Eastern Europe" began to "invade America" and adulterate the great society.[35] "It is safe to say that we invited the evils of the Old World's social, political, and economic disorders by offering our fertile lands and priceless resources," asserted Dies, "as a refuge for the jobless as malcontents of Europe."[36] Like Hamilton Fish before him, Dies built his reputation around a firm stance against immigration. It is no coincidence that many of the "aliens" landing on America's shore from the East happened to be Jews, some of whom would become integral members of the American Communist Party. In singling out his perceived enemies of the state, Dies tipped his hand early in his career and it was no accident that Communists, not Fascists, bore the brunt of the Dies, and eventual Thomas and Wood Committee investigations. Although some, such as Goodman, suggest that Dies was equally if not more interested in fascism, such was simply not the case. Based on his upbringing, attitude, and outlook on American society, the choice between targeting Germans or Jews proved an easy one for Dies, as it would be for the men that nurtured his legacy over the next thirty years.

Dies may have been able to convince Congress that communism posed the greatest threat to American democracy but according to a Gallup Poll taken in February 1939, the American public was not sold. According to the poll, which asked Americans to identify what group they felt posed the greatest threat to internal security, 32 percent claimed American fascism while only 26 percent tabbed American Communism.[37] Amazingly enough, a similar poll conducted less than a year later in 1940 found that 70 percent of the people polled found communism to be the greatest threat versus 30 percent for Nazism.[38] This is a rather incredible turnaround, especially given the rise in German aggression abroad. Such a dramatic shift in opinion begs the question-how did Dies and his Committee both create a popular bias against communism and maintain it throughout the course of the un-American investigations?

Dies and his successors utilized many outlets during the reign of "The Committee." The reciprocal relationship that "investigative agencies" such as the Dies and eventually Thomas Committees and the FBI shared with certain media outlets provided these organizations with incredible manipulative ability. Whether intentionally designed to vilify American Communists or not, headlines that spoke of brewing spy rings and sabotage from within put a scare into the American public that left it searching for answers. The result was a growing popularity for Dies both in the eyes of the American public and on Capitol Hill. A Gallup Poll survey conducted on December 2, 1939, found that 75 percent of those polled felt as though the Dies committee should continue for another year. The same poll also revealed, when asked if "Congress should appoint some other committee to do the work" or should it "provide the money so the Dies committee can continue," 75 percent placed their confidence in Dies.[39] Washington reflected the public's enthusiasm for Dies as Congress, in February of 1939, "voted 344 to 45 to extend the Committee's life."[40] Clearly, at the expense of progressive Americans, Martin Dies' public star was rising.

Articles in mainstream newspapers such as the *New York* and *Los Angeles Times* helped to fuel anti-Communist flames and promote the "imperativeness" of the Committee. For example, an article printed in the *New York Times* on October 15, 1938 ran the headline "The New Deal Is Held Communist Tool: Thomas of Dies Committee Says Reds Have Gained Most in Roosevelt Regime."[41] In the article, Dies Committee member and future committee chair J. Parnell Thomas of New Jersey proclaimed that "New Deal masterminds have pawned themselves out to Communist strategists" and are "so far out on a limb that it is impossible for them to get back."[42] Thomas went on to describe the Party's clandestine nature, likening a Communist to a reptile that insidiously sneaks up on its prey. "They crawl like a snake and creep like a cat," observed Thomas, "until they and their silly dupes have drenched the nation with disaffection."[43] This article, one of hundreds that focused on Communistic activity within the United States printed by the *New York Times*, represents simply a taste of how the anti-Communist machine effectively propagated its campaign through the pages of the press. "The media," writes historian Joel Kovel, "was vital to the maturation of the American inquisition. Inquisitions are pointless without the dissemination of their lessons to society at large."[44] With a paid circulation base of over a half a million readers and with an at large readership (second hand, "on the rack" readers) certain to number in the millions, the *New York Times,* despite its reputation as a liberal literary organ, helped to convey the Committee's message loud and clear.[45]

Communist-themed articles also became regular staples in the *Los Angeles Times* as the Dies investigation of Hollywood heated up in 1939. Although Dies would technically give Hollywood a clean bill of health regarding Communistic activity, the negative attention that he heaped on the industry, simply by poking around tinseltown, set the stage for ensuing investigations and the eventual emergence of the Hollywood "blacklist." "Hollywood Red Hotbed, Ex-Communist Says" sang the headline of an article printed in the Los Angeles Times on August 7, 1940.[46] Based on the testimony of Oregonian and former Party organizer John Leech, the article describes the Party as an underground organization dedicated to the "overthrow of our government."[47] The article fails to note, however, that Leech's appointment as head organizer of the Communist Party of Los Angeles (CPLA) had sparked tremendous controversy among the Jewish members of the Party. It also failed to even acknowledge the existence of a possible link between the testimony of the non-Jew Leech against the largely Jewish CPLA. What it emphasized, however, was the Party's alleged allegiance to Moscow and its designs on American democracy. The Party, according to Leech, was "working always towards a final climax of a blood revolution" by "concentrating its efforts in any place that poverty was prevalent."[48] This statement, however, seems somewhat inconsistent given Hollywood's high concentration of wealth. Perhaps Leech's confusion regarding his own district accounts for his failure as a recruiting boss. Nevertheless, the article, based on the headline alone, was enough to raise eyebrows and stimulate discourse. With its strong anti-Communist slant and bellicose language, there is no doubt that it served a purpose as a powerful propaganda piece.

The growth in the number of newspaper articles featuring Communist "subversion" correlated directly with the rise in popularity and intensity of the anti-Communist movement. It is no secret that the Dies and Thomas Committees along with the FBI had "contacts" in the press. Kenneth O'Reilly notes a corps of "cooperative" anti-Communists writers in *Hoover and the Un-Americans,* many of whom were employed by some of Americas most widely read newspapers.[49] O'Reilly confirms that "a domestic propaganda campaign" was indeed a reality and that via the dissemination of "educational materials" through available channels, the FBI [and other anti-Communist organizations] could mobilize its public relations machinery for the purpose of nurturing an anti-Communist consensus."[50] The effectiveness of this media machine manifested itself in the growing popularity of the Dies Committee. By mid-1941, over 70 percent of Americans wanted to outlaw membership in the Communist Party. Concurrently, Martin Dies, the architect of the campaign, enjoyed an approval rating in excess of 90 percent.[51]

Somewhat overlooked in the discussion of the media and its impact on the anti-Communist purge is the role that popular magazines played in the depiction of Communists as subversives. It is rather clear, based on the numerous published articles, that many of America's most widely read magazines bought into the idea that American Communists were revolutionaries committed to the usurpation of democracy. Not only did magazines such as *Reader's Digest, Life, Look,* and *The Saturday Evening Post* provide a forum for men such as Martin Dies, J. Edgar Hoover, and J. Parnell Thomas to vilify the American Communist Party, they also provided commentary, in the form of editorials and articles written by Communist "authorities," that directly contributed to creation of anti-Communist hysteria. In addition to amplifying the paranoia surrounding American Communism, they also helped to fuel the popularity of the Committee, which, despite its unscrupulous nature, commanded a relatively strong approval rating into the early 1950's.[52]

Magazines in the 1940's and early 1950 were much more than simply sources of entertainment for Americans. In an age when television was still in its developmental stage, the majority of Americans turned to periodicals for their news and entertainment. Although newspapers served as major information resources, magazines provided "unbiased" and "reliable" news and undoubtedly touched a wider range of the population. In 1947, *Readers Digest* alone had a circulation base of over 9 million readers and this figure is based on subscriptions only.[53] There is no telling how many Americans read the magazine second hand. Based on its popularity, the attention that *Reader's Digest* allocated to Communistic activity made it a very powerful "weapon" in the anti-Communist arsenal.

As several other popular magazines waited until the post-war period to earnestly pick up on the anti-Communist momentum generated by the Dies Committee, *Reader's Digest* jumped on the "Red Menace" bandwagon during the formative stages of the campaign. Despite the fact the magazine failed to directly address communism as a "menace" prior to 1940, a series of articles on the Third Reich reveal that editors Dewitt and Lila Acheson Wallace did not perceive fascism in the same light as men such as Sam Dickstein. Although there were "antifascist" articles released in the late 1930's, articles such as "The Common Sense of American Neutrality" by Stuart

Chase published in November of 1939, "Nazi Number Two," contained in the same issue and written by Douglas Reed, and "Could Hitler Invade America," a December article by Hugh S. Johnson, combined to soften the image of Hitler and lessen the seriousness of the German threat.[54]

Reed, in "Nazi Number Two," comes close to lionizing Luftwaffe boss Herman Goring, Hitler's right hand man, in a piece that tainted with apparent pro-German sentiment. "Goring's masterpiece has been Nazi Germany's miraculous rearmament," wrote Reed, "effected at lightening speed with astounding secrecy."[55] A leader without equal in Germany, noted Reed, "Hitler orders the apparently impossible; Goring does it. He is, says Hitler, the best man I have."[56] Author Stuart Chase, in his article "The Common Sense of American Neutrality," argued in favor of isolation as a means of guaranteeing an "economic boom," and to ensure that "we will not be hurled into state socialism."[57] Clearly, driving Chase is a fear that war would engender a domestic purge of German-Americans. "We shall not risk taking on half the world in mortal combat," wrote Chase, "fellow citizens will not be tortured because they were born with German names."[58] Chase failed to mention, however, that war with Germany might also breed insurrection at home given the rising popularity at this time of the fascist German American Bund. Apparently unbeknownst to Chase, Americans with German names had already been targeted, and rightfully so. Unfortunately for men like Sam Dickstein, America's apathy towards German fascism, or in some cases, seeming fascination with it, provided the German Bund with relative impunity while Dies honed in on America's Reds.

By early 1941, Martin Dies was one of the most recognizable political figures in America. His campaign against "subversion" in full swing, Dies had orchestrated a pursuit of potential "insurgents" on a scale without precedent in American history. A beaming success, a "sensational one man show," Dies had arguably accomplished his goal of vilifying the Communist Party.[59] Americans from all walks of life, according to a 1941 Gallup Poll, overwhelmingly agreed that Communists presented a direct threat to American security. The spotlight was so firmly on the CPUSA that a poll on American fascism was not even conducted. By this time, however, Dies was not without a support system. The anti-Communist public relations machine had finally swung into gear in with magazines such as *Reader's Digest* leading the charge.

A series of articles released in 1941 by *Reader's Digest* reflect both the effectiveness of the Dies campaign and the mounting hysteria surrounding communism in America. Although soon to be at war with ever-strengthening Nazi Germany, the threat of domestic communism continued to outweigh, at least according to *Reader's Digest*, the peril of American fascism. With the help of America's most popular periodical, communism had emerged as the embodiment of atheism and the antithesis of capitalism. Communism was "the drug," according to Martin Dies, "which deadens the mind of men to the highest realities of life."[60]

Communism's "threat" to the American economy, not just in a philosophical sense, but in a physical one, had been a constant fear in American society (or at least in the American business world) since the initial "Red Scare" of 1919. Although blue collar workers constituted the lifeblood of corporate enterprise, their welfare was often compromised in the name of industrial efficiency and productivity. Organized labor provided the working man with a voice and helped to prevent the exploitation of America's proletariat. Strikes, however, ground production to a halt and a lack of commodities meant a lack of capital. In a time when the economy was still struggling to regain its footing in the wake of the Great Depression, unionization in the early 1940's was seen by many in the corporate world as a direct impediment to economic growth. White collar capitalists such as Martin Dies and Hamilton Fish had long worn their disgust with Roosevelt's labor-friendly New Deal on their sleeves and their campaign against communism found many supporters among America's economic elite. "There is no denying that within the business community were elements that could never come to terms with the New Deal," asserts historian David Caute, "and [they] saw in anti-communism a convenient weapon with which to smear progressive legislation and to weaken the effectiveness of organized labor."[61]

"Rehearsal for Revolution," an article written by Stanley High and published in the June 1941 issue of *Reader's Digest*, captured the essence of both the anti-labor, anti-Communist mentality of big business America. It also validated the efficacy of the Dies campaign while simultaneously contributing to a burgeoning sense of anti-Communist hysteria. Written in reference to the Aliss-Chambers strike, an ugly incident where management forcibly showed workers the door at the Aliss-Chambers plant in Milwaukee, Wisconsin, High attempted to prep America on the danger that "Communist inspired" strikes could have on war-time production. High took his argument further, however, and implied that American Communists had purposely been initiating strikes across the nation as a means of "displaying their destructive technique and power."[62] High contended that the business of organizing workers was part of a grand "Red" plan designed to "whip rank and file members into submission to the Communist Party."[63] The strike at Aliss-Chambers, an event that slowed work on defense production contracts for the three months that it lasted, "was no mere strike," according to High, "it was a dress rehearsal challenge to the American system."[64] High's manner of sensationalizing the event, turning albeit a more than routine strike action, but an act made in the name of worker solidarity nonetheless, into a "first step" in a Communist plan to overthrow the nation, was a tactic frequently employed by anti-Communist authors. High "capitalized" on the strike and used the "opportunity" to introduce his anti-Communist positions. This article is not simply about organized labor, it is about full blown revolution. *Reader's Digest*, by providing a sounding block for writers like High, brought the exaggerated "evils" of communism to living rooms across America. "That the Communists will strike again where it will hurt most can be depended on," warned High, "But they can be forestalled if the public is awake to Communist aims and aware that our democracy needs defense, not only from foes without but from foes within."[65]

In July, High produced a follow up article titled "We Are Already Invaded" for *Reader's Digest*, once again centered on Communist infiltration of American labor. In "We Are Already Invaded," an article that revealed its intention in its title, High argued that America must act to staunch the spread of this "ominous, Communist army" before it successfully achieved its goal of internal sabotage.[66] With an eye on labor, specifically the Los Angeles section of the Congress of Industrial Organization (CIO), High looked to establish American Communism as anathema to American democracy. With the health of the pre-war manufacturing machine his major concern, High warned that American Communists imbedded in America's industrial arena possessed the capability and the desire to stagnate the production of war-related materials in an effort to render the nation incapable of defending itself against attack. Communists, according to High, "have moved into position from which, on orders from Moscow, can jam the wheels of production and paralyze our national defense."[67]

Although focused primarily on labor, High devoted more than a few lines to the "general problem" that communism posed to the nation. In High's opinion, an opinion readily available to the more than 9 million Americans who subscribed to *Reader's Digest* (and however many more had access to it second hand), the real goal of the CPUSA, through its involvement with organized labor, was to "give Communists practice in the techniques of violence and to create as much dissention as possible in preparation for the armed insurrection out of which the Communists will seize power."[68] High made it a point to note that the Communist presence within organized labor was simply part of a larger plan, initiated "by Moscow," to spark revolution within the United States and overthrow the government from within. "The invasion is on," proclaimed High, "The United

States has become the chief objective for Moscow's disruptive international battalions."[69] Regardless of High's intentions, "We Are Already Invaded," an article defined by its apocalyptic tone, served as a powerful piece of propaganda for the Dies Committee. Facing increasing hostility at the time of the articles publishing, the Dies Committee fed of articles such as High's and used Communist hysteria to fend off attacks from men such as Samuel Dickstein who claimed, in 1941, that there were "110 Fascist organizations in the United States that had the key to the back door of the Dies Committee." [70] Articles such as the ones written by High helped to keep the spotlight on communism and off of fascism. This provided Dies and his committee with the political and popular power to forge ahead in their pursuit of progressives.

The heat on American communism increased in intensity throughout 1941 with *Reader's Digest* continuing to serve as a mouthpiece for anti-Communist "authorities." Jan Valtin (previously known as Richard Julius Herman Krebs), a former German Communist and author of "Out of the Night," a biographic piece detailing Valtin's (Krebs') quest to evade execution first at the hands of the Germans, then the Soviets at the outset of the Second World War, contributed a piece "Academy of High Treason" which played on High's theory of internal invasion via organized labor.[71] Valtin, bitter over his near death experience in Soviet Russia, claimed in the article that there existed a number of "Soviet trained" union leaders within the United States, schooled at "Moscow's Lenin University," who, in 1941, were actively preparing for the "Communist seizure of world power."[72] These "leaders," in the eyes of Valtin, "were highly trained officers of a secret invasion army under the command of a foreign dictator."[73] Valtin continued by declaring that "almost all key positions in the Communist machine in America are held by comrades trained in Moscow," and that nearly all "Communists sent here on subversive missions are likewise graduates [of Lenin University]."[74] It is not difficult to imagine what kind of impression an article like Valtin's would have on an uniformed American mind. As communism remained an enigma for many in America in the early 1940's, those receiving their "current events" from *Reader's Digest* were sure to develop a most unfavorable opinion of the American CP. Regardless of the fact that these articles were overblown embellishments designed to scare rather than educate, the themes they presented resonated strongly within the American public as indicated by popular polls.[75]

"Stalin's American Power," by Max Eastman, was yet another fervently anti-Communist article published in *Reader's Digest* in 1941. Contained in the December issue, Eastman, according to the magazine, published the article in order to educate the American populace on "the insidious techniques by which Communists are hoodwinking millions of loyal Americans."[76] Eastman, a former editor of the Communist publications *The Masses* and *The Liberator* and long time Trotskyist, had come away from a visit to Soviet Russia in the early 1920's apparently "disillusioned" with socialism and eager to contribute to the nascent anti-Communist movement of the 1930's.[77] His zeal to suppress American Communism inspired him to write several books designed to expose the evils of socialism and its perceived threat to democracy. His work, *Artists in Uniform,* spoke of cultural suppression in Russia in the late 1920's and, according to historian Irving Howe, "raised serious problems concerning the nature of Stalinism."[78]

Speaking in general terms and using blanket statements to condemn all those affiliated with the CPUSA, Eastman, in "Stalin's American Power," portrayed America as a land infested with Communist subversives, openly vulnerable to the imminent attack being orchestrated by infidels from within. Eastman linked the CPUSA to a broad range of Americans and powerfully condemned citizens from a myriad of professions, going as far as to indict Eleanor Roosevelt, a leading advocate of socially progressive reform. "Americans see labor leaders, businessmen, movie actors, parsons, government officials, publishers-they have even seen the first lady of the land," charged Eastman, "hoodwinked into giving aid indirectly to a foreign dictator to destroy our democracy."

A scholar familiar with the many faces of the American CP and someone who knew full well that there existed many so-called Communists who were anything but doctrinaire, Eastman chose not to differentiate between Stalinism and communism with a "small c" and, employing guilt by suspicion logic, blasted the CPUSA as a cultivator of sedition. "Check very cautiously on any organization, publication, or meeting which features the name of a known Communist of Fellow Traveler," advised Eastman in his effort to "protect" Americans from direct Communist exposure, "It may be that [the person "associated" with the American CP] does not belong to the party, but wherever their names are played up in a political 'cause,' you may guess that a party nucleus is at work underground."[79] Eastman concluded his tirade against, what he referred to as the "Red Racket," by encouraging Americans to take action against American Communists in order to expose them as the "totalitarians" that he claimed them to be. "Call them what they are," instructed Eastman, "totalitarians, agents of Stalin's power, conspirators against the democratic way of life." [80] Eastman's ardent denunciation of the Party certainly came at no surprise to those affiliated with the American CP. Eastman had long had it out for the organization and the CP, in turn, openly despised Eastman.[81] It may have surprised quite a few of those who came across the article in *Reader's Digest* or the *American Mercury* (where it was originally printed), however, especially those who understood little about the American Communist Party and its intentions. Despite the fact that the Party may have had 50,000 members at most in a country of over 120 million, based on Eastman's tone and fiery rhetoric, the "red" revolution was clearly underway.[82] Although fear of the "Red Menace" would greatly subside later that year with the establishment of the U.S.-Soviet alliance against the Axis powers, articles such as Eastman's helped to stimulate the evolution of the asphyxiating Cold War social "tenor" which drove the "Red Scare."

Following the December 1941 bombing of Pearl Harbor, fear of totalitarianism abroad replaced concern over communism at home. With the United States and the Soviet Union allied against fascism, anti-Communist organs such as the Dies Committee found themselves temporarily removed from the public spotlight. Fear over communism took a back seat to anxiety over "spies," namely Japanese Americans who would soon be destined for internment camps. Dies still, however, refused to take his eye off of the American CP, despite the fact that Communists and Democrats were now technically on the same side. "Dies asked the Department of Justice to register all Communists and Bundists," observes Ogden, "so that they could be prevented from obtaining employment in defense camps."[83] Dies also increased his surveillance of the Congress of Industrial Organizations (CIO), an organization deemed to be inundated by Communists and capable, as High suggested, of retarding the production of war related materials.[84]

Nevertheless, despite his continued angst over the CPUSA, the union between the United States and Russia made it very difficult for Dies and his committee to prosecute his campaign against the "Red Menace." As recognized by Goodman, due to the alliance, "the subject of Communist subversion could not very well sustain him as long as Russia remained in the fight."[85] As a result, Dies decided to turn inward, to Congress, in an effort to use past "sins" to incriminate members of the House and Senate who had at one point in time associated themselves with "front groups." Within the course of this "congressional" investigation, Dies targeted the Federal Communications Commission, specifically broadcast analyst Goodwin Watson who Dies claimed to be a "propagandist for the Soviet Union."[86] Dies also targeted the Office of Price Administration for its supposed "long record of affiliation with Communist organizations."[87] Dies used his attack on the O.P.A and on Watson and the Federal Communications Commission to demonstrate that the Committee still served an invaluable function regardless of the Russian-American alliance. Not surprisingly,

Dies continued to devote as little attention as possible to the Bund. This practice spawned a series of accusations linking him to the Axis alliance. The Federal Communications Commission continued to hammer away at Dies despite his attempts to label the institution Red. "According to the FCC's monitoring service," observed Goodman, "Dies had been the beneficiary of as many favorable references in Axis propaganda as any living American figure."[88]

With American communism enjoying a war-time reprieve coupled with Dies attack on federal agencies, the number of congressional representatives in Washington suspicious of Dies began to grow. By 1942, many began to perceive Dies in the same light as Sam Dickstein and condemned him for failing to target "the true subversives," namely "the real fascists and Nazis of this country that are really the greatest danger to our country."[89] Dies, however, continued to hammer away at American Communism, seemingly oblivious to the fact that "we were at war with Germany and Japan and not with Russia."[90] Dies' strategy, although increasingly controversial, remained both effective and generally popular. He not only won re-election to the House in 1942, but his Committee was re-upped in both 1943 and 1944.

In his eight year run as America's chief "Red hunter," Dies had received over 600,000 dollars in support from Congress, a testament to his manipulative skill and his ability to constantly "maintain a high profile."[91] His support from Congress could also be attributed to the prodigious attention devoted to communism on behalf of the media. Without the support of the public, who, through articles such as High's and Eastman's, received a biased "education" on the perils of the American CP, the Dies Committee would not have lasted as long as it did. Although he passed away in 1944, Dies' death did not stop the investigation of communism nor did it bring an end to the "relationship" that popular periodicals shared with the anti-Communist investigation. If anything, 1944 marked the dawn of a "Cold War" anti-Communist media campaign unparalleled in intensity and vigor. Dies had done his job. He fanned America's anti-Communist flames just long enough for Cold War hysteria to take over. Within three years of his death the nation would once again be gripped by media driven "Red Fever" with "his committee," the infamous House Committee on Un-American Activities, positioned to achieve a level of "success" that not even the old Texan himself could have imagined.

Despite the fact that the United States remained allied with the USSR in mid-1944, fear over communism began to once again build. With the Germans barely hanging on and the Japanese on the verge of collapse, many in America felt rather strongly that an Allied victory was assured. With this in mind, questions surrounding what was to come in the war's aftermath began to confront Americans. As the Dies Committee had kept fear of communism alive throughout the early war years, the thought of the United States and Russia left as the world's only remaining superpowers created anxiety throughout the nation. *Reader's Digest* contributed to this growing tension by continuing to run articles attacking the American CP, depicting it as a lingering evil whose rise in strength would correlate with Soviet Russia's emergence as America's preeminent challenger for global dominance.

"The New Communist Conspiracy," by a reportedly former "high official of the Soviet Government" Alexander Barmine, placed American Communists once again under the microscope. In the article, Barmine alleged that an "insidiously growing menace to free institutions," namely the American CP, remained on the move in 1944, growing in strength as it continued its operations inside the United States.[92] Ironically, despite being a supposed Soviet whose nation remained engaged in war against Nazi Germany, Barmine maintained that fascism stood as the lesser of two evils. Using the term "we" and "our" in reference to the United States, as if he had been a raised in the backcountry of Virginia, Barmine advocated the persecution of American-born citizens for simply embracing certain tenets of an ideology that he had presumably spent the majority of his life promoting. "The totalitarian Communist habit of thought is penetrating insidiously into the body of American democracy," wrote Barmine, "the Communist conspiracy in the United States is vastly more dangerous than the original [Russian] party was to [Russian] institutions."[93] Suggesting that Communists be jailed along with other "high up New Dealers," Barmine warned that the "stage is now set for a seizure of power by a controlling underground group."[94]

Barmine went on to insist that "trade unions, Governmental agencies, the Democratic party, and even the Army and the Navy" had all been infiltrated by Communists, red agents committed to internal sabotage. He concluded by imploring Americans to rally against this "menace" before it dethroned democracy and ushered in an age of repressive totalitarianism. "[The events mentioned in this article] reveal a flourishing conspiracy," stated an increasingly pessimistic Barmine, "helped by influential but foolish people, to undermine democracy and the American state. This conspiracy must be exposed."[95] Barmine's vilification of American communism ominously foreshadowed what was soon to come. His calculated attack reflected the mood of many conservatives in Congress as the nascent Cold War began to heat up. Clearly, a clash loomed on the horizon and there were many in Congress cognizant of what Cold War tensions could do for their careers. As Martin Dies had previously demonstrated, communism could actually serve as a convenient catalyst for one's political career. An opportunity to chase "reds" had once again presented itself and it would not take long for Congress to catch on.

On a typically cold, dark 1946 January day in Washington, D.C., Mississippi Congressmen John Rankin rose up from his seat in the House of Representatives and proposed that the flagging Dies Committee be continued under the infamous moniker The House Committee on Un-American Activities. Rankin, a cunning Southern politician who had earned a reputation as a "student of parliamentary procedure," looked to use the treasure chest of "subversive" information gathered by Dies to spearhead a more intense campaign against American Reds.[96] With the Dies committee on life support following the death of its namesake, Rankin, a devout segregationist and known anti-Semite, looked to carry on the legacy of his fellow Dixiecrat and extend the Communist inquisition into the post-war years. With a booming economy and a fiercely patriotic nation behind him, Rankin capitalized on this "golden opportunity" and incarnated HUAC by a House vote of 207 to 176. Worth noting, out of the 207 congressmen that voted in favor of prolonging the Committee, 137 were Republicans and 70 were Democrats. Of the 70 Democrats, 63 hailed from south of the Mason-Dixon Line.[97] Hence, a Committee composed primarily of Southern and Midwestern conservatives, led by perhaps the most visible neo-confederate of his time, John Rankin, had been brought into existence by a body of Southern and Midwestern Conservatives. One could only image the anxiety that befell progressives across the nation once the "rebirth" of this organization became publicized.

Although Rankin would not formally be named Chair of the Committee, that "honor" would go to Edward J. Hart of New Jersey, his influence would dominate the course of HUAC proceedings for the next decade. Thanks to Rankin, HUAC remained afloat in a time when it was close to extinction. He also kept HUAC in business long enough to see communism emerge once again as the greatest internal threat in the nation in the mid-1940's. Perhaps Rankin's most notable "achievement," however, was his advance on Hollywood. An inquiry first initiated by Dies, Rankin picked up where his predecessor left off an issued a warning to America that Hollywood "served as the greatest hotbed of subversive activity in the United States."[98] According to Rankin, Hollywood was a "tarantula" where "loathsome paintings" hung in the home of its brightest star, a "seducer of white girls," Charlie Chaplin.[99] Given its large Jewish population, it came as no surprise to those who knew Rankin that he would target Hollywood. A vociferous racist, Rankin despised Jews and routinely linked the evolution of communism to Leon Trotsky and his "Jewish Conspiracy" in Russia. "In Rankin's mind, to call a Jew a Communist was tautology," writes

HUAC historian Walter Goodman, "In the halls of congress he called Walter Winchell 'a little slime-mongering kike' and he took glee in baiting his colleagues."[100] Like Dies, however, Rankin's 1946 foray into Hollywood did not bear the results he desired. He would have to wait another year for a full blown investigation of Hollywood to transpire. Nevertheless, he set the stage for the intensification of the "red hunt" and made it known to all those on the left that, no matter how "big a star," there was no eluding the eye of the Committee.

As the nation now faced a new type of warfare, a "cold war" marked by ideological friction and a race for technological superiority with the Soviets, the American press, once again feeding off anti-Communist inertia generated by the Committee, played a crucial role in brewing hysteria among the populace. By early 1946, the Committee had passed into the hands of J. Parnell Thomas, a social conservative from New Jersey and perfect compliment to Rankin and his horde of philistines. To many, Thomas' appointment served as a sign that Congress remained committed to rooting out Red subversion. With a new chair and an expanding budget, the Committee had apparently achieved unquestionable legitimacy. The media only energized HUAC's Communist inquisition as it continued to vilify American Reds through the pages of many of America's most fashionable periodicals.

In the years immediately following the war, *Life Magazine* joined *Reader's Digest* as a forum for anti-Communist propaganda. Though not as widely read, *Life* touted a circulation base of close to 6 million Americans in 1946. Add to that figure the millions of individuals who viewed the magazine while in the doctor's or dentist's waiting room, standing in line at the grocery store, sitting in a chair at the barber shop, or while sipping coffee at the local café and you have a pretty influential information medium. "The U.S. Communist Party," written by anti-Communist "liberal" and future head of the ADA (Americans for Democratic Action) Arthur Schlesinger, came out in *Life* in the spring of 1946.[101] Although Schlesinger had yet to publish his infamous work *The Politics of Upheaval* in which he referred to the American Communist Party as a "pliant instrument of Soviet Policy" and of communism "as evil in the repression and persecution to which it led," his stance on the Red Menace was well known. [102] He had in fact emerged, by the mid-1940's, as the leading figure in the emergence of "anticommunist liberalism," a development driven by former New Dealers who wished to disassociate themselves from so called reds. Led by Truman who realized the political imperativeness of a firm post-war anticommunist position, "Vital Center" liberals, a moniker soon to be coined by Schlesinger himself in his 1949 publication by the same name, endeavored to establish middle ground between left and right.[103] "It was possible, indeed desirable, in fact inevitable," writes Victor Navasky, "to be liberal and anticommunist [in the immediate post war period] at the same time."[104] "Liberals" like Schlesinger understood the ramifications associated with red affiliation and endeavored to make it very clear that their political and social proclivities were distinctly American. As far as Schlesinger was concerned, the left needed to rid its ranks of "doughface progressives," parlor reds "whose sentimentality has softened [them] up for communist permeation and conquest."[105]

In "The U.S. Communist Party," Schlesinger alleges the CPUSA to be a subversive organ of the Soviet Union "here to stay," one "working overtime to expand party influence, open and covert, in the labor movement, among Negroes, among veterans, among unorganized liberals."[106] Referring to the Party as a sanctuary for the disillusioned and downtrodden, Schlesinger suggested that the Party looked to the lowest echelons of American society to harvest its subversives. "The party fills the lives of lonely and frustrated people," Schlesinger contended, "providing them with social, intellectual, even sexual fulfillment they cannot obtain in existing society."[107] He wrote on to label the party as nothing more than an organ of the Soviet Union committed to fomenting unrest and bringing about full blown revolution. These "unquestioning servants of the USSR who strive with fanatical zeal to promote the aims of Russia," noted Schlesinger, "spread their infection of intrigue and deceit wherever they go."[108] Ending with a bang, Schlesinger did his best to instill fear in the hearts of his readers' as he implied that the fate of the nation could be at hand. "Its main objective is by policies of disruption and blackmail to make sure if war comes [with the Soviet Union], that the U.S. is badly prepared to fight it."[109] Coming from the hand of one of America's most recognizable politicians and printed in arguably the most popular American magazine, there is little doubt that this article influenced more than a few Americans.

Life also demonized the Soviet Union and in turn, amplified anti-Communist paranoia at home. A series of articles by John Foster Dulles on Soviet foreign policy proposed that the USSR sought to bring totalitarianism to all corners of the globe. This Communist conquest, according to Dulles, looked to engender "governments everywhere which accept the basic doctrines of the of the Soviet Communist policy and which suppresses political and religious thinking which runs counter to those doctrines."[110] Referencing the ancient Roman Empire, Dulles maintained that the Soviets longed to create what he referred to as the *Pax Sovietica,* a worldwide Communist empire with the USSR at its head. A leading republican and future secretary of state under Eisenhower, Dulles insisted that the Soviet program had achieved "initial success" and that if it went untouched, "it would carry a threat to personal freedoms which constitute out most cherished political and spiritual heritage."[111] With the Committee portraying American Communists as pawns of the Soviet Union, Americans began to establish a link between the members of the progressive left and a worldwide Communist conspiracy.

The *United States News* got into the anti-Communist act as well in the early Cold War period with the release of "US Communists New Line: Open Drive For More Power" in its March 1946 issue. Written without a byline, the article claimed that under postwar leader William Z. Foster, the man who succeeded the more moderate Earl Browder as head of the Communist Party of the United States of America, the party looked to take a "more militant line" in order to "inject itself, more openly than before, into every economic and social issue before the country."[112] According to the magazine, Browder was "not militant enough," so therefore, "Mr. Foster has emerged to change all that."[113] Citing labor unions across America as hotbeds of Communist activity, the article inferred that the party intended to branch out beyond labor into all areas of American life. Strength in numbers, according to the article, served as the postwar motto of the CPUSA. "Where party leaders formerly thought of recruiting ten or twenty members in a shop or area, they now are instructed to think in terms of hundreds."[114] Such words had apparently begun to reverberate throughout America. In a July 6, 1946 Gallup Poll, when asked what to do with American Communists, a shocking 36 percent of Americans said "kill or imprison them." According to this same poll, over 84 percent of the respondents felt as though Communists posed an immediate threat and should be, at a minimum, watched carefully. The numbers provided a convincing vote of confidence for the Committee, which continued to embellish its goals in the 1940's.[115]

As the Committee turned west in 1947 and focused its sights on the bright lights of Hollywood, the voice of J. Edgar Hoover, head of the FBI and virulent anti-Communist, rang loud and clear throughout the country as he continued publicly to blast the American Communist Party. Regardless of the fact the Hoover and the Un-American Activities Committee did not always see eye to eye, there existed a good degree of cooperation between the FBI and the Committee. In fact, the information gathered by the FBI allowed the House Committee to proceed in the fashion that it did. It could be said, as it is suggested by Kenneth O'Reilly, that the Federal Bureau of Investigation masterminded the propaganda campaign against American Reds, which in turn established the contentious atmosphere in which the Un-American Activities Committee, and eventually McCarthy,

operated. O'Reilly observed that in early 1946, then assistant FBI director
D. Milton Ladd "called for a domestic propaganda campaign to dramatize
the seriousness of the threat posed to America's internal security by CPUSA
radicals." [116] Bureau director Hoover, "witch hunter in chief," according to
Sally Belfrage whose father, Cedric, was a former Hollywood director and
brilliant writer turned "unfriendly witness," coordinated the attack on the
CP.[117] Using a variety of tactics, Hoover and the FBI gathered information
on Communists that proved invaluable to the Un-American Activities Committee throughout the course of its investigation. "Hoover's agents, always
in pairs like nuns and with one to cajole and the other to threaten, visited
suspects at offices or homes in a tireless pursuit of names," observed Cedric
Belfrage, who also noted that Hoover's "wire tapping," although admit-
tedly not completely effective, "made heretics act as if walls had ears."[118]

Although often engaged in bureaucratic and often times, personal
war with the Committee, Hoover armed the inquisition with information
and provided it with the popular "credibility" that sustained it throughout
its lifespan. "In contrast to Truman who sought to prohibit congressional
access-particularly Un-American Activities members-to FBI and other loyalty data," O'Reilly wrote, "Hoover required the FBI to provide conservative congressmen and other anti-Communist interests with limited access
to Bureau files."[119] It may not have been a perfect union, but the Hoover-
HUAC connection proved lethal to progressives throughout the nation.
One of America's most powerful figures and possessor of a voice that commanded seemingly consummate authority, Hoover's personal attacks on
Communists resonated strongly. Using mediums that ranged from newspaper articles to feature stories in America's most popular magazines, Hoover
undoubtedly influenced the millions of Americans who came in contact
with his words. With popular periodicals continuing to serve as a vocal
outlet for the anti-Communist right, Hoover gladly graced the pages of
numerous magazines with his diatribes against the "radical" left.

Published by *American Magazine* in February 1947, a periodical with
base of over 3 million readers, Hoover's article "Red Fascism in the United
States Today" announced that the lone goal of the American CP was the
"destruction of the American way of life."[120] In one of the most militant
anti-Communist articles ever to be published, Hoover coupled the American Communist Party with the Ku Klux Klan while referring to it as a
"totalitarian group" home to members "cloaked in stealth and intrigue."[121]
Liberally commenting on American Communists in a blanket fashion as if
they all subscribed to the same militant ideology, Hoover argued that all
those affiliated with American Communist Party were linked through a revolutionary bond. The goal of the Party, Hoover contended, was to destroy

capitalism and establish as Soviet styled Communistic system within the United States. According to Hoover, American Party members were mere pawns in the Soviet struggle to gain global domination. "[The American Communist Party] leads the working class in a fight for the revolutionary overthrow of capitalism," wrote Hoover, "for the establishment of a Soviet Socialist Republic in the United States."[122]

Hoover also addressed the Communist threat to America's religious foundation. A sensitive subject for the millions of churchgoing Americans, the thought of atheistic Communists infecting the nation with their godless ideology proved difficult to stomach for many. With religion serving as the one area where Americans were not willing to compromise, Hoover's strategy of hammering home the atheistic component of communism, regardless of the fact that there existed a good number of religious progressives, played directly into the hands of Un-American Activities Committee and the anti-Communist movement. "The truth remains that atheism is a fundamental doctrine with Communists as the existence of God is to all religious faiths," noted Hoover, "One or the other must inevitably triumph." [123]

Hoover finished his piece by encouraging the use of anti-Communist propaganda to combat the American Communist Party. For Hoover, the only way to eliminate American communism was to expose it as the evil that he claimed it to be. "Truth was our propaganda in World War II," Hoover asserted, "it is the best weapon to use against Red Fascism in America today. A Communist steeped in stealth, trickery, and deceit, cannot long survive the truth. Public opinion focused on communism will have the same curative effect that x-rays have upon a cancerous growth."[124] If "the American way of life is to be preserved," Hoover maintained, "the menace of communism must be met and its march stopped."[125] Ironically, it was Hoover who authorized the use of unconstitutional and "un-American" measures such as unlawful wiretaps, illegal searches, and unmitigated intimidation in the battle with Bolshevism, not the Communist Party of the United States of America. Known all too well to American progressives, Hoover's double standard was consistent with the entire Red inquiry. The hypocrisy of the investigation remained lost on America's most popular magazines, however, as anti-Red articles continued to feed burgeoning paranoia.

Reader's Digest kept up its assault on the American left in 1947 with another round of anti-Communist articles. With tensions mounting in anticipation of the Hollywood hearings scheduled to take place in October, *Reader's Digest* treated the American public to a barrage of anti-Communist commentary that undoubtedly facilitated the Un-American Activities Committee's anti-red quest. "The Red Spy Net," by author of "Our Secret War," Thomas M. Johnson, published in June of 1947, maintained that a Soviet spy ring, namely the Communist Party of the United States of America, had embedded itself deep within the nation and was effectively relaying privileged information to the Soviet Union. This group of "agents and informers" subscribed to a program of internal sabotage designed leave the country vulnerable to a Soviet strike. Johnson, playing on the growing fear of the "Red Menace," declared that "The largest and most threatening intelligence service in the history of espionage is penetrating the country on a scale unimagined by the average American."[126] Targeting immigrants as instruments of the spy conspiracy, Johnson argued that recent Eastern European arrivals to America were easy prey for those engaged in gathering intelligence for the Soviet Union. "The Soviet secret apparatus, comprising thousands of agents and informers, is aided increasingly by American fellow travelers [non-card carrying Communists]," wrote Johnson, adding "and certain members of the two million persons in the United States who were born in countries that are now Russian allies. The Russians are using here every trick they were caught using in Canada but on a far greater scale."[127]

   With the nuclear threat beginning to escalate, Johnson hinted that these so-called spies were on the trail of America's atomic secrets. Citing nuclear espionage, a charge that would plague Communists throughout the early Cold War Period and lead to the conviction of dozens and the execution of the Julius and Ethel Rosenburg on June 19, 1951, Johnson declared the Red reconnaissance effort to retrieve nuclear information to be a legitimate and potentially diabolical threat to American security. As pictures of mushroom clouds and portrayals of complete annihilation began to percolate throughout the nation, insinuating that the Communist Party of the United States of America served as an incubator for traitors undoubtedly intensified anxiety surrounding communism in America.[128] "In the United States some 3,300 Russians, including many experts posing as underlings, swarmed over the country visiting factories, laboratories, and testing grounds," decreed a hostile Johnson, "They were denied little save the atomic secret and other Russian agents were already nibbling at that."[129] Johnson insisted that The American Communist Party, a "subsidiary of the Comintern," served as the sparkplug of Russia's American intelligence program. Through these "agents" on the ground, the Soviets could enact their insidious agenda that included "extraordinary missions such as kidnappings and executions."[130]

   In the end, however, it was the atomic question that dominated Johnson's discussion. Plugging the Un-American Activities Committee as the first and last line of defense against this internal invasion, Johnson delivered a warning arguably intended to send shivers down the spines of *Reader's Digest* subscribers. "The main objective of Soviet espionage has been the atomic bomb," contended Johnson, "the Russians seek information on the B-36, the new bomber that can carry the atomic bomb anywhere on earth. Important materials dealing with guided missiles are said to have been stolen from an experimental laboratory in Virginia. A later double check revealed [the culprit] to be a Soviet spy."[131] Clearly, articles such as Johnson's were sinking in. According to an April 2, 1947 Gallup Poll, a paltry 18 percent of Americans polled felt as though American Communists were capable of being loyal Americans.[132] Suspicion was rising as brewing paranoia, inflamed by periodicals, began to take a firm grip on the nation.[133]

Look Magazine, possessing a subscription base of close to 3 million readers, joined the anti-Communist campaign in 1947 in zealous fashion. In a March 4, 1947 article by Leo Cherne, "How to Spot a Communist," *Look* made clear its position on the Red Menace. *Look* apparently chose to "overlook" the fact that The American CP, or as referred to by Cherne as "our problem," had been slowly declining in strength and numbers in the years immediately following the war.[134] Many "moderate" Communists, men and women committed to the Communist Political Association (as the party was renamed by Earl Browder in 1944), had withdrawn from the party following Browder's ousting from power at the hands of William Z. Foster in 1945. This exodus of "cultural Communists," "Trotskyists," or men and women concerned with social issues such as race relations and poverty as opposed to any type of militant revolution, rendered the party virtually powerless.[135] Unfortunately, for a significant number of these progressives, many of whom resided in Hollywood, the decline in party members ironically correlated with a rise in anti-Communist hysteria. Garish articles such as "How to Spot a Communist" certainly contributed to this phenomenon.

Churne began his treatise by proclaiming that "There is a real Communist problem in America. The real Communist believes in Russia first and a Soviet America and he is prepared to use a dictator's tactics or lies and violence to realize his ambitions."[136] In a virtual guide on how to recognize and report Communists and their associates, Churne provided the reader's of *Look* with a handbook full of all the usual "tell tale" communistic signs. In his "How to Identify a Communist" section, Churne listed sure fire communistic characteristics such as any "reader of the *Daily Worker,* sponsor of civil rights organizations, and anyone who criticizes American policy" among others.[137] Using language clearly designed to inspire anxiety in the hearts of his readers, Churne, the executive secretary of the Research Institute of America, vilified American communism as a "menace" designed "to penetrate, confuse, and facilitate the task of destruction."[138] Suggesting that those opposed to racial segregation in the South belonged to a red conspiracy, Churne revealed a racist edge in claiming that "if a liberal opposes the poll tax, or Mississippi's Bilbo (a racist caricature of a black man with ape-like features), he is sure to find a Communist at his side."[139] In closing, Churne offered advice regarding "How Not To be a Sucker for a Left Hook," a section in which he provided thirteen strategies intended to help unsuspecting Americans avoid "joining or helping any Communistic group."[140] He concluded his harangue by stating that Communists "think differently from other kinds of Americans." According to Churne, "Communists are forceful, aggressive, and ruthless. They are men of weak personality" and "weak personalities" wish to "destroy their own environments by force. "Communists don't wait for developments," warned Churne, "force and violence are their tools."[141] Certainly Churne could not be serious? With party membership under twenty thousand, the brutality of the Stalin regime coming to the fore, and nationalism at a fevered pitch, what "Communist" in their right mind would even consider spearheading any kind of revolutionary "development" in 1947 America? The fact is, no one would. Nevertheless, the idea made for great drama and controversy had magazines flying off the shelves. Clearly, by 1947, HUAC and the press had established a symbiotic relationship. The Committee required a threat and the press delivered. The press needed a storyline and the Committee and its sympathizers provided one. Both entities, in the end, profited from this most convenient relationship, a union cemented in embellished communist controversy that had the nation paralyzed like never before.

The fall of 1947 will permanently be marked by arguably the most significant development in the history of the Committee. September brought the Committee west to Hollywood to hunt Reds in the city of stars. Hollywood set the stage, literally, for both the Committee and its thrust for fame as well as for those technically on trial, namely the "unfriendly witnesses," who seemingly possessed a golden opportunity to expose the Un-American Activities Committee as an unconstitutional body. Standing on the First Amendment and the premise that Congress could not investigate where it could not legislate, specifically in matters of free speech, ten of Hollywood most talented "behind the scenes" figures did their vested best to bring the Committee to its knees.

As author and director Dan Bessie, son of original Ten member Alvah Bessie remembers, the "Unfriendlies" viewed the October 1947 Hollywood hearings as more than simply a means to clear their own names. The spectacle, according to Bessie, presented those in defiance with "an opportunity to make a statement, [Congress] had no authority to pry into personal association or private belief."[142] Perhaps attune to this at the time, the "Unfriendly Ten" stood in position to not only bring the Committee down, but they held the potential to change the course of the entire anti-Communist investigation.

With the bright lights burning and the flash bulbs flaring, "the Ten" had the Committee right where they wanted it. Unfortunately, in typical domineering fashion, Thomas closed the curtain on the Ten and prevented them, by manipulating the hearings and denying members of the Ten a proper forum in which to exercise their voice, from successfully challenging the Committee and its tactics.

In a rather strange development, given an event of such incredible magnitude, popular magazines such as *Reader's Digest, The Saturday Evening Post,* and *Look,* barely gave the Hollywood hearings a mention. It certainly was not due to lack of attention given the coverage allotted to the event by the press. Headlines screaming "Red Conspiracy" graced the covers of papers across the country throughout the fall of 1947. On October 21, the *Los Angeles Times* ran an article "Hunting Hollywood's Red's" that served as a ringing endorsement of the Committee. "[The Committee] has never had more important work to do," stated the *Times,* "Rep. Parnell Thomas' committee, acting properly and without legalistic obstruction, would do a lot for the film center by labeling the guilty and thus absolving the great majority of the innocent."[143]

The *Times* featured "79 In Hollywood Found Subversive Inquiry Head Says" on October 23 as author Samuel Tower clarified that "today, actors, writers, and others in Hollywood were named members of the Communist Party." [144] In the *New York Times,* "Un-American Committee Puts on Big Show" ran on October 26 noting that "what is being heard here is designed for maximum impact on the public consciousness." The article also recognized that "all the evidence heard thus far has been from witnesses chosen to bolster the committee's thesis."[145] Nevertheless, the Committee had seemingly "succeeded" despite its failure to achieve its primary "agitprop" objective. The industry, according to the Un-American Activities Committee, was "Red" and millions across the nation accepted this flawed contention.

The fact that several of America's most widely read publications failed to produce a feature article on the Hollywood hearings remains somewhat puzzling. Perhaps, due to the fact that the Committee failed to produce certifiable evidence of communistic adulteration in film, editors decided to pass on the spectacle. As the Committee had been heralded by most publications as a necessary and pivotal defense mechanism in the battle against internal "Bolshevism," an article suggesting Committee fallibility would have defused, to a degree, the patriotic electricity surrounding the anti-Communist campaign. A clash between "republicans" and "revolutionaries" is what sparked intrigue among Americans.

World War II had shown the media that what America hungered for were tales of American heroism, stories revolving around patriots standing steadfast in the face of tyranny. Such a situation, "cops versus robbers," had seemingly metastasized in the form of the Un-American Activities Committee anti-Communist crusade (only to become even more defined in the McCarthy days). With future profit in mind, many editors arguably balked at covering the Hollywood hearings and instead chose to capitalize with brazen abandon on Red fever mounting in the aftermath of the investigation. Fear, as it does today, sold. Controversy equaled capital. Communism, as the nation was well aware, equaled controversy. Talk of a Soviet conspiracy was undoubtedly more apt to sell magazines that any article even remotely sympathetic to the cause of alleged Reds (via the revelation of committee incompetence). Thus, instead of diffusing paranoia surrounding the "Red Menace" with an article that detailed what truly transpired in Hollywood, major magazines such as *Reader's Digest* decided not to print anything at all.

Life, however, devoted ink to the hearings running a crafty and typically biased feature on the event in their November 1947 issue. This article carefully excluded extracts of the prepared statements that "Unfriendlies" introduced into the record in favor of commentary from the hearings themselves, much of which was understandably harsh in nature. The article, "The Movie Hearings" by Sidney Olsen, featured an exchange between screenwriter Dalton Trumbo and J. Parnell Thomas, one laden with vitriol and customary Communist "defiance." "As photographers moved in and circled him, popping flash bulbs in his face, Trumbo," wrote Olsen, "whirled off the stand shouting 'this is the beginning of American Concentration Camps!"[146] Olsen made it a point to note that Trumbo, quite possibly Hollywood's most gifted screenwriter at the time and a man who would eventually break the blacklist with his work on *Spartacus* in 1960, had possessed a "1944 Communist registration card, made out to Dalt T., 620 Beverly Drive, Los Angeles. Dalt T. was the official Communist Party designation for Dalton Trumbo." [147] Trumbo, in a letter to an admirer written several weeks after the publication of the article, couldn't help but comment on the "strategically" selected transcript clips featured in *Life*. "If you are generally interested in the Hollywood investigation conducted by the House Committee on Un-American Activities," scribed Trumbo, "I suggest that you write the Committee and they will be glad to send you the official transcript of my testimony, which , as you will discover, differs considerably from that reported in *Life* Magazine."[148] Apparently, for *Life* at least, profit transcended professionalism.

Olsen also demeaned screenwriter and Hollywood Party head John Howard Lawson, known throughout Hollywood as a leading advocate for racial equality. A fact excluded by Olsen, Lawson, according to historian

Gerald Horne, "was a man who came to symbolize the Communists' attempt to inject anti-racism into movies." Lawson was a vocal leader for "struggling black writers in Hollywood," someone "who was miles ahead of most of his non-Communist contemporaries" on this issue.[149] Olsen, however, chose to portray Lawson in a different light. "Lawson," Olsen observed, "showed himself the master of Pravada-like prose (referencing the Soviet "propaganda" organ), he said that Chairman Thomas wants to 'drive us into a disastrous and unnecessary war.'"[150] Olsen concluded by disparaging the Ten as he maintained that they were anything but convincing in their attempt to combat the Committee. "In sum, the witnesses who had been labeled pro-Communist were an unimpressive group. They were unsuccessful as martyrs in the cause of communism or Americanism."[151] Olsen carefully omitted commentary on why the Ten were less than successful. Had they not been unjustly muted by Thomas, who Olson claimed to be "as fair as one could expect after nine years of dealing with liars," the Ten would have undoubtedly presented a formidable challenge to the Committee, a challenge that would have certainly come with ramifications for the entire "red" investigation.[152]

Another publication to touch on the Hollywood affair, *Time Magazine,* provided a short blurb in their "National Affairs" section of the November 10, 1947 issue. *Time* noted that neither the Committee nor the Ten were all that effective in conveying their positions. If anything, this article, at a minimum, shed light on the ineffectiveness of the Committee. Ultimately, however, the magazine endorsed the Un-American Activities Committee and its function as America's anti-Communist vanguard. "Congress' power to investigate was not explicit in the Constitution. But it has become implicit. Because such inquiries are not a judicial process, Congress has the right to make its own rules."[153] Certainly, the Ten learned the merit of this argument quickly. With rights normally afforded to "defendants" on trial withheld, the Ten stood little chance of "exoneration."

Choosing to focus on the worth rather than the fallibility of the Committee and the anti-Communist inquisition, popular periodicals, in the aftermath of the Hollywood hearings, kept up the attack on American progressives. If anything, the Hollywood hearings served as a boon to the anti-Communist crusade. The Ten's failure to expose the unconstitutionality of Thomas and his "henchmen" as unjust allowed HUAC to up the intensity of both the "red raid" and its purveying paranoia. Clearly, the Committee had been relying on duplicitous measures to probe in areas of free speech and thought, a fact which placed the Committee and its investigation in violation of the First Amendment to the Constitution.

Thanks in part to the combustible tenor of the time, however, this reality remained concealed. Nevertheless, the fact that it went undisclosed in 1947 did little to deter the likes of screenwriter Albert Maltz from publicly articulating why, exactly, the Ten and their supporters considered the Committee unconstitutional. "I would not go to prison myself, or accept blacklisting in the film industry, to give over the principles upon which I stood," reflected an indignant Albert Maltz in the spring of 1951, "that no American should be compelled to disclose matters involving his freedom of thought and secrecy of the ballot."[154] Unfortunately for Maltz, however, the Committee had indeed placed thought on trial and in doing so, established an "unconstitutional" precedent bound to become a hallmark of the McCarthy age.

With the film industry tainted red and the infamous Hollywood "blacklist" a sad reality, the press, feeding off of HUAC "momentum," ambitiously broadened its coverage of the Red Menace. Shortly following the events in Hollywood, *The American Mercury* published James A. Wechsler's "How To Rid The Government of Communists." Wechsler, a *New York Post* columnist, asserted in language similar to that soon to be employed by Wisconsin Senator Joseph McCarthy, that Communists had nefariously infiltrated Washington. According to Wechsler, HUAC, comprised of "thinking men who are now shaping Government policy in this elusive realm (that of combating totalitarianism without becoming totalitarian)," served as the first line of defense against an "international army of agents organized as native Communist parties."[155] American Communist groups, declared Wechsler, "are organized instruments of Russian espionage, disruption, and in the event of war, full fledged sabotage."[156] Wechsler likened Communists to Nazi's in the fact that they "lead political double-lives," and that unless a firm loyalty-policy is implemented, "some of the most important and elusive Communist operatives might escape."[157] All Reds, according to Wechsler, including so called "Fellow Travelers," were potential spies ready and willing to furnish the Soviet Union with America's most intimate secrets.[158]

"Does Communism Threaten Christianity," by Dorothy Thompson, came out in *Look* in January 1948. Like Hoover and Dies before her, Thompson concentrated on Communistic atheism and attempted to portray the American CP as a demonic organ. "Does Communism threaten Christianity," Thomson asked, and concluded "the answer is yes. Communism threatens the entire established social order of which Christianity is a part. Contempt for Christianity has permeated all Communist thinking."[159] In a tone that borders on aristocratic and somewhat racist, Thompson contended that a society without religion would mean "society without class."[160] Communism, according to Thompson, had caused the Soviet Union, "the only country inhabited by white men" to suffer with "wholesale famine and mass death by starvation."[161]

Thompson concluded by asserting that the Communist presence within America's borders posed a moral threat to the fabric of the nation like nothing that had ever confronted it before. "Christianity faces its greatest crisis in millennial history," decried Thompson, "the Christian faith and the Christian courage have never been more profoundly menaced than they are today."[162] Thompson, however, was apparently not up to speed on her American history. Were not the Founding Fathers enlightened men, aristocratic disinterested republicans who considered the idea of a divine Christ, in the words of John Adams, "awful blasphemy?"[163] Was it not Thomas Jefferson who, according to esteemed early American scholar Gordon S. Wood, had "denounced the 'priestcraft' for having converted Christianity 'into an engine for enslaving mankind?'"[164] Church clergy, proclaimed Jefferson in the early 19th century, had turned the institution "into a mere contrivance to filch wealth and power to themselves."[165] Clearly a "menacing" challenge to "Christian courage" had precedent in America. Nevertheless, in a nation rabid with patriotism and blinded by hysteria, articles such as Thompson's were accepted as "gospel truth."

The Saturday Evening Post, a leading anti-Communist voice, printed "Is America Immune to the Communist Plague" in April 1948. In the editorial by Frederic Nelson, the magazine insisted that there "are soft spots" in America vulnerable to Communist contamination.[166] Keying on Communist threats to capitalism, organized labor, and education, Nelson argued that Reds had successfully pushed the nation toward centralization and greater reliance on federal control. Nelson also claimed that the "red tainted, New Deal intelligencia" had waged a successful propaganda campaign in classrooms across country, which vilified entrepreneurship and bred resentment of capitalism. "The fifteen-year New Deal propaganda against success by individuals is still carried on in too many college classrooms," Nelson asserted, "young people are taught that there is no supply and demand, only the greed of rapacious businessmen. [The Communists] effect in weakening the influence of a capitalist economy has been tremendous."[167] Nelson brought his article to a close with a series of apocalyptic remarks concerning the nation's future and the consequences concomitant to a Red presence within America's borders. "America will not prove permanently immune to the dangers which assail other countries," Nelson wrote, "a continuation of loss of faith in our own principles and infiltration of Communists and their stooges may well lead up to some morning when we shall find ourselves taking orders from mysterious and determined men."[168]

The American Mercury continued its series of anti-Communist articles with its summary of the Hollywood hearings in a 1948 article titled "The Communist Record in Hollywood," by author, friendly witness, and alleged "propaganda expert" Oliver Carson. Carson argued that it came as no surprise to many that "the film industry could have been so much under the influence of foreign-directed totalitarians."[169] Carson made this claim in spite of the fact that the Committee, as recognized by several publications including *Time Magazine,* "had failed to establish that any crime had been committed-that any subversive propaganda had ever reached the screen."[170] Olsen wrote that Hollywood had long been a hotbed for Red activity, serving as a breeding ground for subversives and possessing the potential to disseminate Communist agitprop throughout the nation via the silver screen. "The record of Communist activity in Hollywood is a long one," penned Olsen, "dating back many years and involving some of the industry's most glamorous names. In the past ten years Hollywood has become the mouthpiece, heart, and pocketbook of the American Communist Party."[171] Olsen's claim was bold, especially given the fact that the Hollywood CP was perhaps the most benign Communist organization in the country. This position is corroborated by the simple fact that the Un-American Activities Committee, in close to fifteen years of investigating the film industry, failed to produce any link at all between the presumed pocketbook of the Communist Party and any type of Soviet conspiracy, military, nuclear, or otherwise.

In 1949, a year before the emergence of Joseph McCarthy on the national stage, popular magazines provided another deluge of anti-Communist commentary. The strong rhetoric directed against the American Communist Party and featured in magazines was clearly having an impact on popular opinion and in turn, the popularity of anti-Communist organs. According to a January 7, 1949 Gallup Poll, 63 percent of college educated adults, individuals obviously literate and most likely to read with regularity, felt as though the Un-American Activities Committee was doing an admirable job and should continue. On a national scale, only 11 percent of the nation felt as though the Committee should be discontinued.[172] This can certainly be at least partially attributed to the presence of numerous anti-Communist articles found in the pages of America's most widely read publications. Through its media connections, the Committee waged a propaganda war against alleged Reds that vilified progressive Americans and "exposed" the Communist Party of the United States of America as an instrument of the Soviet Union.

Life continued to print articles designed to exhibit the inimical nature of American Communism. "Dupes and Fellow Travelers Dress

Up Communists Fronts" featured two pages full of "mug shots" of America's leading (allegedly) Red figures. Among those pictured were U.S. Congressmen Adam Clayton Powell, Jr., physicist Albert Einstein, poet Martin Van Doren, feminist and grandniece of the famous suffragist Susan B. Anthony, Susan B. Anthony II, and actor Charlie Chaplin.[173] "Up the Red Flags," an editorial, warned of a Communist conspiracy designed cripple the American economy. "Party members, its stooges and press are enthusiastically plugging party analysis that an economic crisis has begun in the U.S., this depression talk is used for their own ends." [174]

The year 1949 also produced perhaps the most provocative anti-Red article ever printed to date. "Where Our Young Commies Are Trained," written by Craig Thompson and contained in the March 3 edition of *The Saturday Evening Post,* served as an appetizer to McCarthy's famous Wheeling, West Virginia address. The article, arguably designed to strike fear in the hearts of parents across the nation, spoke of a progressive school in New York as if it were akin to a Hitler youth camp. A fitting article given its Nazi symbolism and the fact that the German-American Bund was passed over in the early 1940's in favor of the American Communist Party as the subversive organization of choice for the Committee, "Here's Where Our Young Commies Are Trained" held no punches in its attack.

Touching on what had to be an extraordinary sensitive issue among Americans, Thompson alleged that Reds had turned their attention to the youth of the nation in an effort to cultivate young Marxists. If children were being trained as Reds, what possibly could the future hold? Citing New York City's "Jefferson School of Social Science" as a Red pedagogical factory, Thompson observed that "considered collectively [the students of Jefferson], these shiny-eyed boys and girls furnish solid proof that United States Communism is roping in its new puppets by catching them in their teens."[175] Speaking as though "revolution" was the staple of the Jefferson curriculum, Thompson, in a McCarthy-esque tone, warned that "Red children" would develop into Red revolutionaries determined to undermine democracy and usher in a totalitarian age hostile to the liberties and freedoms synonymous with America. "Communism, encouraging blind hatred toward all who deny the myth that communism offers a better way of life, insulates its victims against truth and reason. The boys and girls of Jefferson school wait for their revolution."[176]

Less than a year after the publication of Thompson's article, Wisconsin Senator Joseph McCarthy, on February 9, 1950, walked into a Republican Women's Club meeting in Wheeling, West Virginia and proclaimed that "I have here in my hand a list of 205 people that were known to the secretary of the state as being members of the Communist Party and are still making and shaping the policy of the State Department."[177] Thus, the age of McCarthy was officially born. The climate that welcomed McCarthy, however, was cultivated long before he stepped up to that West Virginia podium. Thanks in part to over ten years of HUAC, Hollywood, Hoover, and the constant anti-Communist media blitz, the American Communist Party had already been demonized and McCarthy simply capitalized on an extant repressive social environment defined by fear and paranoia. Magazines played an instrumental role in the creation of this combustible climate which continued to intensify under "the reign" of the capricious Wisconsin senator.

A poll taken three months before McCarthy burst onto the scene showed that nearly 70 percent of the nation felt as though communism should be forbidden by law.[178] Clearly, had it not been for the support that the anti-Communist crusade received from both the American press and popular magazines, it would not have been able to generate the momentum that led to the era of suppression known as McCarthyism. With popular support running high, the Un-American Activities Committee exercised its will in an unjust fashion that went virtually unnoticed by a majority of the American citizenry. Pliable Americans across the country, blinded by fear of internal subterfuge, concentrated on the so-called evil of American communism as it was spoon fed to them by such prominent publications as *Reader's Digest, The Saturday Evening Post,* and *Life.* These magazines could have presented a different, more objective picture that may have defused Communist hysteria and allowed the nation to look beyond the menacing shroud cast by the "Red Scare." Instead, they served as a mouthpiece of the Committee and contributed invaluably to the proliferation of "Red" fever. The Committee, along with its investigation, was both corrupt and un-democratic yet it roamed free throughout America's progressive enclaves like a loose cannon persecuting unsuspecting Americans burdened, in many cases, unfairly with the stigma of traitor. Painted Red before they could extol their innocence, hundreds of undeserving Americans fell victim to a purge democratic by design, but despotic in function. No community experienced the potency of this policy more than Hollywood (in the late 1940's), arguably the cornerstone of the Committee's near two decade crusade. It could be said that if not for the Hollywood purge, there would have been no McCarthy. Now more than one scholar may call this a stretch, but there is no denying the fact the damage done in tinseltown sent a signal to the nation that the post-war "red hunt" was on.

Chapter Four
The Communist Conundrum: Moderate Hollywood Communists and Why They Were Subject to the HUAC Inquisition

The HUAC investigation of Hollywood (1938–1951) devastated the film community like no other event in its history. The drive to eliminate Communism within Hollywood touched every corner of the industry and fragmented America's most recognizable enterprise. Spearheaded by soon to be convict J. Parnell Thomas, known racist John Rankin, and "red baiter" extraordinaire Richard Nixon, the 1947 Hollywood Hearings produced drama that could only be found in tinseltown.[1]
With all of its glitz, glamour, and prestige, Hollywood represented a fitting post-war starting point for an attention starved HUAC who translated their film-land success into an escalation of federally prosecuted anticommunist activity. The HUAC-Hollywood hearings also played an instrumental role in establishing the repressive tenor that would come to dominate the McCarthy era. It was a purge justified by the infamous propaganda charge, an allegation that proved nothing more than Committee fabrication. What the Committee did accomplish, however, was the establishment of a "blacklist" for supposed "Red" employees. On that list were names of individuals guilty of nothing more than progressive thinking in a time when HUAC correlated a call for equality with global revolution. The repressive, media driven red scare climate of the time only assisted in perpetuating the "list" which marginalized, ostracized, and, in several cases, ended the careers of several of the industry's brightest figures.

By choosing not to differentiate between the "moderate" brand of Hollywood Communism and the more doctrinaire or hard-line Communism practiced in New York and points further east, the Committee effectively listed all Hollywood Communists under one "subversive" label. Anyone who even remotely challenged the legitimacy of the Committee received the stigma of traitor. Consequently, undeserving moderate members, former members, and party affiliates or "Fellow Travelers," falsely accused of insidiously "propagating" Communism, were unjustly persecuted. A resistant group of Hollywood individuals, however, refused to accept the un-American label sitting down. These men and women sought to illuminate the distinction between progressive and subversive and demonstrate their Americanism in the face of an unwarranted un-American charge.

Making life difficult for progressives who wished to elude the tag of traitor was the intensification of the Cold War. It was no secret to those "connected" to the Communist Party that a corollary between Cold War tension and anticommunist inertia had materialized in post war America. In the aftermath of the Second World War, "the country," according to Gerald Horne, "was moving rapidly away from the relative liberalism of the wartime era to an illiberal Red Scare."[2]American paranoia, energized by Mao Tse-tung's thrust for power in China and Stalin's so called "designs" on Central Europe, only augmented the menacing nature of a "second" American "Red Scare." Equally damaging to the party's image was the ever growing Communist presence in Korea, site of the first legitimate Cold War confrontation. Poised to consume Eastern Europe and China, "empowered" in half of Germany, and ostensibly on the move in Southeast Asia, Communism, in the eyes of Truman and his associates, seemed virtually unstoppable. The American populace, distraught over the possibility of a nuclear confrontation with the Soviets, began to accept the government's position that the need to isolate and eventually eliminate domestic communism would ultimately determine the fate of the nation.[3] As noted by historian Elaine Tyler May, by the late 1940's, Americans had reached the conclusion that Communism stood as the world's most feared and potentially destructive menace. "The United States was now pitted against its former ally, the Soviet Union, as its major foe," writes May, "The Cold War was largely an ideological struggle between the two superpowers, both hoping to increase their power and influence across the globe. The divisions in American society," May continued, "along racial, class, and gender lines [ostensibly precipitated by the introduction of progressive Communist societal values into mainstream American life via the CPUSA] threatened to weaken society at home and damage its prestige in the world."[4]

Although a broad range of alleged American communist "organizations" came under attack as a result of mounting paranoia, Hollywood, with its large number of Communists and "Fellow Travelers," emerged as the Committee's prime post war target. Despite the fact that the majority of "Reds" in Hollywood had distanced themselves from the Party by 1947, HUAC moved into tinseltown bent on exposing a full blown revolutionary conspiracy. The investigation dealt the community a devastating blow based on the large number of "moderate" Communists within the industry and the influential roles that party members, former members, and "affiliates" played in film production. Communists pervaded all facets of the film industry, from screenwriters and cartoonists, to actors and musicians. In fact, many of Hollywood's most gifted artists were either party members or had attended party meetings by invitation from active community members. In essence, the Hollywood division of the Communist Party played a central role within the film industry and, in turn, its eventual liquidation proved utterly devastating.

The Un-American Activities Committee's fears, while exaggerated, were not totally unfounded concerning the Hollywood Communist Party's attempt to insert a piece of its ideology into film. It was the nature of the message, however, that the Un-American Activities Committee misunderstood. Moderate Communism in Hollywood (and throughout Southern California), was not driven by a revolutionary Leninist agenda to usurp American democracy.[5] Moderate Communists in Hollywood or "cinema" or "parlor" Reds possessed a collective belief that socialistic change would bring about a better society for all. As members of an elite "star powered" fraternity, many felt a sense of guilt regarding their economic status and looked for an avenue to give back. The Communist Party was a "nebulous thing," declared screenwriter Robert Rossen to the Committee during his 1951 testimony, which contained "many in its ranks" that were not "hard core Communists" but social progressives.[6] Liberals, according to Rossen, committed to social reform and who "find in the Communist Party an outlet for a sense of grievance."[7]

Consistent with Rossen's rationale, the Hollywood Communist Party had emerged in the 1930's as a proponent of social change and many believed an active role in the party to be analogous with philanthropic humanitarianism. "Whatever else may be said of Communists and the goals they pursued," declared Dalton Trumbo, "I think you can agree that those who joined the party were animated by a sincere desire to change the world and make it better. The impulses which caused them to affiliate with the CP were good impulses, and the men and women who acted on them were good people."[8] Trumbo's justification for party membership was shared by other Southern California progressives. Historian Gerda Lerner, forced to flee Nazi Germany as a child, found companionship in the Communist Party. A woman whose childhood had been plagued by vehement discrimination and extreme poverty, Lerner used the Communist Party as a vehicle to champion humanitarianism in America. "My attitude toward the Soviet Union was never an important aspect of my decision about being a Communist," remembered Lerner, "What was important to me [along with her fellow members of her Southern California branch] was the fight against racism and the resistance to nuclear war. The price of a hamburger, the availability of decent housing, adequate low-cost childcare, those were my issues. I was proud," declared Lerner, "to become part of a collectivity that I believed would make my country more just, more democratic."[9]

Besides its star-studded membership and its popular appeal, what made the Hollywood party unique was that it was much more than merely a political organization. Politics, although regularly discussed at meetings, was never the preeminent issue among Hollywood Communist Party members. Because the organization was not designed to cultivate revolution (in a physical sense), its members focused on societal issues, promoting community, and extending democracy. Dan Bessie, Hollywood director, producer, and son of blacklistee Alvah Bessie recalls, "The Hollywood Party wanted to make sure that people practiced what they preached. If a group promoted racial harmony, such as a school PTA, we wanted to make sure that racial discrimination was non-existent in their organization. It was about forcing people to live up to what they claimed to believe in."[10] Actor Larry Parks, hauled before the Committee during its second round of Hollywood hearings in 1951, described party meetings as social rather than revolutionary gatherings. "For all intents and purposes," declared Parks during his March twenty-first HUAC testimony, "it was more of a social occasion than any kind of unusual meeting."[11] The Hollywood Communist Party, according to Parks, "Fulfilled the needs of a young man who was liberal in thought, idealistic, and for the underdog."[12] The party also provided a sense of family within the film industry, offering many who had traveled to Los Angeles from other regions of the country and the world the opportunity to attain friendship as well as a forum within in which to discuss personal, political, and economic issues with peers. As many within the industry were transplants, the party lured hundreds of perspective members based on its social principles alone. "In a world without roots, peopled by orphans from urban centers and European refugees, the party provided a family of sorts," observed historian Nancy Lynne Schwartz, who also pointed out that due to the "party's progressive attitude towards women," it "fostered better male-female relationships."[13]

Moreover, because of its opposition to discrimination, the party was a sanctuary for the traditionally marginalized. The party, for example, provided an arena in which gender equality became a prominent issue. As women were pressed into "male roles" during World War II (such as working in factories and on assembly lines), they asserted themselves outside the domestic sphere in American society. Although there was a call in the immediate postwar period for the return of women to the household, feminism (spawned in the mid-1800's, forwarded in the late teens, and further cemented by progressive organizations like the CPUSA in the 20's and 30's) stood poised to explode.

In the early years of the Cold War, some American women were no longer satisfied with their role as homemakers. "The year 1945 was a watershed for American women," notes historian Kate Weigand, "At the beginning of that year, many believed that women's participation in the war effort had permanently altered their role in U.S. society [a shift for some women from the household to the workplace]."[14] The sense of confidence gained by many women during the war years would inspire progressive women throughout the fifties and set the stage for the emergence of the postwar American woman as a vital contributor to both the Civil Rights and Free Speech Movements of the 1960's. In the words of Susan Lynn, "The postwar progressive coalition played a crucial role as a bridge that linked the prewar progressive work of woman reformers with women's activism in the movements of the 1960's."[15] The Communist Party, home to more than a few independent women, was certainly not void of gender discrimination. "They [certain members of the Hollywood CP] were just a chauvinistic as anyone," maintained Hollywood progressive and female activist Jean Rouveral Butler, "They didn't think the 'woman question' applied to them."[16] Nevertheless, based on the farsighted nature of the majority of its "membership," the Hollywood CP played a critical role in Lynne's "progressive coalition" calling for greater gender equality.[17] "American Communism empowered women," Ellen Schrecker observes, "encouraging them to become politically active. Though the Communist Party's top leadership remained overwhelmingly male, women also had considerable influence within the Party."[18] The idea of greater equality among the sexes resonated strongly in Southern California, a region with a long progressive history. Gerald Horne has noted that, by 1940, the progressive Communist Party was one of the fastest growing organizations in the state. "The Great Depression, the specter of fascism, the widely shared perception that other organizations were ill equipped to combat racism, an upsurge of labor, and the defense of immigrants" all contributed to the popularity of not just the CP, but of progressivism in California.[19]

Dorothy Healy, who headed the Southern California Branch of the Communist Party throughout the "blacklist period," became attracted to Communism as a young girl growing up in Northern California. Healy admired its stance on extreme poverty and unemployment in the wake of the stock market crash of 1929. Healy became a member of the Young Communist League (YCL) as a student in the 1930's not because it presented her with a means to threaten the security of the nation, but because it offered both a sense of community and the opportunity to address the many socio-economic maladies plaguing the San Francisco area during the Depression. "The mood of Americans who were unemployed was the feeling that it was all their fault," explained Healy, "What was important to me, and again, of significance to the rest of my life, were the impressions that were accumulating, to see this shift in consciousness."[20]

Healy took pride in the Young Communist League's quest to assuage the effects of pervasive unemployment in the Bay Area. Her efforts to assist the less fortunate infused her with a sense of purpose and desire to do more. Through rallies and demonstrations, the Berkeley Young Communist League petitioned the government, on both a state and federal level, to liberate the thousands of homeless and hungry from the chains of poverty. Healey took special notice of the many young parentless boys and girls struggling to survive on the street. "There were tens of thousands of transients who would just tramp the country riding roads, hitchhiking, anything because they couldn't stay home; there was no way to live. So we organized a group, a movement known as the League of Homeless Youth."[21] Utilizing the experience gained as a YCL member and relying on her socialist instincts, Healy forged an altruistically oriented community determined to defy destitution. "Everybody would chip in money and we would rent one big home that everyone would live in, what today would be called a commune. During the unemployed activities, we would organize the neighbors to put back furniture of homes where the family was evicted, teach them how to turn on the electricity when it was turned off. We never philosophized," remembered Healy, "if we had, we would have disdained the idea of being pacifist or non-violent.[22]

A leader within the Young Communist League at a very young age, Healy did not regard her gender as a symbol of inferiority or incompetence. Due to the party's progressive views on women within society, Healy flourished in her leadership role. She remembered the respect she had received during an Imperial Valley labor organizing venture: "There was a great deal of male-female equality among the organizers. I can't remember then or in any other activity," asserted Healy, "where there was any attitude of male supremacy, any challenging because I was either a young woman or just a woman-just a total unconcern with it. If you seemed to know what you were doing, if you had something to say, there was respect."[23] For Healy, being treated as an equal at a time when gender discrimination was still very much a part of mainstream society gave her a feeling of self-worth and imbued her with sense of independence. The Communist Party gave women such as Healy an opportunity to escape the "domesticated" stereotype. Early feminist Betty Friedan, author of *The Feminine Mystique,* the famed progressive manifesto, shared Healy's perspective concerning

Communism and its role within women's liberation. "I am not advocating that women become Communist sympathizers," announced Freidan, "but I am expecting that progressive women be so labeled."[24] Historian Ellen Schrecker has also recognized the Communist Party's role in advancing the cause of women. "American Communism empowered women. There was a kind of 'popular front' Feminism that expressed itself in the activities of a strong cohort of talented women."[25] Moderate Communism, as recognized by feminists such as Healy and Friedan, nurtured the dream of a society absent of gender bias.

Healy, through the confidence that she gained as a Young Communist League member, proved that it was possible for a woman to succeed in a "man's" role as she eventually ascended to the head of the Southern California Party. Her success as a leader within the Southern California Communist Party became a recruiting tool for the party as many Hollywood progressives believed in greater equality among the sexes. Party members such as screenwriter Abraham Polansky, who routinely cast women in prominent roles in his scripts, and Paul Jarrico, the driving force behind the powerfully progressive film *Salt of the Earth,* embraced a progressive position on gender.

The liberal position on gender embraced by several influential progressive Hollywood figures would go as far as to eventually contribute to the emergence of the feminist component of the student movement and the subsequent propulsion of women into the American mainstream. Such far-sightedness regarding the sexes became a valued staple of the late 1960's and early 1970's progressive movement. "Their bold new thinking about the independence of gender, race, and class, and about the personal and cultural aspects of sexism, shaped modern feminism-both directly and indirectly-and laid absolute critical groundwork for the second wave," comments historian Kate Weigand, "Since its emergence in the 1960's the modern women's movement has transformed gender relations and women's status in the United States. The issues Communist and progressive feminists raised in the decade after World War II still reverberate throughout American society in the twenty-first century."[26]

The efforts of moderate Communists such as Healy, Abraham Polansky, Paul Jarrico and others forwarded the goal of bringing about a society that embraced gender equality.[27] It is also clear that this progressive stance regarding women (and all oppressed groups), espoused by many of those who resisted the Hollywood inquisition, was something that the Committee feared might evolve into a broader movement for women's rights. Despite the fact that the Committee never formally stated that early feminism threatened the stability of the nation, preserving the male order, a principle tenet of the status quo, was part of its agenda. As expressed by May, "Single women [following the war] now became targets of government sponsored campaigns urging women back into domestic roles."[28] Added May: "The sources of popular ideology insisted that male power was as necessary in the home, as in the political realm, as the two were connected."[29] It is rather easy to conclude, given the ultraconservative character of the Committee, that the idea of gender equality inspired nausea among its members. If Jews were "Kikes" and blacks sub-human, where do you think women ranked in John Rankin's social hierarchy?

Although it may never be definitively proven that the Committee targeted the Hollywood CP in part because it harbored members who believed in equal rights for women, the fact that it targeted the Congress of American Women (CAW), an organization that was both supported and inspired by the American Communist Party, lends credence to the theory that the party's position on gender equality may have instigated HUAC. Regarding the relationship between the Communist Party and CAW, Kate Weigand has observed that "Between 1946 and 1950 Congress of American Women leaders were able to build on the Communist Party's discussions of women from the 1930's and, using insights from [American Communist and author of *In Woman's Defense*] Mary Inman's work, developed a sophisticated analysis of women's oppression that recognized both the importance of women's race and class differences and the need for women to unite on the basis of gender to fight for their own emancipation."[30]

In 1948, the Un-American Activities Committee listed CAW as a "subversive" organization and targeted CAW within the scope of its anti-Communist campaign. As a result, the Committee was able to tie the Congress of American Women to the American CP, correlating feminism with a Soviet plot to subvert the nation. "The U.S. government dealt the final blow to the Congress of American Women when the House Committee on Un-American Activities published its scathing *Report on the Congress of American Women* in October 1949," asserts Weigand, "HUAC's report concluded that the purpose of the organization was not to 'deal primarily with women's problems, as such, but rather to serve as the specialized arm of Soviet political warfare in the current 'peace' campaign to disarm and demobilize the United States and democratic nations generally, in order to render them helpless in the face of the Communist drive for world conquest."[31]

As seen through the persecution of the Congress of American Women, the Committee targeted progressives and progressive organizations. Since Healy, Polansky, Maltz, and other members of the Hollywood Communist Party who believed in gender equality were hauled before the Committee, it seems clear that their social positions were on trial alongside their political ones. Ironically, in a society where all are technically equal, those possessing progressive social views, such as a vision for a society free of discrimination, were among the first to be targeted by the Committee.

Whether those who named names were aware of the true nature of the Hollywood CP may never be fully determined. What is clear, however, is that the party was prevented from exhibiting its actual orientation during the hearings. As a result, its progressive platforms remained concealed. Silencing the voice of those "on trial" during the 1947 Hollywood hearings, however, allowed the Committee to associate moderate Communism with subversion and effectively facilitated its inquisition. Dan Bessie, whose father Alvah was one of the few members of the Ten allowed to read a portion of his statement during his 1947 House Committee on Un-American Activity appearance, observed that, "Of course, had Lawson and Trumbo been allowed to read their statements a better understanding would have emerged regarding the party and its principles. What they got instead was a group of justifiably indignant men. The fact that they were denied basic liberties infuriated the Ten, especially Lawson-he was mad."[32] Albert Maltz, a man censured by the Committee during his hearing commented: "The Communist Party on the American scene stood for humanity's hope for world brotherhood and peace and social progress; my conscience made me join despite whatever anxieties I had."[33] This view, however, was never publicly expressed as the Committee successfully muzzled Maltz and his fellow party members. As Maltz later told an interviewer, "We were forced to keep quiet our opinions and our viewpoints concerning society."[34] It was not until long after the blacklist had ruined hundreds of careers that the progressive views of the moderate Communist Party began to emerge.[35] "Yes, that is the unfortunate reality of it [that the voice moderate Communism was successfully muted], to a degree, it is still that way," Dan Bessie recently remarked, he continued "People focus on the hearings and never learn the real reasons behind why those men and women stood "trial."[36]

To this day, both the moderate position and the mission waged by Hollywood moderates to dissolve the Committee remains somewhat of a mystery. Kevin Starr, in *Embattled Dreams,* refers to the Hollywood Communist Party as a propaganda organ for the Soviet Union during the Second World War (thus hinting that the purge may have been justified). This illustrates a gross misunderstanding of moderate Communist principles and incriminates all those who belonged to the party, regardless of their patriotism. Writes Starr, "When Hitler invaded The Soviet Union in June 1941, it became time once again to crank up the anti-fascist, pro-Soviet propaganda machine."[37] Using convenient discretion, Starr cites Donald Ogden Stewart's *Keeper of the Flame* for evidence, ignoring the dozens of pro-American wartime works completed by members of the Hollywood CP. According to Ellen Schrecker, however, Communist propaganda never found its way into film. "The producers controlled the final product and, though happy to use the talents of their left-wing writers, they were not going to let anything subversive on the screen. At best, the Hollywood Communists could cast a few black actors or write war movies that stressed cooperation rather than individual heroics."[38] Albert Maltz, commenting on the nonsensical nature of the propaganda charge, has noted that Communist propaganda was readily available at any bookstore in America. After all, Maltz explained, Karl Marx's works had sat on bookstore shelves for years. "It was further a part of said conspiracy that said defendants would publish and circulate books, articles, magazines, and newspapers advocating the principals of Marxism-Leninism," stated Maltz, "Here is a volume of literature [the Communist Manifesto] that has been in existence for a hundred years and has been circulating in this nation for that length of time. If the principals of Marxism advocate a violent overthrow of the US government as alleged, why has it taken a hundred years to discover it?"[39]

Maltz and his fellow progressives in the Hollywood Communist Party were "moderate" because they sought not militant revolution, but the chance to encourage social change in America in a subtle fashion. They shied away from focusing solely on producing scripts documenting the plight of the upper class. "What we wanted to exhibit was a more humane attitude towards human beings-humanistic values," maintained Paul Jarrico, "We wanted a fairer picture of women and for minorities to be represented with greater dignity."[40] Dan Bessie echoed Jarrico's sentiments "We were trying to make films that reflected the lives of real people. Hollywood was a dream factory, we wanted to represent ordinary America."[41] Paul Buhle and Dave Wagner note that Hollywood Communists, "Second to none in promoting the war effort" may have inserted a "glimpse of anti-capitalism," but making a political statement was never a key issue."[42] Challenging conservatism, eventually in the form of taking on the anti-Communist crusade, defined the moderate agenda. "Firm challenges to racism and sexism were more than just benevolent "do-goodisms" [for Hollywood Communists], stated Gerald Horne, "overcoming bigotry was at the core of repulsing reactionary anti-Communism or anti-Semitism for that matter."[43] Jarrico, looking back on the HUAC accusations, stated that he and many of his fellow blacklistees were insulted by the manner in which the Committee refused to look beyond the Communist stigma in order to see what the men and women before them actually represented. "I felt I was on the left of American politics, but I certainly didn't feel like I was some foreign agent," Jarrico resolutely asserted, "not just in the conventional sense of some spy for Russia but, you know, in the sense of some man from Mars who was not really connected to what was happening in his own country. I don't say this as an apology," declared Jarrico, "I think we accomplished a number of good things, or things that I for one am certainly not ashamed of." [44]

If incorporating roles for minorities in film was propaganda then most of those who challenged the Committee stood guilty as charged. Gerald Horne has noted that John Howard Lawson, the same man demonized by the Committee as the epitome of Soviet treachery, took a stance on race that assuredly did not help his cause with the Committee. Horne observes that Lawson utilized the political forum presented by the Communist party to advocate racial equality. "He [Lawson] became one of the first white American writers in the 20th century to involve himself directly in the actual struggle of American Negroes for legal and political justice."[45] What progressives like Lawson wanted to illustrate is that in America, humane ideals should have been embraced, not criminalized.

The propaganda charge proved problematic for the Un-American Activities Committee as well, despite its manipulative abilities. The Committee found that trying to blur the line between propaganda and progressivism was a difficult task, especially when dealing with witnesses capable of differentiate between the two. Time and again the Committee relied on "friendly" witnesses who, unable to support the subversive charge, directed the Committee's attention to the party's position on social issues. Friendly witness and composer David Raskin, in a post-testimony statement, remarked that "The whole thing was some kind of insane ritual. I said to myself, 'this is like the Spanish inquisition, so maybe the best I can do is come out of it alive.' I didn't want people to think that this brand of progressive ideology was something I was ready to destroy myself over. I did what I thought I had to do."[46] As Raskin put it "the progressive ideology" was, at least for him, not worth going to jail for. Clearly, Raskin felt that progressivism was a crime alongside propaganda. Of course the Committee never formally established that progressivism was on trial, but failing to deny it certainly helped establish the convenient intimidation factor.

In many cases, even an attempt by a Communists screenwriter to challenge the social status quo via the insertion of a "progressive" component into a script (such as Polansky's inclusion of a white-collar woman or Trumbo's persistent inclusion of minorities) would have been thwarted by studio executives who operated in the interest (both politically and economically) of conservative America. In a period when the banks that loaned the studios money to produce movies were very sensitive about Communism, film moguls were forced to cater to their conservative restrictions. The competition from television also hurt the progressive cause. With the number of television sets in postwar American households increasing, competition for entertainment dollars intensified. Banks wanted movies that would appeal to mainstream America. Essentially, any script containing content even remotely out of the ordinary was shelved. "By the late 1940's, bankers became intensely concerned with audience decline," writes Gerald Horne, "This drop influenced the kind of films that could be made. Allegations about Red labor leaders in the industry repelled capital, for there were many other less 'tainted' areas in which to invest."[47]

A *Daily Variety* article on September 19, 1951 featuring "friendly" witness Leo Townsend's testimony captures the frustration of those who appeared before the Committee. It was virtually impossible, Townsend contended, to integrate propaganda into film: "The steps are many, there are many phases of editing that occur between the presentation of a script and the production of finished picture. Communists would have to indoctrinate directors, producers, and in some cases, executive producers and studio heads in order to insure that a slanted film reached the screen. Studio heads are not now or ever have been members of the party. The Communists never got one step towards first base."[48] In light of Townsend's revealing remarks, one has to wonder what was so threatening about scripts produced by Hollywood CPers. If propaganda was absent from film, what precipitated statements such as the following one in the Tenney Commission report of 1948: "Motion pictures are particular targets for Marxist infiltration because of their propaganda value."[49] Clearly, movie moguls, intimidated by the Committee, feared the progressive themes inserted into screenplays written by members of the Hollywood CP. Controversial scripts that dignified the "liberated" woman (*I Can Get It for you Wholesale*) or attacked anti-Semitism (*Crossfire*) worried the Hollywood brass based on their threat to the "status quo." "Though moguls spared no expense in producing extravaganzas such as *Gone With the Wind* that were criticized as racially insensitive, the presentation of contrary images was seen as more problematic," maintained Horne, "Reducing the overall level of bigotry [in Hollywood] was hard when anti-Negro racism was blithely tolerated. Moreover," Horne continued "the fact that some of the most insistent investigators of Hollywood also happened to be stolid conservatives-and anti-Semites-was difficult to ignore. HUAC's council, Robert Stripling, 'was a southern white supremacist.'"[50] Producers realized that the Un-American Activities Committee purge was not only a campaign designed to eliminate Communism, but also a crusade to control film content. Cooperating in the effort to preserve conservative American ideals was the only way for producers to maintain their status in the industry.

The question surrounding whether Hollywood Communist Party members actually integrated propaganda into their scripts was addressed by journalist Charles Champlin in a 1985 article written in memory of legendary Hollywood screen writer and Hollywood Ten member Ring Lardner Jr. Looking back on the controversy, Champlin offers similar commentary to that of Townsend regarding the Hollywood Communist Party and propaganda. "The notion of even the subtlest treasonable ideas slipping past such watchdogs of public morality as Louis B. Mayer and Jack Warner and Walt Disney was ludicrous."[51] Commenting on the inquisition at large, Champlin observed "At the Committee hearings, it was invariably the writers' and actors' private beliefs rather than their scripts and public performances that were on trial. In a country based on freedom of though and expression," stated Champlin, "it was a shocking and demeaning spectacle, with strong undertones of cynicism, hypocrisy, and anti-Semitism, and it can only be explained by the pervading climate of fear, manipulated for political and economic ends. It was a failure of national confidence."[52]

Paul Jarrico's observations mirrored both Townsend's and Champlin's regarding Communist propaganda in film. Jarrico noted that the Committee's labeling of progressive themes such as the advocacy of women's rights or the fair treatment of African Americans as propaganda illustrated its obtuse sectarianism.[53] "We realized that we could never have anything radical on screen," explained Jarrico, "We did think that we could have a more humane attitude towards human beings in general and as individuals-humanistic values. We did think that we could have a fairer picture of women and of their capacities, of their value, and not just that women were solely sexual objects. We did think that minorities could be represented with greater dignity."[54] Screenwriter Larry Parks shared a similar sentiment and clarified that that the men and women on trial were in the "entertainment business," although if an opportunity to address "social ills" presented itself, progressive screenwriters would often capitalize. The task of entertaining, however, always transcended any social agenda. "This is a great industry, It has a very important job to do to entertain people," recalled Parks, "in certain respects to call attention to certain social evils, but mainly to entertain. In this," continued Parks, "I feel that they have done a great job."[55] Agitprop, according to Parks, was nonexistent. Not all films are equal and many produced suffered from poor storylines, sloppy direction, or a lack of character chemistry. No film or filmmaker, however, could be considered guilty of actively sponsoring tyranny via the creation of a film oriented around a clear revolutionary line. "I think this is the proof of what I say," proclaimed Parks, "That you can not find one film that had been slanted adversely deliberately."[56]

Dorothy Healy, who remained in close contact with many Hollywood Communists during the HUAC purge, also offered pointed commentary on the spurious nature of the propaganda charge. "The charge against them, that they were trying to get Communist propaganda into the movies was poppycock," railed Healy. "The kind of examples used were so fantastic and silly, especially the Rodgers line 'Share and Share alike, that's America to me' (referring to a line delivered by Ginger Rogers in Dalton Trumbo's *Tender Comrades,* insinuating that all Americans shared equally in the scarcities of World War Two)."[57]

Given the absence of propaganda, why, one must ask, did Hollywood emerge as a prime HUAC target? Many, such as Healy, have suggested that the Thomas Committee's purge of Hollywood was not about eradicating "propaganda" but was motivated by a desire to gain national recognition. HUAC, argued Healy, sought to use the visibility of Hollywood to highlight the patriotic nature of their quest. Ellen Schrecker shares this opinion: "HUAC well knew the publicity value of the film world and had been looking for Communists in the motion picture business ever since the late 1930's."[58] Historian Carey McWilliams attempted to flush out the impetus behind the Hollywood investigation as well. The "propaganda" charges levied against Communist screenwriters, he criticized, were simply conjured up in an attempt on behalf of Committee members to garner a piece of the national spotlight. In *Witch Hunt,* McWilliams perspicaciously concludes that Committee member John Rankin had always harbored a thirst for attention and longed to ascend the political ladder in Washington. By attacking Hollywood, the city of stars, Rankin could draw on the media attention and publicity radiating out of Southern California to propel himself into the national limelight. He also saw a corollary between congressional support and control over the production of film. Propaganda did not sound like such a bad idea after all. The *right* kind of propaganda, that is. "The strategy of the campaign required the propagation of a myth, namely, that a subversive minority controlled or insidiously influenced the production of motion pictures," wrote McWilliams, "On this foundation of straw and dust, Mr. Rankin could then build a mansion of lies. Once voiced in Hollywood," continued Williams, "the charge could then be officially taken up in Washington. The inference would be that unless the producers initiated a purge and ceased production of such "evil" films as *North Star, Casablanca,* and *Mission to Moscow,* a frontal attack could be expected."[59]

McWilliams further observed that, through the establishment of the Motion Picture Alliance for the Preservation of American Ideals, formed in the early 1940's and home to high profilers like director Sam Wood and mogul Walt Disney, the Committee obtained a vehicle through which to exercise its will. The Alliance became HUAC's puppet, providing it with an interior presence within Hollywood that the Committee used to acquire "incriminatory" information ("hearsay" accepted regardless of how erroneous it may have been) on suspected "subversives."[60] The Alliance also empowered the Un-American Activities Committee with the manipulative ability that it used (via fear and paranoia) to perpetrate its conservative purge. "The leaders of the Alliance invited J. Parnell Thomas and John Rankin to impose a Fascist censorship on the motion Picture industry in the name of preserving American ideals. An absurd and revolting spectacle indeed; but a dangerous one, also. For the Alliance itself," McWilliams maintained, "is shot through and through with self hatred, the blind mole like fear of change, the deep-seated social envy and sense of personal inadequacy, the cheap cynicism and the pseudo-hardboiled know-nothing-ism of those who cannot imagine the existence of values really worth defending and who traduce, by their every act and statement, the basic American ideals."[61]

As Communism was clearly placed on trial during the pre and post war years nationally, the Un-American Activities Committee's targeting of the moderate branch of the party in Hollywood, a culturally oriented group, exposed a potential "hidden agenda." It slowly became clear to "Unfriendlies" that the Committee was not out solely to persecute Communists for political reasons, but for social ones as well. Dan Bessie remarks that "Undoubtedly, progressivism was a target. The humanistic position assumed by Hollywood Communists was obviously viewed as highly controversial."[62] Many moderate Communists singled out by HUAC as subversive valued others for their character not their color and were out to challenge discrimination in society. Operating with a philosophy built upon equality, where blacks and whites, men and women, rich and poor, were all accorded due dignity, moderate Communists embraced a highly controversial outlook on America in a time when such a view was not widespread. "Screenwriters [such as Maltz, Trumbo, and Jarrico] became a topic of intense concern [for the Committee] for many reasons," confirms historian Gerald Horne, "including their attempts to affect the content of movies and their anti-racist activism."[63]

There is little doubt that the position on race was one reason why the party received so much attention from the Committee. "From the start, reactionaries had been quick to see Red in supporters of Civil Rights," explains Griffin Fariello, "The racists of HUAC tied their kites to the national storm and defended American apartheid under the guise of national security and patriotism."[64] Ellen Schrecker, commenting on the conservative reaction to

Paul Jarrico's *Salt of the Earth*, states: "The enormous opposition to the film reveals how powerful the anticommunist crusade was and how strongly it was committed to suppressing unorthodox views."[65] Gerald Horne clarifies that efforts made by party members to promote tolerance intensified HUAC's investigation of Hollywood. Racist HUAC members, such as John Rankin and Robert Stripling, undoubtedly feared the progressive stance assumed by members of the Hollywood CP. According to Horne, "Communists in Hollywood had to bear the double burden of existing in an environment that was almost casually anti-black, while seeking to conduct a determined anti-racist fight. These communist initiatives on race were not viewed so benignly by Congressman John Rankin of Mississippi and his Un-American Activities Committee."[66]

Most of the men and women of the moderate wing of the Hollywood Communist party or the "Browder" Communists were attracted to the party's progressive societal stance. "I wanted to believe that Russia was very sincere in wanting peace, and I didn't feel the Communist Party in this country was any particular menace," commented director Edward Dmytryk in his April 1951 HUAC testimony.[67] "Our line," insisted Dmytryk in reference to his decision to join the CP's ranks, "was that communism could work with capitalism. There was no need for revolution."[68] Screenwriter Robert Rossen, in a statement to the Committee, provided a window into the mindset of the many "moderates" who joined the party in the 1930's. "The Communist Party draws into its ranks many who in no sense seek the revolutionary overthrow of our institutions as does the hard core of the Communist Party."[69] It attracted men and women, asserted Rossen, "who look to the Communist Party as a method of reform which will cure evils. Many [found] in the Communist Party an outlet for a sense of grievance but they [were] not in reality agents of a foreign principle, nor [did] they entertain treasonable plans. The difficulty," Rossen concluded, "is how to distinguish one from the other."[70] Clearly, the Committee did not possess such foresight.

Many of the Hollywood Party affiliates, such as Abraham Polansky and Paul Jarrcio, were ethnic minorities who had either personally experienced or had witnessed virulent discriminatory acts against American Jews. Thus the party, grounded in egalitarianism, proved very appealing. The Soviet Union's actions against the fascist dictator Franco in Spain also encouraged many in the Hollywood community to join the party. The Soviet stance in Spain illustrated to those fearful of anti-Semitism that Communism was the world's anti-fascist vanguard. "My reason for joining the Party," stated screenwriter Roy Huggins, "was a great despair for the democratic system. I began to think that the choice might not be democracy versus fascism but maybe fascism versus communism. So I was in a great state of despair for the democratic system in 1940, as a good many people were."[71] The fight against fascism consumed many on the left in the late 1930's and early 1940's. For men like Huggins, along with Polansky and Jarrico, if the Communist Party stood as the most outspoken opponent of the ideology, joining its legion instilled in many the confidence that fascism's spread could and would be stopped.

The Communist position regarding organized labor and civil rights also attracted members of the progressive Hollywood left. The bargaining power gained through unionization enabled film employees to petition production companies for higher wages and benefits. Efforts to feed the hungry and house the poor in the aftermath of the Great Depression furnished the party with the philanthropic appeal that many in Hollywood admired and wished to emulate. The party's challenge to Jim Crow in the American South, such as its attempt to demonstrate the innocence of the "Scottsboro Boys" in 1930's Alabama, highlighted its stance on civil rights. Resisting the sectarian nature of both the Smith Act and the Truman "Loyalty Program" further galvanized the community around a call to uphold the pillars of American democracy. Screenwriter and Producer Sidney Buchman, drawn to the party based on its both its anti-fascist position and its promotion of a broader distribution of both equality and opportunity, explained the Hollywood Party's appeal. "My entrance into the Communist Party was of an emotional character. I joined the party when the world was troubled by Fascism, by the rising tide of Fascism abroad. We in America were wondering about the many problems like economic and political inequality. The Communist Party," explained Buchman, "seemed to be the only political force both concerned and willing to take action against Fascism abroad. Another factor was ideological," continued Buchman. Communism seemed to be an ideal experiment to try and achieve a state where all persons have greater democracy. I was worried about the future of our many citizens and myself."[72]

In the end, it was the party's progressive ideology and its desire, as noted by Buchman, to "create greater democracy" that not only drew Hollywood progressives into its community, but also solicited the potent ire of the Un-American Activities Committee. Such a reality served as testament to the climate of the times. Fear of communism had begun to permeate America and "change" slowly became a synonymous with chicanery. The Committee stood as the guardian of the status quo and clearly the Hollywood left constituted a challenge to that sacred equilibrium. It is for this reason that several who defied the Committee actually welcomed the hearings as an opportunity to showcase their desire for overdue social change before an attentive public. Freedom only extended so far in 1940's America and to recognize that was not a symptom of un-Americanism. Unfortunately for those on "trial," however, "red" paranoia had a majority of Americans believing that it was.

There were many reasons why the Committee targeted Communism in America during the early Cold War years. The rapid spread of Communism abroad had both the government and the nation terrified that the "Red Menace" was on course for a global takeover. A highly religious nation, America feared the atheistic element of Communism (although there were religious members of the Communist Party of the United States of America), prompting pious members of society to declare Communism a haunting evil. The role the party played in organizing labor troubled corporate America as well, forcing, in some cases, big business to pay their laborers an honest day's wage.[73] In Hollywood, however, certainly "propaganda" stood as a concern, but it was not the Committee's lone justification for targeting the Hollywood Communist Party. Many moderate Hollywood Communists challenged the "status quo" and advocated greater social and economic democracy by integrating progressive themes into their scripts. Commitment to their farsighted convictions, lost amidst the both the hysteria and the "subversive" charge, is why Hollywood progressives defied the Committee. More was at stake than simply a job for many "Unfriendlies" in Hollywood. The Committee represented elitist, sectarian America and successfully undermining it would not only halt its purge of progressivism, but would send a message to the rest of the nation that the time for change had come. Many of those who resisted realized that if the Committee was not successfully confronted, the assault on democracy would escalate. As seen by those who cooperated with the Committee, however, combating the anti-Communist campaign was not something that many had the resolve to do.

Chapter Five
Communism on Camera: *Ninotchka* and the Cinematic Representation of the Communist Left

It is relatively clear that the American Communist Party posed little threat to the security of the United States in the 1930's and 1940's. The organization was highly factionalized and lacked the sturdy leadership required to remove the party from the political shadows. Although the emergence of Earl Browder in the mid 1930's provided a spark to the flagging CP, the party lacked the numbers, political connections, and overall appeal to mount any type of socialist offensive within the US. The party, in essence, continued to live in a world of dreams, one where Lenin and Stalin were "men of the people" and where the Russian revolution stood as the supreme example of good over evil. Ironically, party members in the United States were victims of their own medicine. Propaganda emanating from Russia provided a false perception of the "heroes" of the revolution which American progressives, in general, swallowed wholesale. "Western communists dutifully followed the lines of the picture supplied from Moscow," writes Robert Service, "Lenin was depicted as a heroic figure, laden with unconditional praise. His humanity as a comrade, a husband and a Marxist had to be extolled. No blemish on his record was tolerable."[1]

"Propagating" the virtues of the great Soviet Society and the men that produced it became the primary "responsibility" of Western communists as Moscow continued to work towards global communistic uprising. America, with its "open" society, provided the CP with a vehicle through which to disseminate its message and attract potential members to its ranks. As Robert K. Murray has observed, as early as the mid 1920's, the Communist Party boasted "a large variety of Communist publications which, while having no official status, still rabidly preached the communist doctrine."[2] In addition to reaching its patrons, however, the communist message was also received by the United States government. Conservative officials had long pointed to Communist propaganda as a conduit to revolution and looked to censure the party before it precipitated a popular attack on democracy. The propaganda charge became a rallying cry for the Committee as it continued to cite publications such as the *Daily Peoples World* and *The New Masses* as instruments of insurrection. Where the government fell short, however, was in Hollywood. Unable to produce a legitimate strand of communist propaganda in the movies, the House Committee on Un-American Activities led a frustrating purge against the Hollywood Left built primarily on fabrications and sensationalized "events." Strangely enough, if any group was guilty of placing propaganda in the movies it was the anticommunist right. The release of *Ninotchka* in 1939 (re-released in 1947) dovetailed with America's growing fear of the "Red Menace." Playing on the peril of "imminent global revolution," the film became arguably the most notorious in a number of conservative attempts to cultivate anticommunism through the powerful medium of film.

The year of *Ninochtka,* 1939, was a difficult one for the communist left. On January 3, 1939, the infamous House Committee on Un-American activities officially came into existence. Although congressional bodies had been investigating "subversive activity" since the early 1930's, the formation of HUAC under the direction of Martin Dies served as a sign that the government was now firmly committed to suppressing so-called un-American activity. No longer would the campaign against anarchists, radicals, and "reds" be a small budget, isolated effort. The campaign against sedition would now have Washington's full backing and would extend to all four corners of the United States.

With the racist Dies at the helm, a man who had long been a proponent of segregation and who wore his anti-Semitism on his sleeve, the crusade to eradicate "extremism" became an all out purge of all those deemed a threat to the nation's social and economic status quo. "Foreign governments are influencing, if not directing, policies and activities of certain organizations in the United States," wrote Dies in an August 24, 1938 letter to President Roosevelt, "those foreign governments are using these organizations in the United States as fronts to advance their causes and interests in the United States.[3] It is apparent," Dies continued, "that these foreign countries have succeeded in transferring their quarrels and "isms" to our shores."[4] As a result, Dies maintained, "the situation is sufficiently serious to justify a thorough and fearless investigation."[5] Liberals, leftists, communists, "anarchists," immigrants, and feminists were among the many "groups" targeted by Dies as he sought to propel himself into national prominence in the same fashion as Mitchell A. Palmer had done nearly twenty years before.

The creation of the Committee also signified a rise in national anxiety regarding "alien" activity within the country. Throughout the late 1930's, radical organizations such as the Communist Party of the United States of America had begun to grow in prominence. The Civil War in Spain had galvanized leftists around a call for American intervention on behalf of the Loyalists as they continued their effort to combat Franco and his German-aided fascist forces. In fact, many Americans, such as Hollywood screenwriter Alvah Bessie, volunteered to serve the Loyalist cause as a member of the renowned Abraham Lincoln Brigade. Support groups such as the Hollywood Anti-Fascist League also emerged which not only mobilized those concerned with the spread of fascism, but also introduced many for the first time to the concept of communism.

With Soviet Russian engaged on behalf of the Loyalists, the CPUSA had taken on an active recruiting role within the United States energetically pursuing individuals intimidated by the prospect of global fascism. Thousands joined up during this period, including hundreds in Hollywood who not only feared totalitarianism, but who also despised the social and economic inequality prevalent in 1930's America. "Well, during the Spanish Civil War I had a very strong feeling for the Loyalists," stated Meta Rosenburg, former story editor for Paramount, "and I was interested in hearing the point of view of any organization or finding out information that I could regarding the Loyalist fight.[6] I found it necessary," Rosenberg asserted, "to make the American people aware of the nature of the fascism in Germany and the menace to peace and people all over the world."[7] Hence, Rosenberg, along with many like minded progressives in Hollywood, gravitated towards the CP and its many "front" organizations, namely the Hollywood Anti-Nazi league.

With fascism clearly on the move, joining colleagues who shared a similar concern for global welfare in an organized venture to stem the spread of the evil ideology came naturally. Of course, becoming affiliated with the CP came with consequences. Many who joined in the late 1930's, including Rosenberg, did not understand the vicious nature of Soviet totalitarianism. They were also removed from east-coast dealings which tended to be more straight-lined than anything one would find out west. In many of the so called "cultural" bands, such as the Hollywood CP, an egalitarian ethos reigned supreme as new party members entertained utopian dreams inconsistent with Kremlin-based reality. Nevertheless, they joined just the same and numbers grew exponentially. As Elia Kazan explained in an opening statement to the Committee in 1952, the CP was synonymous with philanthropy and with the creation of a "better world" for many who joined its ranks in the mid and late 1930's. It was an organ to fight Hitler abroad and poverty and discrimination at home. "I felt that by joining, I was doing something to help them," wrote Kazan in reference victims of the depression, "I was [also] going to fight Hitler, and, strange as it seems today, I felt that I was acting in the good of the American people."[8] Regardless of the intentions, however, Rosenberg, Kazan, and nearly everyone else who joined during this period were quick to realize that their commitment to the CP raised the Government's solicitous brow. With numbers up, justification existed for a through inquiry of Communistic activity. Dickstein was first to issue the call in the early thirties, only to be overshadowed by Fish and eventually Dies who pioneered the creation of HUAC. With the Committee came the evolution of the "menace" moniker which affixed itself to all associated with communism throughout the second "scare" era. The press began to take notice, articles were produced, magazines ran features, and the country began shiver as the reality of a communist uprising seemed not only possible, but imminent.

Dies did not waste any time going for the CPUSA juggler as his first round of 1939 hearings featured the Party's leading men, Earl Browder and William Z. Foster. Added motivation for his blitz of the CP stemmed from a Washington "discovery" of what was deemed to a Red-Jewish plot to "take over the government in August."[9] According to historian Walter Goodman, the government intelligence agencies had ascertained credible information regarding an army of communist "mercenaries from Spain and elsewhere" comprised primarily of Jews who planned to assault the capital, "depress the value of stocks and bonds and foment strikes."[10] A rabid anti-Semite, Dies arguably welcomed the news and looked forward to putting the CP on public trial.

Browder, a mild mannered country boy from Kansas but equipped with an intellect that had the Committee baffled, took the stand on September 5 and put on an impressive performance. In fact, Dies and friends had a difficult time debating with the cerebral Browder as he articulated party positions in a careful, calculated manner. "Several exchanges [with Browder]," recognized Historian James G. Ryan, "reinforced liberal notions that the committee was a band of yahoos."[11] Browder lectured on the shortcomings of capitalism, noting that "a small fraction of the population" held in its possession the lions share of American capital.[12] "Browder proved a suave witness," observed historian August Raymond Ogden, "and insisted that they [the CP] supported anything that tended to improve the conditions of the majority of the people."[13] Unfortunately for Browder, however, his admission to traveling to Moscow on a foreign passport provided the committee with the final laugh. Although he took the fifth and refused to divulge details regarding his overseas adventuring, his affirmative response to the passport question posed by Committee council Rhea Whitley revealed Browder's insidious side. This is the image that the committee wished to present to the public. Although ever so eloquent during his testimony, the Committee was able to use Browder's slip to portray the future CPA head as a leading representative of a most un-American organization.

Foster's testimony on September 29 went more according to plan for the Committee. The renowned labor organizer portrayed the party as a Soviet pawn as he unequivocally underscored the importance the CPUSA's relationship with the USSR. Despite being able to navigate the committee's questioning rather effectively, Foster eventually succumbed to his feverish admiration of the USSR and provided the Committee with the anti-American ammunition required to vilify the American CP.

Prior to his testimony, Foster, the long time CP boss, had been dealing with the ramifications of a heart attack and asked the Committee for leniency during the inquisition. Dies agreed to limit his testimony(ies) to two hours at a time as a result. Foster, who had represented the party as its presidential candidate (1924, 1928, 1932), admitted, to the delight of Dies, that he had been a frequent visitor to Moscow. Dies pounded away at the witness, asking for exact dates of his visits while reprimanding the party chief as he fumbled to remember the business details. "Would it refresh your recollection if I told you the records of the executive committee of the Communist International show that you made a speech in Moscow on March 18, 1925?" snapped a clearly agitated Dies.[14] "Probably so" retorted Foster as he slowly began to recognize the intensity in voice of the Committee chair.[15]

As was costmary for a HUAC "courtroom," the atmosphere was electric as the Committee stared down on the witness with a collective gaze designed to intimidate and eventually, manipulate. Foster, however, refused to buckle in the face of Committee pressure. He was a tenacious individual and had fought through the worst of times as both a noted labor leader and throughout his tenure as CP head. He also clearly possessed the courage of his convictions which proved a catch-22 for the American left. Deceived by the propaganda emanating from Moscow, Foster, along with most American communists, believed the state to be a workers utopia, a true dictatorship of the proletariat, a pure manifestation of Marxist socialism. The horrors of "Red Terror" under Lenin and Stalin (with greater intensity) had been shelved by Soviet propagandists in favor of a glorified image of the Bolshevik state complete with Lenin and Stalin as benevolent "humanists," mere instruments of the masses. Operating under such an impression, Foster found it virtually impossible to admit even a hint of Soviet fallibility. This played into the hands of the Committee as Dies looked to represent the party head as a revolutionary conduit. "Mr. Foster, I would ask you to please identify some of your publications," spoke the solicitous Committee

Council J.B. Matthews, a controversial figure in his own right who possessed close ties to the Fascist German-American Bund. "Is that book written by you, "Towards Soviet America?" "I wrote it," responded a defiant Foster. "And this one," pried Matthews, "From Bryan to Stalin?" "I wrote it also, your questions answered?" shot Foster.[16]

Foster went on to steadfastly defend the Nazi-Soviet Pact, signed in September, and "agreed that any Communist who differed with the party's explanation of the pact would be expelled."[17] This marked an issue of great contention with the Committee and they refused to let Foster off the hook concerning such a hard-line stance. Foster, however, accurately observed that "there was no united front between Communism and Fascism."[18] Emulating Lenin, who engineered Brest-Litovsk in order to put the pieces of his revolution together, Stalin "allied" with Hitler as a means of buying time to get better organized for an inevitable clash between the two nations. "The Soviet Union is not cooperating with the Nazi government," stated Foster, "The Soviet Union has stopped Hitler in the East and every serious political thinker in the world realizes that fact at the present time."[19] Becoming more animated, Foster turned the tables on Dies and excoriated the Chair for contributing to what he contended to be a more glaring issue than Russian actions in the east, that being racial segregation and economic exploitation in the American South. When referring Soviet involvement in Poland, Foster hinted that the Poles had been released from "feudal" bondage by the Bolsheviks. When Dies asked if Foster maintained that "Poland was under a feudal system," Foster responded with "Just like some of the people in this country are under a feudal system, in your part of the country [east Texas] almost."[20]

When the bickering subsided, however, although Foster had arguably chinked the Committee's armor, Dies got out of his witness what he had originally desired. Somewhat frustrated with the intense nature of the proceedings, Foster decided to "open up" regarding his perception of American capitalism and its salient shortcomings as compared to Soviet socialism. His forthright commentary enlivened the courtroom as Foster admitted his devotion to the worker state. When asked if he "owed his allegiance to Russia, Foster answered "only in the sense that it is a Socialist country, a country of workers, that it represents a new stage of society that is going to abolish misery and suffering."[21] The Committee viewed his comments as an open invitation to attack and proceeded to grind away at Foster's patriotism, or lack there of. Foster, however, remained rather controlled and did not offer up much in the way of anti-American fodder. He simply maintained his original position that the Soviet state represented a society built for and governed by the people in the purest sense. Although his image of the USSR was grossly skewed, Foster held his ground and continued in his defense of Soviet socialist utopia.

Refusing to give ground regarding the Hitler-Stalin pact, Foster deemed Allied efforts overseas imperialist and insisted that he would not be privy to such utilitarian action. It was at this time, late in the trial, that Foster's "anti-Americanism" emerged. "If the United States entered the present war, you would not support the United States?" posed an agitated Dies. "If it is an imperialist war against some other country," spoke Foster, "I will not support it." Dies fired back, "you would not support the United States?" "Not in such a war," announced Foster.[22] Committee council J.B Matthews then introduced excerpts from a prior Foster testimony before the Fish Committee, words which undoubtedly portrayed the Communist as an international conspirator. When Fish asked Foster if the "workers of this country look to the Soviet Union as their country," Foster replied "The more advanced workers do." The workers of this country and the workers of every country have only one flag, and that is the "red flag," the flag of the proletarian revolution."[23] This was all the Committee needed to hear as Dies ended the testimony on this most incriminating note. Cleary, Foster took his cue from Moscow and directed the party accordingly. As far as Dies was concerned, Foster along with his band of American communists were nothing more than Soviet hocks determined to foment political and social upheaval.

This rather shocking revelation provided the Committee with all the evidence it felt necessary to call for the dissolution of the American Party. Foster's hazardous claims also the misrepresented the party, as many American "satellite" bands, such as the Hollywood CP, had little or no contact with either Foster or the Kremlin. Foster did not speak for all American progressives as there were many "communist" sects throughout the country that retained the pacifistic element of the American Socialist Party. Communist "clubs" scattered around America may have identified with the Bolsheviks in an anti-capitalistic sense, but these organizations certainly did not subscribe to a revolutionary agenda. "Cinema Rebels," writes John Cogley, "had not the remotest idea of what communism was in terms of economic structures or political super-states. For nearly all of them," continued Cogley, "it was an intoxicated state of mind, a glow of inner virtue, and a sort of comradeship in super-charity."[24] Screenwriter Roy Huggins, who initially joined the Party in 1940 after becoming fascinated with Marx as a student at UCLA, highlighted the autonomous nature of the Hollywood CP in purporting that "The Hollywood group was only interested in Hollywood and they never, as far as I know, had discussions of world politics."[25] Nevertheless, Foster's contention that the American CP was simply

an instrument of the Soviet Union, despite its various sects, inflamed Dies
and prompted the chairman to demand the extermination of the organization. As Goodman recorded "When Foster was done testifying, spectators
cheered Dies' proposal, to be raised innumerable times thereafter, that the
Communist Party be disbanded."[26]

With the Party on trial, the Committee also expanded its investigation
of American Communism to include selected "front groups," organizations
"infiltrated" with Reds that served the party's revolutionary (in many cases
in a social sense) purposes. The Committee's attack on the Federal Theatre Project in 1938 signified the Committee's growing interest in America's entertainment sector. Dies fully recognized the potential of the party
to reach Americans through stage and screen and sought to deduce the
extent of Communist influence in both areas. Film had become a powerful
medium, one that had expanded its influence and possessed the potential to
manipulate thought throughout the globe if used effectively. If Hollywood
was indeed infected with Communism, Dies found it conceivable that the
film industry could easily be converted into a factory for producing Soviet
agitprop. With the stage in New York already inundated with "progressives," it was only a matter of time, according to the Committee, before
Bolshevism moved west and commandeered the screen. With a Hollywood
"survey" forthcoming, Dies set his sights on the Federal Theater Project in
an effort to quash Communist "entertainment" in the east in hopes of preventing its spread west.

The FTP, part of the New Deal's larger Works Progress Administration, provided employment to actors, writers, and directors who had felt
the squeeze of the depression. It was a vehicle through which to keep the
arts alive and provide light hearted relief from the reality of mass poverty.
By the mid 1930's, the project had successfully sponsored hundreds of performances while providing a career avenue for many of New York's most
gifted artists. Plays that had previously been shelved based on their "controversial" themes, such as Marlowe's *Dr. Faustus,* T.S. Elliot's, *Murder in
the Cathedral,* Sinclair Lewis' *It Can't Happen Here,* and W.H. Auden's
Dance of Death, now graced the stage as millions of American's reaped
the fruit of such creative brilliance.[27] What constituted "controversial"
material according to the Committee, however, bordered on the ridiculous.
As Ogden illustrated, HUAC chocked up "a Negro asking a white girl for
a date" as Communist agitprop.[28] Ogden also pointed out that the 1939
investigation of the FTP made for great headlines which certainly captured
the attention of millions. The Dies purge was growing in popularity and as
the Gallup Polls demonstrated, Americans were attuned to the "communist threat." Seventy-Five percent of those polled in late 1939 believed that

Congress should provide money to continue the Dies Committee.[29] It was apparently a resounding success. Dies had begun to realize that targeting the entertainment world correlated with heightened public interest. There is no doubt that a seed had been planted.

It came as no surprise, however, that the FTP had come under the Committee microscope. The project had become known as a heaven for "progressives" who, as Eugene Lyons pointed out, had begun to "feel dissonance between their gin-drinking self indulgence, which most of them could [hardly] afford, and the grim depression world."[30] Elia Kazan, one of New York's most talented writers, fell into this category and began to gravitate toward the left in the early 1930's. Before long, Kazan found himself not only a member of the Communist Party, but an outspoken Marxist intellectual who gained inspiration from Soviet directors such as Vsevolod Meyerhold. Kazan went as far as to become an instructor at the New Theatre League, "a communist front organization" according to historian Kenneth Lloyd Billingsly.[31]

Like Roy Huggings, who became attracted to the CP for its stance against global fascism, Kazan appreciated the economic components of socialism, especially in a time when poverty gripped the land. Many who participated in the FTP, including the future leader of the Hollywood CP, John Howard Lawson, shared Kazan's sentiments and looked to the CP and its progressive ideology as a means of fostering change. Of those who joined during this time, the majority would experience tremendous shock upon discovering the true nature of Soviet tyranny in the late 1940's and 1950's. At the time, however, in the aftermath of Lenin's revolution, the USSR was viewed as the world's first true worker's state, a nation progressing towards a classless society with little government, no poverty, and unlimited social and economic potential. For Kazan, like many "parlor reds," joining the CP was not about turning one's back on his or her own country. It was about belonging to a fraternity of like minded individuals who perceived flaws in America's capitalistic system and looked to bring about change via peaceful avenues. The theatre group (along with other "cultural" sects) represented an isolated "band" that received discussion material from periodicals such as the *Daily Worker* and remained almost completely out of touch with daily happenings in Moscow. "I want to reiterate that in those years, to my eyes, there was no clear opposition of national interest between the United States and Russia," observed Kazan in a April 10, 1952 statement to the Committee, "It was not even clear to me that the American Communist Party was acting as a Russian agency in this country. "On the contrary," continued Kazan, "it seemed to me at the time that the party had at heart the cause of the poor and unemployed people whom I saw on the streets about me."[32] The Committee, however, massed all Communists and so-called "front groups" under one insidious label and refused to differentiate between those like Foster and others like Kazan, Maltz, and Huggins. The FTP provided a perfect target as it served as a bridge to the core of America's Communist intelligencia. Replete with, as Albert Maltz recognized, "highly intelligent people," the FTP along with other "cultural" or moderate Communist originations and "front groups" (like the Hollywood CP) emerged as leading targets for HUAC.[33] "Practically every play presented under the auspices of the project is sheer propaganda for Communism or the New Deal," lambasted HUAC member and vociferous opponent of the Theatre Project J. Parnell Thomas.[34] With Dies growing in popularity, anticommunism had become somewhat trendy as the media, and even Hollywood, where production on *Ninochtka* was well underway, saw Red as the color of money.

With the Dies Committee enjoying the national spotlight coupled with shock emanating from the infamous the Hitler-Stalin Pact, the CPUSA found itself on shaky ground by the end of 1939. Leadership sill remained an issue for the crippled organization as Foster proved unable to bring his vision of a socialist America to fruition. His polemical style and strict allegiance to Moscow contributed to the formation of a party image inconsistent with anything American. "Everywhere since the Nazi-Soviet pact," writes James G. Ryan, "the CPUSA had encountered mistrust."[35] The 1939 hearings did nothing to assuage fear of seditious activity. In fact, Dies had succeeded in reviving the image of the "Red Menace," absent from the American spotlight since the Palmer raids of the early 1920's.

The press also did its part in adding fuel to the anticommunist fire. Articles featuring the Dies committee and the menace of Communism became ever-more prevalent as 1940 approached. "Uproot the Seeds of Totalitarianism" printed in the October 1939 edition of *Reader's Digest,* reflected the national mood. "Communism is not the antithesis of Nazism but the twin of it," charged political commentator and renowned author of "Our Times" Mark Sullivan, "Communism is fundamentally identical with Nazism and also with Fascism; the three are not three new states of society but one."[36] Highlighting the manipulative potential of the communist presence within, Sullivan proclaimed that "certain ideas toward which America is being led are common to Communism in Russia. Each of these advances," contended Sullivan, "has the effect of choking the American system further and further."[37] In an article which served as a sign of things to come for *Reader's Digest,* Sullivan concluded by warning Americans against imminent action from within. The New Deal, according to Sullivan, reeked of Communism and held the potential to "bring death to the American system." "If we let a part of Nazi-Communism take root here and grow," cautioned Sullivan, "we shall presently get the whole of it."[38] Given that *Reader's Digest* was the nation's most widely read magazine in 1939, it is not a stretch to assume that many concerned with the "red" spread took Sullivan's warning to heart.

With the tenor becoming ever more contentious, the time to "capitalize" on growing paranoia had arrived. Hollywood, soon to be the site of arguably the most destructive HUAC investigation, had yet to thoroughly immerse itself in anticommunist filmmaking. Nevertheless, it had produced a number of anticommunist films throughout the 1920' and 1930's, some of which proved more successful than others. With "Red hysteria" beginning to dominate the social climate of the mid and late 1930's, however, it became clear that a market now existed for the production of a large scale anticommunist film.

Ninotchka, although clearly the most successful and arguably the most provocative "anticommunist" film ever produced, was not Hollywood's fist attempt at portraying communism as the fiery "Red Menace." Hollywood had released several films, beginning with a 1919 four-reel comedy centered on the moral transgressions of a young Bolshevik titled *Bullin' the Bullsheviki,* designed to illuminate the menacing nature of Communism. *Fighting Youth* (1935), written and directed by Hamilton MacFadden (with Henry Johnson), featured a gang of turbulent "reds" intent on overrunning a quiet University in bucolic America. Later that year, *The Red Salute* (1935), written by Elmer Harris and Humphrey Pearson and directed by Sidney Lanfield, graced the silver screen with another classic campus confrontation between hostile red agitators against ultra-nationalistic frat boys. In 1936 Paramount released *Once in a Blue Moon,* the story of a clown's abduction by a gang of unruly Bolsheviks. *Tovarich,* the screen adaptation of Jacques Deval's successful Broadway production, hit the box office the following year. *Spawn of the North,* by Jules Furthman and Talbot Jennings and directed by Henry Hathaway, came out in 1938 and served as somewhat of a thematic prequel to *Ninotchka.* With *Spawn,* the most intensely anticommunist film to date, there is little doubt that Talbot and Jennings, sought to capitalize on what was clearly becoming, by the time of the films release, a developing anticommunist market.

Despite the fact that these titles did not achieve *Ninotchka's* level of success, they certainly amplified anticommunist fear. *The Red Salute* proved particularly polemical as its clear cut anti-radical, anti-youth message provoked unrest within liberal communities throughout the nation. In fact, a substantial amount of hostility greeted its initial screening in New York as students from local high schools and universities, angered by the film's

depiction of student "radicals" as communist seditionists, united in opposition to the clearly political piece. The fanfare surrounding the film's initial
screening at the Rivoli theatre was well documented by the New York press
and subsequently picked up by news agencies from coast to coast. *The
New York Times* took a particular interest in the reaction to Red Salute
and printed a series of articles documenting what the paper referred to as a
student "riot."

The students, many belonging to one of two (or possibly both) "com-
munist front" organizations, the National Student League (NSL) and the
Student League for Industrial Democracy, made quite a scene in front of the
Rivoli on October 4, 1935. Confident that Red Salute constituted an attack
on "liberal discourse," the indignant students encircled the Rivoli using
"Boycott the Red Salute" as their marching cry.[39] According to the Times,
the students had marched over to the theatre after a brief meeting of the
National Student League at the Union M.E. Church on West Forty-eighth
Street. The meeting had been organized by the so-called ringleaders of the
action, George Watt, 20, president of the National Student League, and
Robert Joseph, 20, and James Wechsler, 19, both National Student League
members. The three men, along with their fellow NSL members, symbolized a growing number of "alienated" American youths frustrated with the
state of the national economy and ubiquitous discrimination.

The National Student League was known to be a left-wing, intellectual student group which concerned itself with racial inequality and economic exploitation. The group served as an arm of the Young Communist
League (YCL) and attracted a good number of intellectual campus leftists.
Operating on the supposition that students represented a repressed "class,"
the organization attempted to add a student component to the larger concept of class struggle. "The National Student League," asserted historians
Irving Howe and Lewis Coser, "worked on the assumption that the class
struggle raged as actively, if not quite as violently, in the classroom as in the
factory."[40] According to Howe and Coser, members of the NSL despised
the notion that a college campus represented a safe haven, an island, a
detached sanctuary removed from the ills and challenges of every day life.
These young intellectuals furthered the contention that universities were
in fact part of the mainstream. Students, in the eyes of NSL leaders, were
not necessarily out of touch with daily reality but in fact a product of the
"outside" or "real" world and its many complexities. "Starting with the
plausible notion that the university could not be isolated from the major
conflicts of society," wrote Howe and Coser, "they drove toward the dubious conclusion that ideas in the university were merely a reflex of events
taking place beyond its walls."[41]

Although privileged in the fact that these students possessed an educational opportunity afforded to few during this time, they wished to collectively consider themselves as one with the masses. In their minds, members of the NSL shared a similar plight with the penurious majority in the fact that "youth" stood as a synonym for dependency. "Students," in the minds of many 1930's "adults," lacked the "maturity" and experience to think and act independently. When one attempted to challenge this notion, he or she became radical or revolutionary, an instant target of ridicule and an "object" in need of rehabilitation. This trend would continue throughout the 1930's and culminate in the late 1960's when the youth of America exploded in the face of such insularity through the prism of the radical/anti-war movement. In this light, it is rather easy to perceive why *The Red Salute* elicited such a determined response from New York's student left. Its primary currents led the viewer to the conclusion that the "liberal" constituency on campus represented an intellectual channel to revolution. The students who comprised this radical band epitomized the "red menace" in one of its most diabolical forms. Successfully controlling the mind eliminated the need for a physical assault on the body. *The Red Salute,* in essence, communicated this fallacy to its viewers in an attempt to demonize progressive thought and all those intelligent enough to nurture it on campus.

Times columnist Andrew Sennwald exposed the glaring shortcomings of "Red Salute" in his piece titled "On the Anatomy of Americanism" printed in the *Times* on October 6, 1935. In an article that certainly could have peeked the interest of America's growing contingent of anti-communists, Sennwald dissected the film's underlying themes as a means of uncovering its ultimate motive. Sennwald verified that the filmmakers clearly had a political agenda, an agenda oriented around a drive to generate militant patriotism in the face of growing un-Americanism. "[Once] "Red Salute" has completed its definition of Americanism," wrote Sennwald, "it has come to represent the glorification of war as an outlet for the nervous energy of our young men, the suppression of political thought in our universities, the abolition of the Bill of Rights with the connivance of the U.S. Army, and several other doctrines which are less than completely democratic."[42] Of course, Sennwald did not go without taking the customary mainstream journalistic shot at the American CP, referring to it as a "vicious propaganda machine."[43] Nevertheless, his review is candid and his analysis objective as he accurately pinned the propaganda tag on a most unimaginative film. "The film is so obviously propagandizing for the Americanism of the patrioteer and the zealot that it loses all usefulness as a defense of American institutions," Sennwald observed, "By the time "Red Salute" is through using Americanism as a shield behind which to launch its attack on radical and liberal thought in American colleges, most of us who are not professional patriots are bound to decide that the film has worked a positive injury to the cause for which it is fighting."[44] Regardless of its obvious partiality, however, "Red Salute" was certain to cause a stir among its viewers, especially those "patriots" beginning to sense "red" around every corner.

Another 1935 release, *I Stand Condemned* starring the popular Laurence Olivier, contributed yet another title to the growing list of anticommunist films. With The Great War as a backdrop, *I Stand Condemned* portrays Russian tsarist society as one riddled by social and economic unrest. Amidst the turbulence stemming from the war, the Russian people struggle to come grips with its ravages and the crippled condition of the Russian state. Directed by Anthony Asquith, the film details the plight of "new money" merchant Peter Pertovich Bruikov (Harry Baur) and his attempt to transcend the chains of his peasant past and embrace his newly acquired parvenu status. After falling in love with a lovely Russian nurse (Penelope Dudley Ward), Bruikov learns that the apple of his eye is interested not in his companionship, but in his money. As the nurse stems from an impoverished peasant family, she is under tremendous pressure to "marry up" and alleviate financial burdens at home.

The ultimate object of her affection is the young, charismatic army captain Igatoff (Laurence Olivier) who quickly finds himself on trial for treason. After losing eighty-thousand rubles to none other than Bruikov in a gambling venture, Igatoff is forced to borrow money from the one person in town that he knows has access to such capital, Madame Sabine. Unfortunately for Igatoff, Sabine just so happens to be an enemy spy and plots to exchange the debt for critical Russian military information. Luckily for Igatoff, the Russians raid Sabine's quarters before she is able to act on her duplicitous intentions. Nevertheless, a link between Igatoff and Sabine is drawn by Russian authorities and the captain faces a trial with his life and reputation on the line. Ironically, it is Bruikov who ultimately comes to Igatoff's rescue. In an act of great magnanimity, Bruikov comes forward and explains the origin of Igatoff's debt to Russia authorities who ultimately acquit Igatoff of all wrongdoing. The development allows Igatoff and the Russian nurse to marry while Bruikov is forced to take solace in the fact his actions symbolized the birth of the "urban, sophisticated man" that he had long wished to become. Although the story seems innocent enough, its depiction of war-torn, instable, erratic Russia "portrays," writes Michael J. Strada and Harold R. Trooper, "the Russian people as rent by social conflict and by the forces of good and evil."[45] It is a grim portrayal and given its 1935 release, with the Fish-McCormack committees on the move and with anticommunist fears beginning to crescendo, only added to the "alien" image of the Soviet State.

In 1936 Paramount produced *Once in a Blue Moon,* an anti-Bolshevik "comedy" written and directed by Ben Hecht, known throughout Hollywood as an ingenuous yet capricious talent. The film documents the travels of "Gabbo the Great," a peripatetic clown looking for respite from the chaos surrounding the Russian Civil war. Gabbo is victimized throughout the duration of the film by the Bolsheviks, "the heavies," who harass and ultimately imprison the clown for possessing counterfeit rubbles.[46] Once "liberated" by a group of admiring children, the clown proceeds to utilize his freedom to spring a group of "White" soldiers previously detained in a Bolshevik camp.

From a critical standpoint, the film was rather unheralded and received a number of negative reviews. With a plot deemed more suitable for children and a cast lacking star quality, *Once in a Blue Moon* certainly did not qualify as a "blockbuster" production. Its limited appeal also diminished its effectiveness as an anticommunist piece. There is no arguing the fact, however, that it did contain a storyline designed to demonize the "Red" menace in Russia and its appeal to young adults arguably influenced more than one impressionable mind. Frank Nugent, the *New York Times* chief film critic, caught the film at a children's matinee at New York's Plaza Theatre in early 1936. Despite not being afraid to admit that the film was not Hecht's best, Nugent refused to condemn the film entirely and noted that the picture still managed to reveal signs of Hecht's cinematic brilliance. "In a sense, the picture was worth waiting for," wrote Nugent in his February 1936 review, "There isn't a line of brittle dialogue in the piece, not a hint of satire, not a trace of impish impertinence."[47] While lighthearted in nature, Nugent had little difficulty identifying the film's rather political primary thrust. "[Hecht and MacArthur] have placed their fable in Russia at the time of the Red revolution. A Family of aristocrats is hunted down in the forests by red revolutionary soldiers. Their only escape," scripts Nugent, "is offered by the fortuitous appearance of Gabbo the Great, [a clown] whose troupe has deserted him."[48] Although the movie, according to film historians Michael J. Strada and Harold R. Trooper, is void of a "political statement" and offers nothing more than a "mild endorsement of the Whites over the Reds," it provides, nonetheless, a sinister portrayal of Bolshevism consistent with its growing reputation as a menace.[49]

Arguably a prelude to its more famous "sister" film *Ninotchka* of 1939, *Tovarich,* spawn from Jacques Deval's incredibly popular Broadway production, hit the big screen in 1937 as a another in a line of "comedic" anticommunist pictures. Similar to what Hecht and MacArthur accomplished in *Once in a Blue Moon* and what Lubitsch would eventually do with *Ninotchka*, director Anatole Litvak, a Russian, conceals his anticommunist positions behind a comedic veil. It is conceivable that Litvak, a German exile who, like Lubitsch, fled Hitler's wrath, viewed the production of Tovarich as an opportunity to prove his "patriotism" to the increasingly powerful anticommunist contingent in Washington. Headed by Hamilton Fish and the young Texan Dies, who would shortly take the reigns of the infamous House Committee on Un-American Activities, Congress' investigation of seditious activity within the U.S. was in full swing by 1936. The Committee on Rules, chaired by John McCormack, had been conducting executive hearings throughout 1936–1937 in an effort to discern the extent of communist and, to a degree, fascist activity in the United States. An increase in "anarchist activity," which included the attempted assassination of Franklin D. Roosevelt and the emergence of a leftist, anti-fascist coalition in support of the Loyalists in Spain, amplified congressional concern on Capitol Hill. American Communism, according to the "McCormack Committee," "was not sufficiently strong to do harm to American institutions at the actual time, but its growth did present a definite danger to the country."[50] In fact, by mid 1936, Dies had begun to make considerable noise within the halls of Congress lobbying for the passage of anticommunist legislation. It remained the hope of the growing anticommunist congressional contingency that the party eventually be outlawed and its members deported.

Litvak, as well as Lubitsch, was undoubtedly aware of the rise in anti-communist concern in both Washington and amongst the general populace in the mid 1930's. A film designed to exhibit his anti-Bolshevik inhibitions would certainly deflect attention away from his Russian roots (and Jewish ancestry). *Tovarich,* with its anticommunist undertones, allowed Litvak to produce a "comedy" which in actually generated more than simply laughs. Although the film does not constitute an outright condemnation of Bolshevism, its subtle anticommunist hints resonate strongly with the analytical viewer. A product of staunchly anticommunist Warner Brothers Production Company, it is no surprise that *Tovarich* stands as one of Hollywood's earliest attempts at "big budget" anticommunist entertainment.

The plot, similar to *Ninotchka's,* centers on aristocratic Tsarist exiles (played by Claudette Colbert and Charles Boyer) reduced to menial laborers in Paris as they seek sanctuary from Bolshevik retribution. Products of the Tsarsit "feudal" system and guardians of the Tsar's forty-billion franc fortune, Prince Ouratieff (Boyer) and Grand Dutchess Tatiana (Colbert) are entirely out of place in the ever-cosmopolitan Paris. Refusing to touch the money, the two struggle to navigate the hustle and bustle of the city in an attempt to survive as members of the societal "class" that they once commanded. Like Garbo's *Ninotchka*, Ouratieff and Tatiana eventually morph into warm, "concerned" characters who represent, according to Strada and Troper, "charming and high minded" individuals.[51]

Opposite the two Tsarists is the film's Soviet "villain," the insidious Commissar Gorotchenko (Basil Rathbone) "whose brutality towards aristocrats knows no bounds," and "whose cold, incisive persuasions do not fail to arouse fervor in Russia."[52] In fact, Rathbone does such an effective job playing the role of the "Red" scoundrel that film historian David Shipman has referred to the character as the "best all around villain the movies ever had."[53] It is the chore of Gorotchenko to "convince" the two Tsarists to use the monarchial fortune to feed Russia's hungry. Ouratieff and Tatiana, however, are bound to a pact that they share with Nicholas II who entrusted them with the cash to revive the monarchy. Ultimately, the two are wooed by Gorotchenko's "charm" and agree to provide the Bolsheviks access to the money as a means of assuaging the ills of Soviet Russia's hunger epidemic. Similar to the "feel good" ending provided by *Ninotchka*, the manner in which *Tovarich* concludes leaves one with the sense that Russians are indeed compassionate at heart. Not lost on the viewer, however, is the impression left by the Soviet Commissar, a man who represents all that Americans feared concerning the "Red Menace." Heralded as one of the "most important pictures of the year" by the *New York Times, Tovarich,* with its anticommunist underpinnings, reflected growing anxiety regarding the mystery of Communism and its potential both abroad and within.[54]

Although *Ninotchka* enjoyed more success at the box office and generated more publicity given the star-appeal of Greta Garbo, *Spawn of the North,* released in late 1938, was an Academy Award winning production (special effects) and boasted a star studded lineup of its own. Garbo may have been a bigger name, but Henry Fonda, the protagonist in *Spawn,* was certainly a well respected actor and generated quite a buzz with the movie going public. The movie was also heralded for its spectacular scenery as its Alaskan setting provided the picture with breathtaking aesthetic quality. Scenery aside, however, taking center stage in the film is a quintessential Russian who plays the part of villain with a most malicious air. Sporting the name "Red" (Akim Tamiroff), as if a Bolshevik could be referred to by anything else, the Russian raider is a source of malevolent chicanery as he plots throughout the film to divest honest trappers of their hauls through trap raiding. It is a classic case of the upstanding westerner in Fonda versus the ever mendacious easterner in Red punctuated by an epic ending with Red eventually meeting his demise at the hands of Fonda's old friend turned schemer Tyler (George Raft).

Although the political commentary is kept to a minimum, *Spawn* is not void of its fair share of anticommunist quips. One exchange between the unruly Red Skain and a couple of American "good old boys" proved particularly chilling. After consuming several shots of Vodka at the port bar, Red becomes agitated with two Americans "advising" the Russian against his duplicitous ways. Red, who is completely at ease with his role as a bandit, believes the sea and its inhabitants to be open game. According to Red, the first to any trap has the right to the fish it contains. The ocean can not be fenced in and his practice of raiding the traps of his fellow fisherman is justified in his mind based on his "open water theory" (undoubtedly a metaphorical reference to Communism). Of course it also helps that he had yet to be caught. With his temper at its limit and the Vodka heating his veins, Red turns to the two men at odds with his policies and proclaims "they [the fish] don't belong to Alaska, that's the one thing you Yankees couldn't steal from my country. You got everything else, but you don't get the fish."

A classic confrontation between Jim (Fonda) and Red (Tamiroff) highlights the latter half the film as tensions between the Russian and the patriot take center stage. Earlier in the film, unbeknownst to Jim, Red had recruited Tyler to join his venture as a trap raider. This reality confronted Jim as he led a mid-movie expedition to hunt and kill the perpetrators of the trap crimes. It was during an open ocean battle that Jim caught site of Tyler manning a harpoon gun on one of Red's crafts. Jim, acting in the interest of those threatened by Tyler's actions, shot and injured his good friend.

With Tyler held up in bed and Jim at his boiling point over Red's exploits, the two adversaries meet at the lobby bar and produce arguably the films most intense moment. With Red once again saturated with Vodka, Jim approaches from an upstairs loft and greets the Russian at his bar stool. The two lock eyes in an electric stare as Red, in characteristic "Bolshevik" fashion, reveals his colors as a cold, brash, sadistic Easterner. "This bay, she's too small for the both of us," announced Red, "If I catch you out there, I look for you with my harp gun." Jim, stoic and possessor of a cool confidence, responded "too bad you had to say that." Now, with more vigor and vitriol, Red boils over and shouts "keep off the bay or I'll kill you on sight!" Thanks to Jim's old friend Tyler, however, Red would not get that chance as his opportunity was spoiled by Tyler's cunning. With Red and Jim near an epic showdown on the water, Tyler, stowed away on Red's boat, locks the Russian in his cabin and steers the boat into a glacier. The two vanish into a wall of ice leaving Jim alone as master of the sea, savior of the seaside Alaskan town.

Although the film was a modest success at best at the box office, it was well reviewed and highly acclaimed for its cinematic quality. The fact that it was awarded an Oscar certainly reveals something about its appeal. There is little doubt that Hathaway had a target audience in mind as *Spawn's* political message was certainly powerful enough to resonate with a right-leaning viewer. With the market established for anti-Soviet, anticommunist filmmaking, *Spawn of the North* proved a timely piece that garnered significant attention in film circles throughout the country. "*Spawn of the North*" is a satisfactorily wild eyed tale of the Alaskan salmon fisheries," wrote *New York Times* film critic Frank S. Nugent in his September 1938 review, "when Russian pirates raided the fish traps and looked as menacing as Akim Tamiroff with a stubble of a whisker."[55] Marveling at the film's aesthetic splendor and rough and tumble action sequences, Nugent praised *Spawn* as a visual tour de force. "The bloodshed is beautiful in Technicolor [and] there are some impressive shots of crumbling icebergs and of the salmon run."[56] According to Nugent, despite its shortcomings, particularly its failure to develop the relationship between Fonda and his love interest, Diane (Louise Platte), *Spawn* represented a "brawling" and "robustious" melodrama definitely worth the price of admission.

Favorable reviews of *Spawn* foreshadowed the coming of the most successful anti-communist film of the pre-Cold War era. The debut of *Ninotchka* in November of 1939 served to signify that filmmakers now recognized the existence of a sizeable conservative market ready to be tapped. Films such as *Red Salute, Tovarich,* and *Spawn of the North* symbolized a growing effort on behalf of production companies to channel anticommunist emotion in to revenue but no film prior to *Ninotchka* reached its level of success. In fact, Greta Garbo, one of Hollywood's most recognizable starlets, received more praise for her role in *Ninotchka* than for any other film in her career. *Ninotchka,* based on Garbo's glittering performance, effectively became known, in film circles throughout the globe, as the film in which the ever stoic Garbo actually "smiled." Although the Academy award nominated film was not a runaway success a the box office, its over two-million dollar gross combined with the Oscar hype that it generated made *Ninotchka* a resounding cinematic success and a powerful conduit of anticommunism.

Although director Ernst Lubitsch received much of the "oscar" attention for *Ninotchka,* Billy Wilder and Charles Bracket, known as Hollywood's "dynamic duo" writing tandem, provided the screenplay which ultimately made the film a resounding success. Wilder, a Polish immigrant, came to the United States in the early 1930's after having fled Hitler's Germany. In Berlin, Wilder had established himself as one of the brightest minds in the UFA (Universum Film Aktien). He had also made a name for himself in Paris, a stopover on the way to the United States, where he co-directed the film *Mauvise Graine,* a critically acclaimed effort that garnered him worldwide recognition. When asked why he left behind such a promising career in Europe to head overseas, Wilder calmly responded "I came because I didn't want to be in an oven."[57]

Where the eccentric Wilder was somewhat progressive politically, his partner Charles Bracket was, according to Hollywood historian Sam Staggs, a "polished republican" who stemmed from background literally foreign to his immigrant counterpart.[58] An old money eastern patrician, Bracket was a blue-blood and the benefactor of an aristocratic upbringing. After attending the snobbish Williams College in western Massachusetts where he was known as "the richest young man in his fraternity," Bracket headed off to law school at Harvard where he excelled.[59] During his collegiate years, Brackett discovered a love of fine prose and became determined to become a master novelist. His dedication reaped early rewards as several of his initial attempts met wide praise, including his novel *Weekend* which became an instant favorite of Harold Ross, founding editor of the *New York Post.*[60] Having recognized Brackett's considerable literary skill, Ross appointed Brackett as the magazine's drama critic, a position that he commanded from 1926–1929.

In 1930, Brackett decided to try his hand at Hollywood. The industry had been soliciting stories from the writer throughout the 1920's and he figured the time had come to seek his fortune in the city of stars. He began his Hollywood career at RKO with a short stint as a writer but quickly became disillusioned with Hollywood's "assembly line approach to writing."[61] After a brief return home, Brackett was once again lured west, this time by Paramount, which immediately paired him with the affable Wilder. Little did the executives know at the time, but the pairing of the two most unlikely partners marked the forging of one of the most successful writing combinations in Hollywood history. The two would go on to collaborate on a number of films, several of which have etched their place in Hollywood lore. In addition to *Ninotchka,* Wilder and Bracket's *A Foreign Affair* (1948), *The Emperor Waltz* (1948) and *Sunset Boulevard* (1950) have all been recognized as screen classics. *Sunset Boulevard,* the duo's last collaborative writing effort, remains popular to this day and is widely recognized as a groundbreaking film that "led Hollywood from the pre to the post war era."[62]

Wilder and Brackett, despite their many achievements, could not, however, accept full credit for *Ninotchka's* screenplay. The script had originally been the work of renowned playwright Melchior Lengyel, a talented

Hungarian who had envisioned a film featuring "a Russian girl saturated with Bolshevist ideals [who] goes to fearful, capitalistic, monopolistic Paris. She meets romance and has an uproarious good time. Capitalism not so bad after all."[63] Lengyel's piece, however, was seen as overly dry and lacking the comedic flair that came to define *Ninotchka*. In Lengyel's version, the Soviet commissars commissioned with the task of pawning the infamous Tsarist jewels are "played straight," whereas in Wilder and Brackett's rendition, the commissars serve as a source of comic relief throughout the duration of the film. Although Lengyel's vision for *Ninotchka* was well received, his "flat script" kept the film off of the production line.[64]

In 1938, Gottfried Reinhardt worked with *Tovarich* composer Jacques Deval on a revamped version of the script but still did not insert the comic panache synonymous with *Ninotchka*. It was also at this time that Garbo, the film's targeted star, issued an ultimatum to MGM. She would only work with an "artist," which eliminated, in her mind, most of the directorial field. The company had to make a choice between Ernst Lubitsch or Edmung Goulding. If neither of those two sufficed, then she would walk. MGM decided to pass on Goulding, despite his a resume of successful films, in favor of Lubitsch. Although his MGM project *The Merry Widow* did not succeed at the box office, his genius was well known to the company and he undoubtedly possessed the creative ability to rework *Ninotchka* into the classic that it became.

Hence, the fragments of the *Ninotchka* screenplay left over from Lengyel, Reinhardt and Deval passed into the hands of Lubitsch. The director, however, was not impressed. It was at this point that Wilder and Bracket entered the *Ninotchka* scene. Possessor of a script that held tremendous potential but remained unquestionably flat, Lubitsch realized that Bracket and Wilder's collective charm is just what the film needed. Lubitsch, however, remained closely involved with the screenplay's revision effort. Although Brackett, Wilder, and Walter Reisch would receive official writing credit, Lubitsch biographer Scott Eyman recognized that "all three writers felt Lubitsch was more entitled to a credit."[65] Lubitsch knew that *Ninotchka* presented him with a terrific opportunity and with Garbo in the lead role, a successful production would provide the man known to Hitler as "the archetypal Jew" with just the boost that his promising Hollywood career needed.

The final product was clearly a collaborative work. Wilder's sharp wit and humor is evident in the film's clever dialogue and humorous punch lines. The movie's clean presentation and free flowing style can be attributed to the editorial hand of Walter Reisch. Where Brackett's influence is felt is in the film's anticommunist commentary. Although a "comedy," there is no disguising the film's political undertones. "The film can be considered [an] "overtly political" satire," writes film historian Nora Henry, "as a contemporary political conflict, the opposition between capitalism and communism is not only background but also a part of the story and the dramatic conflict."[66]

Lubitsch's influence on the screenplay is also evident in the scripts political content. A Jewish refugee of Russian ancestry, there is little doubt that questions surrounding "subversive" activity swirling around Hollywood in 1939 had caught the attention of the director. As the man ultimately responsible for the finished product, it is conceivable that Lubitsch encouraged or perhaps personally inserted political lines into the script as a means of diverting HUAC's penetrating gaze. In fact, Lubitsch had recently been to Moscow to visit family in 1936. His trip, highlighted by his stay at the Hotel Metropole, Moscow's "best hotel," featured an engagement with an old friend Gustav Von Wangenheim, a Russian actor who had appeared in Lubitsch's direction of two Shakespearean spoofs, *Romeo and Juliet in the Snow* and *Kohlhiesel's Daughter.*[67]

Following their encounter, Von Wangenheim and his wife, Inge, both committed communists, had Lubitsch and his new bride, Vivian, over for a lavish dinner at their home, a meal complete with "ham and caviar so good it melted even Vivian's formidable resolve."[68] Once seated, Inge went into a long diatribe condemning capitalism while extolling the virtues of her beloved Soviet state. According to Inge, America, the "dream machine lubricated by dollars, seemed a paltry, insufficient world in which to spend one's life."[69] Lubistch politely swallowed Inge's political commentary but was not amused. For Lubitsch, Soviet restraints on creativity prevented true genius from manifesting itself in any artistic capacity. This was not a world in which Lubitsch could live. If anything, having experienced Nazi repression, Soviet Russia represented all that Lubitsch despised as a totalitarian system built by tyrants and controlled by terror.

Despite the extravagant meal, Lubitsch left the Von Wangenheims with a sour taste in his mouth. His trip to Russia had introduced him to the intricacies of Bolshevism, an ideology anathema to his westernized political proclivities. Nevertheless, he did not leave the nation empty handed. A country known to suppress ideas, Russia had imbued in Lubitsch perhaps his most ingenious of all. Inge, with her militant mannerism and calculated political acumen, planted a character seed in Lubistch. Her personality would undoubtedly drive *Ninotchka,* a film that presented the director with an opportunity to denounce the Soviet state while at the same time demonstrate his Americanism to those who may have held his loyalty in question. As someone who felt compelled to send J. Edgar Hover a 1935 letter describing his willingness to "cooperate fully at all times with this bureau," it is clear that Lubitsch was more than a little concerned.[70]

Although heralded as a comedy of epic proportion, a quick glance at the screenplay and *Ninotchka's* political appendages emerge. As far as the overall plot is concerned, the story revolves around Ninotchka, a Russian envoy sent to settle a dispute over Tsarist Jewels destined to be sold in Paris for the benefit of of starving Soviets. Played by Greta Garbo, arguably Hollywood's most graceful actress, Ninotchka represents the quintessential comrade: cold, stoic, and businesslike. It becomes her responsibility to unravel the mess created by three of her fellow countrymen entrusted originally with the task of pawning the merchandise. Obstructing the sale is the presence of Grand Dutchess Swana (Ina Claire), of the former Tsarist regime, who learns of the jewels' hotel location and insists that they belong to the former Russian crown. Facilitating her effort in the face of the Bolsheviks is Count Leon d'Algout (Melvyn Douglass), a French charmer who eventually mediates between the two camps. It is the romance that flourishes between the amorous Frenchman d'Algout and the increasingly sunny Ninotchka that takes center stage, however, as the love struck Russian slowly morphs into capitalistic putty in the hands of the ever suave French aristocrat.

For the analytical viewer, however, the political punch lines which dot *Ninotchka* command as much attention as the blossoming romance between the two lovers. Although most contend, such as Michael J. Strada and Harold R. Troper, that Lubitsch avoids any "hard edge political message," a more thorough analysis of the script reveals a vested political effort on Lubistcsh's part.[71] The first of such lines come from Ninotchka following her initial arrival in Paris. After disembarking from the train, Ninotchka responds to "how are things in Russia" with "Very good. The last mass trials were a great success. There are going to be fewer but better Russians."[72]

Upon reaching the host hotel, a grand establishment that prompted the commissars to note that "nothing like it exists in Russia," (despite the fact that Lubitsch had stayed in Moscow's luxurious Hotel Metropole, a hotel that currently runs 300 Euros a night for a single, 1600 for a suite, during his 1936 visit to the Soviet Union), Ninotchka fires off another chilling line. After noticing the "ridiculous" design of a woman's hat for sale in a lobby shop, Ninotchka quips "Tsk, Tsk, Tsk, how can a civilization survive which permits women to put things like that on their heads. It won't be long now, comrades."[73] Ninotchka's reference to pending revolution serves as a rather provocative line given the contentious American social tenor of the time. The Dies Committee had been up and running for nearly a year by the time *Ninotcthka* hit the screen and a 1939 Gallup Poll showed overwhelming popular support for the investigative organ. With fear of seditious activity on the rise coupled with the headlines garnered by Dies and his Committee, even a line spoken in jest was enough to raise concern among Americans. Although meant to be humorous, simply hinting at internal revolution placed in the context of 1939 America undoubtedly fueled the fire of those in support of the Congressional investigation of the "radical" left.

Despite its increasingly comedic tone, *Ninotchka* retains its anticommunist edge throughout its duration. In the first of several romantically charged scenes with d'Algout, Ninotchka reveals her detestation of capitalism and her confidence in Lenin's promise of global revolt. While d'Algout helps Ninotchka locate the Eiffel Tower on a Parisian map, she cannot but help notice his flirtatious forwardness. Seemingly annoyed by his unsolicited advance, Ninotchka scolds the count in bitter "Soviet" fashion. "You are very sure of yourself, aren't you," spouts Ninotchka, "Nothing has occurred recently to shake my confidence," replies the ever imperious d"Algout. "I have heard of the arrogant male in capitalistic society," the Soviet shouts back, "It is having a superior earning power that makes you like that." Discovering that she is indeed a Soviet, d'Algout answers back "A Russian! I love Russians! Comrade, I have been fascinated by your Five-Year Plan for the last fifteen years!" Ninotchka, now clearly offended, delivers the conversation's deciding blow, "Your type will soon be extinct."[74]

Miraculously, despite the abrasive tone of their roadside exchange, d'Algout is able to talk his way into escorting the Soviet beauty to the Parisian landmark. Upon arrival, however, the mood once again turns "red." After the count announces that he feels fortunate to have looked upon the city one more time from the tower "before becoming extinct," Ninotchka sets off on a miniature tirade in defense of her positions. "Do not misunderstand me, I do not hold frivolity against you. As basic material you might not be bad, but you are an unfortunate product of a doomed culture. I feel sorry for you." Again, placed in the context of 1939, with fear of sedition on the rise and steady growth (pre-Hitler Stalin pact) in the American Communist Party, such a line was certain to elicit an impassioned reaction. Comedy aside, as seen in the intensified post-war investigation, the communist "threat" to the United States was no joke and repeated references to revolution were bound to hit home.

Although the film eventually evolves into the romantic comedy it was presumably destined to be, *Ninotchka* does not conclude without leaving the viewer with at least something to think about concerning the militant nature of Soviet society and the threat that communists across the globe posed to the security of the Unites States. For those that argue that its anticommunist quips represent simple comedy, lines of a similar "comedic," "political" nature (from the opposite perspective) created by liberal screenwriters in the 1930's and 1940's garnered them a place on the blacklist and in some cases, a cell in jail. Continued references to "Siberia," "execution," and "firing squads" further enhance the USSR's image as the manifestation of ultimate evil. Late in the movie, a Soviet immigration official, one who would eventually deny d'Algout passage to Russia to see his beloved Ninotchka, is positioned at his desk when the phone rings. "Yes," aswers the official, "Comrade Cazabine? No I'm sorry, he hasn't been with us for six months. He was called back to Russia and investigated. You can get further details from his widow."[75] The line may represent comedy, but with a price. With thousands attempting to demonstrate their loyalty in the face of a burgeoning HUAC investigation, even remote affiliation with a nation as seemingly ruthless as the Russia of *Ninotchka* warranted, in the eyes of the concerned conservative majority, a traitorous stigma.

The overall reception of *Ninotchka* was incredibly positive. Such publicity made it an even more pervasive anticommunist piece. "*Ninotchka* rates as the best Ernst Lubitsch picture since the days of love parade," proclaimed Edwin Schallert in his review for the *Los Angeles Times,* "It is one of the most enjoyable pieces of entertainment offered in any year of the movies and besides, marks an important transition in the career of Greta Garbo."[76] Citing the film as a product of both "comedy" and "satire," Schallert dismissed the notion that the film constituted an anticommunist "propaganda" piece. "Never in a million years could you regard *Ninotchka* as propaganda," wrote Schallert, "It is too deft and unconcerned for that."[77] The film, according to the critic, is generally without fault and represents a work of pure genius unrivaled by any 1939 production. "Virtually all of *Ninotchka,*" concluded Schallert, "is in the A plus bracket for cleverness. The actors practically achieve stardom."[78]

Schallert was not alone in his praise for Lubitsch's "masterpiece." *Time Magazine* offered similar commentary in its November 6, 1939 review. The film, according to *Time,* is a clever satire that mocks the Soviet system in a manner too comical to be considered propaganda. It is a witty piece that relies on its subtle humor to maintain an apolitical line. If anything, it is a good humored spoof of the USSR, not a work intended to maliciously tarnish the image of the Soviet state or its citizenry. "Unlike most pictures about Russian Reds, this one is neither crude clowning or crude prejudice," noted *Time,* "but a literate and knowingly directed satire which lands many a shrewd crack about phony five-year plans, collective farms, Communist jargon, and pseudo-scientific jab where it will do the most good-on the funny bone."[79]

There existed one critic, however, who at least recognized the anticommunist element buried within *Ninotchka's* humor. Frank Nugent, of the *New York Times,* summed up the film's anti-Soviet line with a simple quote: "Stalin won't like it." [80] If the anticommunist component of the picture is so well masked by its comedic element, it would only be fair to assume that Stalin himself would have received a kick out of the picture. The reality, however, is that many blatantly anticommunist lines do appear in the film and not all of them are shrouded in humor. One cannot argue the fact that the picture is more parody than propaganda. Nevertheless, given the release date combined with growing communist fears, clearly on the rise in the wake of the Hitler-Stalin pact, *Ninotchka* certainly "ruffled the feathers" of more than one concerned American. *Ninotchka* alone is a fascinating film which has entertained millions throughout the globe. In 1939, however, with Dies perusing leftist enclaves within and the Soviets "aligned" with Hitler abroad, *Ninotchka* undoubtedly proved to many that communism was no laughing matter.

The last, and perhaps the most viscous pre-war anticommunist film to hit the big screen, *Comrade X,* released in 1940, unabashedly vilified the Soviet system in a picture deemed "contemptuous of the Soviet citizenry and of the Soviet system" by film historians Michael J. Strada and Harold R. Troper.[81] Starring the ever-popular Clark Gable, the plot centers on an American agent, McKinley B. Thompson (Gable), undercover in Moscow as a reporter, who is blackmailed into escorting the beautiful, but outspoken daughter of a hotel porter to the United States. The young woman, a train operator who has taken the name "Theodore (Hedy Lamarr)," is a communist "with ideas" and ideas, according to her father, "get people shot." With a screenplay by Ben Hecht, a man who "has always tasted bile at the thought of Comrades," *Comrade X* is replete with anticommunist dialogue.[82] Unlike *Ninotchka,* however, most of the commentary is not veiled in humor as the film clearly represents a pointed attack on the Communist left.

Separating *Comrade X* from similar films of its era is its salient anticommunist edge. Director Ben Vidor in no way attempts to disguise the film's political intentions as strong anti-Soviet dialogue flows throughout. Beginning with the opening scene, which features a "typical" Soviet hotel (nothing is working), *Comrade X* attempts to introduce the viewer to the "realities" of communist Russia. Talk of execution, secret police, espionage, and murder dominate conversation throughout the film. Speaking of a recently executed Soviet foreign press agent,

Gable quips "every time they throw another liberator in the ground they throw another banquet. Vodka, champagne, caviar, stuffed goose, more vodka." Referencing the Stalin "trials" and the attack on engineers or "wreckers," the hotel porter notes that the elevator is out of service due to the fact that "we are looking for the hotel engineer but nobody knows where he is." Later in the film, Gable comments on the hysterical state of Soviet society. "I haven't seen a Russian yet that wasn't suspicious." In a telling revelation, Gable observes that if they keep on "killing Russians," it will "be a great country." The film also hints at an "internal invasion" of America, undoubtedly directed at "Reds" within. When asked whether or not she was packed (for her American venture), Theodore responds with "I took only my motorman's uniform in case we want to bore from within."

The clear political tenor of *Comrade X* was not lost on critics. Clearly a product of the anti-Soviet hype emanating from the non-aggression treaty of August 1939, the film constitutes a propaganda piece that unquestionably contributed to billowing American anticommunism. "Seldom has a film satirized a nation with such grim and malicious delight as does this Yuletide comedy," asserted Bosley Crowther of the *New York Times,* "diplomatic relations between the United States and Russia have been in bad shape for many years, but now that Metro and Capitol Theatre have celebrated Christmas by presenting *Comrade X,* non belligerency is at an end."[83] Although many parallels between *Ninotchka* and *Comrade X* exist, the presentational differences, noted Crowell, are impossible to overlook. "Unlike *Ninotchka,"* Crowther observed, "*Comrade X* lacks even a comic pace. [Much of its "comedy"] is too grim for enjoyment since it has to do in a jesting vein with assassination and political execution. Even in Russia, that isn't funny."[84]

Nevertheless, the film proved to be a resounding success at the box office. Given its Christmas-time release, thousands flocked to the theatres to catch a glimpse of one of Hollywood's brightest stars in Gable. According to the *Los Angeles Times,* the film "played to record audiences at Grauman's Chinese and Loew's."[85] The *New York Times* also reported that record numbers turned out for the picture as nearly 80,000 New Yorkers flooded the theatres over Christmas weekend to take in *Comrade.* [86] Cleary, anticommunist films had become valuable revenue sources for production companies as Americans continued to absorb the media's representation of the "red menace." With more Americans becoming "familiar" with the peril of the Soviet Union, the anticommunist domestic milieu continued to strengthen. Although the official purge would go on hiatus during the war years, the pre-war anticommunist hype was enough to keep the image of the "menace" alive just long enough for it to be revived in full during the pre-dawn days of the Cold War.

In 1941, the United States and the Soviet Union engaged in an alliance that effectively quashed the pervasive spread of global fascism. For four years, the relationship between the U.S. and the USSR quieted anticommunist critics at home, sending the Dies Committee into hibernation. Following Yalta, however, the threat of communism once again came to the fore. As Roosevelt (soon to be Truman) and Stalin continued to quarrel over the fate of liberated territory in Europe, conservatives at home looked to resurrect HUAC and continue the pre-war investigation (or attempted liquidation) of American Communism. Spearheaded by insular, attention starved individuals like John Rankin of Mississippi and J. Parnell Thomas of New Jersey, HUAC regained its pre-war momentum and set out on a purge that would eventually lead the nation into the epoch known as McCarthyism. Ironically, the issue of propaganda in film and the potential of the American CP to adulterate American minds via the screen became a pivotal issue. In fact, the Hollywood hearings, beginning in 1947, were arguably the most important in the history of the Committee. What stands as truly ironic is that starting with *Bullin' the Bullsheviki* in 1919, Hollywood screenwriters, producers, and directors released over twenty-five "anticommunist" films designed to demonize the "radical" left. From *The Red Salute* to *Spawn of the North,* to *Ninotchka,* anticommunist films directly contributed to the cultivation of the "Red Menace," and in turn, to the evolution of a "super-patriotic" social milieu that had Americans across the country "red" with rage. These films, amazingly enough, along with the men that produced them, were conveniently "overlooked" once the HUAC spotlight intensified over Hollywood.[87] The committee, however, in the heat of their investigation, forgot to consider one integral point. Propaganda was certainly present in a number of film, films, that is, of the anticommunist variety.

Chapter Six
The Right to Remain Silent: Hollywood, Albert Maltz, and the Post-Hearing Resistance

On October 18, 1947, Jack Warner, vice president in charge of production for Warner Brothers Pictures Inc., stepped in front of the House Committee on Un-American Activities (HUAC) armed with information that would decimate Hollywood's "radical" community. Facing a conservative panel bent on rooting out "subversive" elements in American society, Warner was extended the dubious honor of being HUAC's first high profile "friendly witness." A man that had made millions off the scripts written by several soon to be blacklistees, Warner blissfully provided "names" of so-called Hollywood Communists to protect his financial interests. Warner's testimony spawned the evolution of the infamous Hollywood "blacklist" and the subsequent purge of progressivism within the film industry.

In the years that followed there were many who acted in Warner's likeness and chose to overlook the unscrupulous manner in which the Committee conducted its investigation. There existed a small faction of Hollywood "Reds," however, who refused to compromise their principles and sought to uphold the integrity of the Constitution by exposing the Committee as an arm of oppression. Although their effort did not achieve its ultimate aim, the "Hollywood Ten's" quest to unmask the Committee's undemocratic nature could have potentially dealt a decisive blow to the entire course of the conservative anticommunist campaign. With HUAC derailed in Hollywood and the validity of the "red menace" in question, the anticommunist crusade would have been divested (somewhat) of the hysterical inertia critical to its subsistence. Hollywood stood poised to catapult the Committee into anticommunist eminence. The Ten, however, refused to allow the industry to serve as political springboard without a fight. As fate would have it, to the dismay of those steering the anticommunist investigation, the resolve displayed in Hollywood was not waged in vain. The "legacy" of the "Unfriendly" resistance lived on to inspire a "new" generation of "left" aisle Americans who, like the Ten, recognized the "un-Americanism" of the Un-American Committee.

The Hollywood "resistance" consisted of a small number of defiant members of the Hollywood CP who refused to "name names" during the HUAC investigation of Hollywood. The Committee, which furthered the contention that the Hollywood CP was merely an instrument of the Soviet Union, became the target of this "Unfriendly" coalition of alleged Hollywood "Reds" (a label attached to communists, former communists, and perceived communists, a.k.a. "Fellow Travelers") determined to expose its illegitimacy. Within their effort to resist the Committee, defiant Hollywood "radicals" attempted to use the forum afforded by the investigation to showcase their respect for democracy. The Committee, however, determined to maintain the image of these men as "subversive" so as to justify its inquisition, silenced the voice of the "opposition" and prevented the intentions of those in defiance from emerging. By examining the "unheard" words and "disallowed" statements so conveniently omitted by HUAC over fifty years ago, a window into what was left undisclosed at the 1947 Hollywood Hearings is opened offering an in depth look at the despotic nature of a most undemocratic exercise.

With a panel that included Chairman J. Parnell Thomas (R. NJ.), Chief Investigator Robert E. Stripling, ranking Democrat John Rankin (D. Miss.), John McDowell (R. Penn.), J. Hardin Peterson (D. Fla.), Herbert C. Bonner, (D. NC.), Richard B. Vail (R. Ill.), John S. Wood (R. Ga.), and Richard M. Nixon (R. CA.) presiding, Jack Warner stood firm amidst the sights and sounds of HUAC's Washington spectacle. One of the most influential men in the film industry, Warner flew to Washington in October of 1947 to participate in what he believed to be a most critical exercise. The "Red Menace," according to Warner, had reared its ugly head in tinseltown and the only thing between the communists and the camera was the Committee. "Our American Way of Life is under attack from without and from within our borders," declared Warner in his opening statement, "Ideological termites have burrowed into many American industries, organizations, and societies. Wherever they may be, I say let us dig them out and get rid of them. I believe it is the duty of each loyal American to resist those attacks and defeat them." [1]

Providing twenty-seven names including Alvah Bessie, Gordon Kahn, Dalton Trumbo and Albert Maltz, Warner, fearing the crippling economic consequences certain to befall anyone or any organization that refused to cooperate, took dead aim at the Communist Party and its supposed influence in the film industry.[2] "Subversive germs breed in dark corners," cautioned Warner, "let's get light into those corners. That, I believe, is the purpose of this hearing and I am happy to have the opportunity to testify."[3]

Ironically, despite all the talk of conspiracy, espionage, revolution, and sedition on the 18th and 19th of October, Warner and his band of "Friendlies" were unable to assist the Committee in achieving its ultimate objective.

To the embarrassment of Thomas, evidence linking the Hollywood CP to Communist propaganda in film failed to materialize. In fact, not a single witness presented a tangible example of propaganda finding its way into a script. "There is no proof about it," proclaimed the cooperative Louis B. Mayer of famed MGM, "when I look at pictures that they [members of the Hollywood CP] have written for us, I can't find one where they have written something like that." [4] In fact, Mayer reveled that he had absolutely no fear of communists in tinseltown given the fact that "they can't get a single thing into our pictures or our studio under our set up. The only ones I would have to worry about," Mayer continued, "are the producers, the editors, the executives because our scripts are read and re-read by so many of the executive force, producers and editors that if you looked carefully at 1,200 or 1,500 pictures you would be surprised how little you could possibly point to." [5] Friendly witness and actor Adolphe Menjou further substantiated this contention, claiming, "I have seen no Communistic propaganda in pictures." [6] Warner himself admitted that if any agitprop "found its way into a film," he was there "to cut it out." [7]

Actor turned Hollywood historian Robert Vaughn weighed in on the Committee's failure to successfully connect the Hollywood CP to a Soviet propaganda effort as well. "The Contention that those identified as being affiliated with the Communist Party were capable of subverting the American moviegoer by injecting pro-Soviet propaganda into their work was never proved by the Committee." [8] Ronald Reagan, a man who would soon become the face of American conservatism, added "I do not believe that the communists have ever at any time been able to use the motion picture industry as a sounding board for their philosophy or ideology," stated Reagan to the Committee in 1947. "I think that will continue as long as Hollywood people continue as they are," Reagan explained, "which is alert, conscious, and fighting." [9]

The inability to unearth any tangible "propagandic" evidence proved both problematic and somewhat humiliating for Thomas and his Committee. So certain of Hollywood's subversive nature heading into the hearings, his failure to expose the presence of agitprop forced Thomas to concentrate on the character of the men on trial as opposed to the content of their films. The "degradation ceremony" that ensued, dependant upon on false accusations accepted due to the explosive climate of the time, revealed the Machiavellian tactics of a Committee manned by ultraconservatives and determined to stain Hollywood "red" at any cost. [10]

The Committee clearly used the October hearings to address more than simply agitprop in film. The Hollywood investigation was also a personal attack as those "on trial" carried a progressive ideology that threatened the "traditional" socio-economic foundation upon which the Committee stood its ground. Committee member McDowell's comments regarding immigration spoke to the Committee's collective conservatism. Blame the presence of communists in America on a porous border and you have a ready excuse to place the nation under lock and key. "I have been examining the borders of the United States," snapped McDowell, "and I would like to tell you that within weeks, not months but weeks, bus loads of Communists have crossed [into the country]."[11] HUAC, however, masked its hidden agenda behind its "legitimate" inquiry. Although somewhat sidetracked given the failed attempt to produce propaganda, the Committee held a trump card. In the absence of agitprop, HUAC shifted its attention to names. The more so called "red" names acquired, the easier it would be shroud its deficiencies. Names would also serve to validate the Committee charge of Red subversion in the industry. Names of "communists" signaled the presence of a revolutionary element, a threat that justified the full scale Congressional investigation that Thomas, Rankin, and the rest of the HUAC band so desperately sought.

The quest for "names" however, began well in advance of the 1947 hearings. The Committee, thirsty for fame, took whatever means necessary during the months prior to the investigation to ensure that they achieved a result that would justify its endeavor. For example, illegal wire taps and unjustified surveillance, courtesy of the FBI, provided the Committee with the means of accumulating "dirt" on hundreds of individuals allegedly connected to Communism. Illustrated by historian Ellen Schrecker, "Agents resorted to illegal wiretaps and break ins and leaked materials from the FBI's allegedly confidential files to sympathetic politicians."[12] The Committee, as seen through the building of the blacklist, equated a name with the certified existence of a Communist. A name provided the tangible evidence that the Committee required to wage and eventually continue its investigation. If there were Communists in Hollywood (and according to Warner, Meyer, and others, there were) then the Committee believed its purge of the industry was not only justified, but necessary. "As a result of the many revelations [of names] from persons who recognized the traitorous nature of the Communist Party," stated the Committee's 1952 annual report, "it was ascertained that the Communists efforts to infiltrate the industry had been a full scale and carefully planned operation and that the Communist party had been successful in recruiting individuals in important and strategic positions in almost all phases of movie production."[13] As misleading as this statement may be, it affirms the Committee's need to uncover a "Communist conspiracy" to validate its campaign to eliminate not only Communism, but the Hollywood Communist Party's progressive agenda.

Eradicating the Hollywood "radical" left in the absence of any legitimate incriminating evidence, however, called for a little "undemocratic improvisation" on the Committee's behalf. With its back against a wall, HUAC revealed its true colors and compromised the rights and integrity of those deemed subversive to attain its aims. Men such as Rankin and Thomas, known for their social insularity and salient racism, were determined not to let a group of "liberal Jews" off the hook. In *Time of the Toad*, Dalton Trumbo revealed that the Committee's collective prejudice and utilitarian ideology was not lost on the Ten. How could the Ten expect fair treatment, noted Trumbo, with men like "Rankin, who has used the words 'Kike,' 'Jew-boy,' and 'Nigger' in open debate on the floor of Representatives," leading the charge against them?[14] Griffin Fareillo, after quoting Rankin as stating that "Slavery was the greatest blessing the Negro people ever had," weighed in on Rankin's racist nature. "Rankin pushed for the resolution to transform HUAC into a permanent Committee. He contended that segregated blacks had been happy until stirred up by "Communist agitators." He was also quite friendly towards the Ku Klux Klan," observed Fariello, "which he endorsed as an "old American tradition.""[15]

Such sentiment manifested itself numerous times throughout the course of the hearings. For instance, during the testimony of Adrian Scott, a committed antifascist who had worked on the anti-anti-Semitic film *Crossfire,* Thomas came off as particularly caustic. Perhaps he (along with Rankin) was outraged that a non-Jew such as Scott had demonstrated such admiration and respect for a race that faced, in the aftermath of the war, compete dissolution. Upon asking Thomas if he could read a prepared statement, Thomas, in a most degrading fashion, chastised the screenwriter. "This may not be the worst statement we have ever received but it is almost the worst," smacked Thomas, "Therefore, it is clearly out of order, not pertinent at all, hasn't anything to do with the inquiry, and the chair will rule that the statement will not be read."[16] Coldly shot down, Scott's statement remained excluded from the record.

Jewish screenwriter Samuel Ornitz shared the Ten's collective concern regarding the presence of known racists on the Committee panel. In an inadmissible statement to the Committee, Ornitz observed: "Is it mere coincidence that you chose to subpoena and characterize as "unfriendly" the men who produced, wrote, directed, or acted in feature length films and short subjects which attacked anti-Semitism or treated Jews or Negroes sympathetically? The eyes of the world are on this committee," trumpeted Ornitz, "let them not see that civil rights have become a mockery in America in a congressional caucus room of all places!"[17] Historian Kevin Starr, a man who remains generally unsympathetic to the Ten's "cause," echoed

Ornitz in recognizing that more than simply communist propaganda was at issue in Washington. "Anti-Anti-Semitism, for sure, had gotten Hollywood into trouble with HUAC in 1947, the same year that President Truman recognized the newly formed state of Israel. Two films," maintained Starr, "had proven especially galling: *Crossfire* (1947), directed by Edward Dmytryk, and *Gentleman's Agreement* (1947), directed by Elia Kazan and starring Gregory Peck as a gentile reporter who passes as a Jew in order to research an article on anti-Semitism. Kazan," Starr asserted, "also directed *Pinky* (1949) starring Jeanne Crain as an African American passing for a white who returns to the south and encounters the realties of racism. The Right," concluded Starr, "considered such films propaganda, and John Rankin delighted in baiting the Hollywood delegation."[18]

Ornitz' statement, in particular, hit at the heart of the "Unfriendly" resistance. While the Ten wanted to clear their names, their main goal was to expose the conservative nature of the Committee and prevent it from continuing a saliently unjust Congressional purge of the American left. The Ten and those who followed as "resistors" did not think solely in terms of the Committee's impact on Hollywood. As appraised by Ornitz, HUAC's investigation of the film industry provided those who resisted it with the chance to reveal to the public the threat that the Committee posed to civil liberties. Thomas, however, made such an endeavor nearly impossible. "Yes or No" answers served as his defense mechanism during the Ten's attack. "Can I answer the question in my own way please, may I have that right? Can I have that right?" pleaded Lester Cole during his September 28 testimony in response to the $64 question. "It would be very simple to answer," retorted Thomas. "At times," replied a demoralized Cole, "when I feel it is proper I will but I wish to stand on my rights of association." Thomas barked, "We will determine when it is proper. Next witness."[19]

The Committee also denied the Ten a multitude of privileges enthusiastically extended to those who cooperated. The Committee rejected the requests of selected members of the Ten to read prepared statements, failed to allow the Ten's attorney's to cross examine friendly witnesses, denied the Ten's request to present evidence in the form of scripts and writing samples to demonstrate their innocence, and refused to allow the Ten and their lawyers to examine the evidence presented against them.[20] As noted by Trumbo, out of 549 pages of text devoted to courtroom dialogue, only thirty-seven were dedicated to the "Unfriendlies."[21] It is a rather elementary situation to analyze. The Ten were simply not provided with the opportunity to state their case and as a result, the Committee virtually had its way with the accused.

The Committee justified its actions by citing Public Law 601, a derivative of the Alien Sedition Act of 1798. Robert Kenney, an attorney for the Ten, attempted to rebuke the Committee based on its failure to observe basic constitutional rights only to be blasted by Thomas. "We operate under Public Law 601," railed Thomas, "we cannot set aside this law to suit the convenience of certain witnesses or their counsel."[22] When John Howard Lawson, the first of the "Unfriendlies" to testify, was denied his request to read a prepared statement illustrating his belief in American democracy, Lawson shouted back, "You have spent one week vilifying me before the American public, and you refuse to allow me to make a statement on my rights as an American citizen. You permit us to cross-examine the witnesses that testified last week and we will show up the whole tissue of lies."[23] By denying Lawson the right to read his statement and the collective group the opportunity to cross examine, refute testimony, and question the character and intentions of those deemed "friendly," Thomas prevented the American public from gaining insight into the mindsets and motivations of those on trial.

Had Lawson been afforded a moment to share his emotions with the American public, those following the hearings might not have seen him as so utterly subversive. However, in order to maintain the legitimacy of his investigation, Thomas knew the "Unfriendlies" must appear to be genuine threats to American security. Lawson was denied the basic privileges extended to cooperative witnesses, liberties that men such as Warner used to demonize communism in the United States. Thomas, however, took one look at Lawson's statement and set the tone for the entire interrogation. "I read the first line and the statement will not be read," Thomas announced to a stunned Lawson.[24] It is completely understandable, in light of the treatment that he received, that Lawson would become agitated. Thomas treated him with little respect and Lawson, known for his quick temper, reacted in a fashion that unfortunately played directly into the hands of the Committee. His typical "communistic" petulance served as a sure sign of his un-Americanism, or at least that is what most of the solicitous public naively believed.

Dalton Trumbo, who followed Lawson, suffered a similar fate. After submitting his statement to Thomas for review, Thomas rejected Trumbo's request to present it before the Committee. Trumbo's statement, although never read, was printed in Gordon Kahn's *Hollywood on Trial*. It stands as true testament to Trumbo's respect for both the nation and its defining principles. "We must furthermore remember always that the defense of constitutional rights is not simply a convenience to be invoked in a time of need, but a clear and continuous obligation imposed equally on us at all times. We as citizens," declared Trumbo, "are to protect the Constitution against even the slightest encroachment upon the protective barrier it interposes between the private citizen on the one hand and the inquisitors of government on the other."[25] Such a statement would have effectively provided a window into the supposed "red tainted" soul of a presumed insidious communist. Trumbo's words, however, were clearly inconsistent with his Committee tagged malevolent label. Trumbo was in fact a proud American, as were all of the men paraded in front of the Committee in September of 1947. The freedoms concomitant to democracy afforded each man the liberty to create. Such a luxury translated into the cinematic brilliance that each brought to the film industry. Their patriotic sentiments, however, remained concealed as Thomas prevented the Ten from showcasing their collective "loyalty," a revelation that would have gone a long way towards discrediting the "Hollywood as a subversive hotbed" contention. For the Committee to "succeed," the Ten had to appear as advertised. A steadfast Thomas made sure that they did.

Scholars such as Victor Navasky have cited the combination of personal loyalty and economics as the driving force behind "unfriendly" efforts to defy the Committee.[26] What has been overlooked is the effort waged by Hollywood Communists to fight the emergence of fascist tendencies in American government. Spanish Civil War veteran Alvah Bessie, a long time antifascist, seized a rare opportunity to actually read a statement and attempted to illuminate the Committee's ultraconservative orientation during his September 28 testimony. "I will never aid or abet such a Committee in its patent attempt to foster the sort of intimidation and terror that is the inevitable precursor of a fascist regime."[27] Bessie recognized the importance of the Hollywood hearings to HUAC's goal of building anticommunist hysteria as a means of establishing conditions propitious to their ultraconservative aims. Taking his cue from his predecessor Dies, Thomas captured the media spotlight by placing Hollywood on trial in Washington and amplified national paranoia regarding communist infiltration. "The true purpose of this committee," announced Bessie, "is to provide the atmosphere and act as the spearhead for the really un-American forces preparing a fascist America."[28] Demonstrating foresight beyond the Committee's comprehension, Bessie issued a portend that manifested itself in the form of Joe McCarthy.

Trumbo also perceived the conduct of the Committee to be fascist in nature. In *Time of the Toad,* Trumbo declared "As a matter of general policy, the Committee has flouted every principle of Constitutional immunity, denied due process and the right of cross-examination, imposed illegal sanctions, accepted hearsay and perjury as evidence, served as a rostrum for American fascism, and instituted a reign of terror over all who rely in any degree upon public favor for the full employment of their talents."[29] Although Trumbo would later declare that "heroes" were not present at the 1947 hearings and that he and his compatriots did not have the destruction of the Committee at the forefront of their agenda, his words in the immediate aftermath of the "trials" speak for themselves.[30] Clearly, the Committee and the threat it posed to civil liberties represented a target. Perhaps in hindsight Trumbo wished to remember things differently but at the time, in the heat of the 1947 trials, a quest to challenge the legitimacy of the Committee was clearly underway. HUAC, according to the "defendants," represented the exact form of un-Americanism that it was supposedly established to attack. "The rights of American citizens are important in this room here, and I intend to stand up for those rights Congressman Thomas," stated a dogged John Howard Lawson, "I am not on trial here, Mr. Chairman. This Committee is on trial here before the American people."[31] Echoing Lawson, "HUAC," announced Alvah Bessie, "had no legal right to pry into the mind or activities of any American who believes, as I do," Bessie affirmed, "in the constitution."[32]

Products of the age that produced Adolph Hitler, those who resisted viewed the Committee as an extremist organ designed to attack liberalism under the aegis of anti-Communism. The "Unfriendlies" saw more than just Hollywood's "radical" community threatened, but the entire American left. The crux of HUAC's attempt to stagnate the evolution and growth of post war progressivism in America is best surmised by Albert Maltz. Reflecting on HUAC (as well as the broader anti-Communist campaign) and its intentions years later, Maltz remembered "For this is the purpose behind the blacklisting of a university professor or of ten men of Hollywood, or forty postal employees or eighteen county workers or a dozen scientists. The purpose," Maltz propounded, "is the regimentation of all professors and government workers and all film artists. One is destroyed in order that a thousand will be rendered silent and impotent by fear. Through fear and hysteria Americans are to be induced to give up their rights as free citizens."[33]

As unjust as they may have been, the 1947 hearings represented an opportunity for the Ten. Although they faced vicious persecution, the hearings provided the Ten with the prospect of exposing the government's failure to respect the Constitutional rights of those deemed subversive. The fact that members of the Ten were not even afforded the luxury of reading a statement ironically demonstrated the illegitimacy of the organ. To the dismay of the Ten, however, the public did not correlate censorship with a constitutional conspiracy. In effect, the muzzling of the defendants ultimately cost the Ten the chance to reveal HUAC's ultraconservative ambition. Had they been presented with an adequate forum, they may have been able to alert the nation to the threat that the entire anticommunist campaign posed to America's openly democratic way of life. HUAC's unjust trial practices, however, remained (for the most part) concealed.

In the process of preventing the Ten from expressing their convictions, the Committee equated forced "silence" with an indication that the Ten were instruments of the Soviet Union. Silence, however, according to indignant members of the Ten, did not equal subversion. Standing on the First Amendment, the Ten, in absence of the right to speak to the charges levied against them, resisted in the only effective way made available to them. Ironically, their only weapon was not to say anything at all. If they couldn't attack the Committee verbally, they would happily deny HUAC the very words that they so desperately coveted: yes or no.[34] As John Howard Lawson observed, it remains the right of every American citizen to keep his or her political beliefs to themselves. "If Congress can't legislate in the area of free speech," remarked Lawson, "neither can it investigate."[35] In unison with Lawson, Alvah Bessie, speaking in response to the Committee's obtrusive invasion into the political beliefs of the "defendants," observed: "Mr. Stripling and gentlemen of the Committee. Unless it has been changed since yesterday, in our country we have a secret ballot, and I do not believe this Committee has any more right to inquire into my political affiliations than I believe an election official has the right to go into a voting booth and examine the ballot marked by the voter. General Eisenhower himself," recalled a defiant Bessie, "has refused to reveal his political affiliations [Ike had yet to declare as a Republican] and what is good enough for Eisenhower is good enough for me."[36]

The First Amendment provided all of those who resisted with the right to remain silent along with the right to keep concealed their political affiliation. More importantly, remaining silent allowed the "Unfriendlies" to protect the names of those they knew to be Party members or affiliates ("Travelers"). Trumbo revealed the intention of not just the Ten, but of all who refused to name names. "It is no exaggeration to say that the case of the Ten represents a landmark. It is a direct challenge to the censorial power of government over the human mind. If it is lost," Trumbo announced, "the customary rights of free speech-provided the government chooses to use the power bestowed upon it, and governments rarely seek power for idle purposes-may legally be abrogated. If it is won," continued Trumbo, "then the sinister twins of compulsory confession and political censorship, will, at the very least, have been stunned; not forever certainly, but long enough to give free men respite. The case," warned Trumbo, "is the immediate outpost in a long line of battle. If its holds, all will hold, and even advance a little. If it falls, all will share in the defeat and in the harsh years of struggle to make up for it."[37] To the demise of Trumbo and his allies, however, it was the Committee that ultimately held as its grip locked the nation in constant fear for the next decade.

Following the 1947 trial, the Hollywood CP began to fragment. There remained, however, a small faction of Hollywood Communists and former CP members who continued to defy the Committee. Albert Maltz emerged as the leader of the post-hearing Hollywood resistance. Maltz worked assiduously in the aftermath of the trial to expose the illegitimacy of the HUAC campaign and gain exoneration for the Ten.

Maltz had appeared in front of the Committee as the third "unfriendly" witness in the second round of the 1947 hearings behind Lawson and Trumbo. Unlike his two confidants, however, the Committee allowed Maltz to read his trenchantly prepared statement. It was a moment that Chairman Thomas would live to regret as Maltz painted a picture of the Ten unreflective of their "subversive" label. Pronouncing his strong belief in American democracy, Maltz stated "I am an American and I believe there is no more proud word in the vocabulary of man. Whatever I am, America has made me. And in turn, I possess no loyalty as great as the one I have to this land."[38]

A man who had proven his patriotism, Maltz struggled with the same confusion regarding the Committee's accusations that plagued many innocent men and women who went before the Committee. If the Committee was ostensibly designed to promote and protect American democracy, how was a man who clearly harbored the utmost respect for the fruits of liberty a threat to the American way of life? Maltz noted his long resume of patriotically themed works created not to subvert democracy, but rather to amplify its merits. As he told the Committee, "My novel, *The Cross and the Arrow,* was issued in a special edition of 140,000 copies by a war time government agency, the Armed Services Edition, for American servicemen abroad. My film, *The Pride of the Marines,* was premiered at 28 cities at Guadalcanal Day banquets under the auspices of the United States Marine Corps. Another film, *Destination Tokyo,* was premiered aboard a United States submarine and was adopted by the Navy as an official training film."[39] In scribing patriotically-oriented scripts celebrating the Allied war effort, Maltz had demonstrated his loyalty to the nation.

Following his testimony, Maltz, in the spirit of both Lawson and Trumbo, refused to respond to questions regarding his political affiliations. The Committee subsequently cited him for contempt. Maltz knew that remaining uncooperative could subject him to possible incarceration as well as cost him his career, yet he stood by his fellow accused and remained defiant. In fact, on his way out of the hearing room, Maltz glared at Committee investigator Robert Stripling and proclaimed "I have answered the question Mr. Quisling [a globally recognized synonym for traitor]."[40]

Maltz' case was unique both for the role he played as a leader of the Hollywood resistance following the hearings as well as the destructive manner in which the blacklist decimated his screenwriting career. Unlike many of his fellow screenwriters who waited out the blacklist period and found work following its evaporation, Maltz' career was virtually destroyed by the HUAC campaign.[41] Maltz sacrificed all that he had worked so hard to achieve in the film industry in order to take on the Committee. Unfortunately, Maltz' role in resisting the Committee after the 1947 hearings and in the time before his period of incarceration has gone virtually unnoticed.

Maltz joined the Communist Party in the early 1930's. Like many in that era, Maltz was disillusioned with socio-economic inequality in America and viewed the Communist Party as a means of actively assisting those in need. The Communist Party of the United States of America (CPUSA) provided Maltz with an arena to share his thoughts on poverty and discrimination. Maltz admired the proactive manner in which the CPUSA attacked deprivation. Maltz recalled an instance where his membership in the American Communist Party inspired him to act on a philanthropic impulse and lend a helping hand to a New York theatre facing bankruptcy. "I was asked to go make a speech to the Finnish Cultural Club in Brooklyn," Maltz recalled, "I traveled an hour on the subway and found myself in a hall were there were fifty people and yet [I knew that] those fifty people might take a benefit and sell 200 tickets. [My presence] was undoubtedly a tremendous help to a struggling theatre."[42]

Maltz found a sense of belonging in the party since it consisted of men and women who shared his progressive mentality. Maltz, however, proved to be, like many in Hollywood, an "atypical communist" as he demonstrated that he was not afraid to speak his mind regarding party doctrine. In 1946, he temporarily broke with party leadership over the the Foster-Duclos hard-line "art as a weapon" position.[43] In response to the straight-jacket philosophy, Maltz published a letter in *The New Masses* attacking the policy as sectarian. "The source of the problem is the vulgarization of the theory of art," penned Maltz, "which lies behind left-wing thinking, namely 'art as a weapon.'"[44]

Although he would eventually succumb to Party pressure and "recant" his statements, his willingness to challenge party dogma was reflective of the ideological chasm that existed between the Hollywood CP and the "parent" New York organization. Foster had gone "Stalinist" and clearly totalitarianism did not appeal to Maltz. He saw in the American CP an organization that sought a more equitable distribution of wealth and opportunity, a party which embraced Marx's utopian dream of an egalitarian society. Obviously, the party had abrogated its moderate, war-time "Browder" agenda in favor of a hard line position that insisted on conformity.[45] Those unwilling to "fall in line," such as Maltz, became victims of verbal abuse, physical threats, and ultimately, expulsion. The party under Foster had gone "doctrinaire" and not surprisingly, began to lose its appeal within the nation's progressive circles. Due in part to the party's shift coupled with McCarthy's rise, the CP faced virtual extinction within a few short years of the Maltz-*New Masses* "incident."

The fact that Maltz challenged the party openly signified his disillusionment with the CP's sectarian policies. Maltz undoubtedly spoke for many in Hollywood who had long embraced a communist vision that was clearly inconsistent with what existed in both Moscow and New York. Maltz, in many ways, refused to come to terms with the fact that the utopian dream formerly synonymous with Communism had become somewhat of a nightmare. Stalin was a dictator. The purges were reality. The Soviet Union clearly did not represent "a better world" and Maltz, understandably, had a difficult time digesting this. His *New Masses* article represented a test, and perhaps, a plea. Had the party truly morphed into something completely inconsistent with his own personal perspectives on life, society, and politics? Had it truly become "Stalinist?" Maltz got his answer and "cravenly" went back on his words. There is little doubt that the incident impacted him dramatically. The party had changed, the dream was over but Maltz, determined as ever, refused to give up. "Maltz continued to believe," asserted biographer Jack Salzman, "that the social injustices of America could only be changed by radical means."[46] Maltz may have "lost face" in his spat with the party, but his commitment to a "better world" remained in tact.

First on Maltz' post hearing agenda was to wage an attack on Truman's Loyalty Program (Executive Order 9835), put into effect in March of that year. To Maltz, the order represented a direct challenge on behalf of the government, an assault on the rights of those simply exercising their constitutionally guaranteed privileges. Additionally, the "loyalty oaths" reflected a shift. Now, the democratically-led federal government had aligned itself with conservatives in the battle against Communism. Maltz was not alone in his critique of the Truman's actions. "Truman touched off the worst witch hunt in the last quarter century by signing the loyalty order on March 22, 1947," observed historian Carey McWilliams.[47] McWilliams broadened his contention to trenchantly conclude that the oaths were reflective of a larger, government-fed anticommunist effort intent on dragging the entire nation into the "Red scare" controversy. To McWilliams, the complete McCarthy phenomenon "was a direct outgrowth of the President's loyalty program."[48] Griffin Fariello offered a similar perspective to McWilliams, "[With Executive Order 9835] President Truman brought his anti-Communist war home to America. With the stroke of his pen Truman had sowed the ground from which would spring the worst excess of the Red Scare. Within time," observed Fariello, "it became the yardstick of loyalty in almost every area of American life and operated, in effect, as a presidentially approved blacklist."[49]

Maltz saw the order as a political ploy rather than a security concern and viewed its issuance as an attempt on behalf of Truman to salvage some of the Democratic power base lost to the Republicans in the 1946 Congressional elections. "It was a demagogic attempt on Truman's part to repair the results of the 1946 congressional election, which swung votes to the Republicans based on the grounds that the Democrats were soft on Communism," noted Maltz, "In a larger part, I believe that it was designed to create in the country a cold war psychology that would support larger military budgets, military aid to selected countries abroad, the creation of the Central Intelligence Agency, and the establishment of military bases."[50] The "Red Scare," had emerged as the dominant force within America's social climate and Truman's action, according to Maltz, was not only a product of the phenomenon, but stood to increase the intensity of the incendiary milieu. "Furthermore," continued Maltz, [the order] created and atmosphere in which any criticism of Truman's foreign and domestic policy would be made difficult and to seem disloyal."[51]

Alongside the establishment of mandatory loyalty oaths for all government officials came the full fledged reemergence of J. Edgar Hoover as a central player in the post-war anticommunist effort. As was the case during the Dies days, his organization, the Federal Bureau of Investigation, served as the vehicle through which "subversive" activity would be monitored and eventually attacked in the United States. A time when Truman feared "losing" China to Communism and when the Soviet Union was rumored to be experimenting with atomic power, the rush to quell the spread of Communism both abroad and at home took on an unparalleled degree of urgency. Truman looked to Hoover to lead the domestic quest to uproot American Communism. "It is hard to overestimate the importance of J. Edgar Hoover and the FBI in creating the anti-Communist consensus," argues Ellen Schrecker, "[The Bureau] took control of the administration's anti-Communist effort and managed to infuse its own right wing concerns into what otherwise might have been a narrow program of security."[52] In fact, Maltz placed just as much responsibility on Truman and Hoover as he did on Dies or Wisconsin Senator Joseph McCarthy for the evolution of the postwar anti-Communist crusade. In Maltz' opinion, "These must be called the Truman-McCarthy years, because it was Truman's loyalty oath that created the atmosphere in which McCarthy flourished. During this time (the late forties), anything left of center was considered Red."[53]

It was in this context that Maltz saw the Ten as democratic martyrs. To him, those "on trial" placed their livelihood, and all the comforts that Hollywood afforded, on the line to undermine HUAC's attempt to ravage the progressive left. Reflecting on the freedoms threatened by the Committee, Maltz remarked "The most American of all American rights is the right of any man to think as he pleases and to say what he thinks. That right is protected against congressional interference by the American constitution. The question before the country" suggested Maltz, "is can a committee of Congress do indirectly by inquisition into a man's beliefs, what the Constitution forbids the Congress to do directly? And, if it can, what is left of the Constitution and the freedom it protects?"[54]

Maltz knew, like all artists, that artistic beauty can only truly manifest itself in an environment free of creative obstacles. In Soviet Russia, for instance, Stalin had forced all artists to work within the confines of a party agenda (a policy that Maltz was clearly opposed to). As a result, artists, no longer empowered by their passions, subordinated their artistic visions to party propaganda. In tyrannical states, art for public consumption is the product of not an artist, but a politician looking to mold the minds of the citizenry through a most intimate medium. "All those active in literature and the arts [in the time of Stalin] had to adopt a single creative method," writes Soviet historian Edvard Radzinsky, "They must follow the party's example. Every departure from it had to be punished, like factionalism in the Party. The method," continues Radzinsky, "was called 'social realism.' Only works that served the Party had the right to exist."[55] Cognizant of the threat that dictatorial regimes posed the creativity, Maltz passionately embraced democracy. He was fully aware that living in America was a dream for any artist. However, due to the anti-Communist campaign's intensity, times had changed.

No longer could Americans think "freely" without fear of consequence. America was slowly evolving into a quasi-fascist state where "the walls had ears" and "spies" lurked behind every corner. On eggshells, like Germans in the time of Hitler, Americans were suddenly terrified to speak their minds and art, certainly not immune from this reality, was slowly becoming a product of hysteria rather than a release from it. Critical political discourse was discouraged as conservative agencies, such as the Committee, employed artists to breed paranoia and foment unrest.[56] Maltz agonized over this verity and saw HUAC as the driving force behind the societal shift. "A truly Jeffersonian society would, of course, never punish people who had radical ideas," Maltz contended, "the society, if it were truly Jeffersonian, would follow his principle that all ideas have the right to be heard."[57] In HUAC's America, however, if it was merely assumed that you harbored a certain position, the Committee targeted you as if you did. This "guilt by suspicion" stance allowed the government to blanket all Communists and "Travelers" as subversives. "The most prevalent injustices," Schrecker notes, "occurred as a result of [the loyalty] program's essentially ideological definition of what constituted unacceptable 'association.' Because the executive order did not specify the exact nature of that association, the criteria were vague and came to be applied to a wide range of political beliefs and activities."[58]

Knowing full well that HUAC had instigated an ultra-conservative socio-political swing, Maltz attempted to use the 1947 hearings as a vehicle through which to expose the Committee's unconstitutionality. Denied this opportunity by a malicious Thomas and his refusal to provide the Ten an adequate forum, Maltz engineered a two-and-a-half-year post-trial crusade to gain exoneration and destroy HUAC before it destroyed the American left. "We stood on the First Amendment (during the hearings) to try and destroy HUAC and not merely for expediency," wrote Maltz in a 1976 letter to his attorney Ben "Charlie" Margolis, "I clearly recall our meeting at your home, Charlie, in which you suggested that we take the fifth as well as the first so that there would be no risk of our going to jail. But we turned it down."[59] The Fifth would have muzzled the Ten. Maltz and his fellow Ten members realized that to damage the Committee's credibility, they needed to speak. They also knew that a public hearing did not constitute a healthy environment for their attack. Only by taking the Committee to court would the Ten ascertain a medium amenable to their cause of exposing the Committee as the undemocratic body that it truly was. "If we took the Fifth," asserted a determined Maltz, "we could not get the Committee into the courts. There is no doubt in my mind that one of the major considerations was what action would be most effective in undermining and hopefully destroying the Committee and its power."[60]

Maltz initiated a public relations campaign in the hearing's aftermath to gather support for the resistance effort. He called for the establishment of a unified public front to oppose the Committee and its abuse of federal authority. Maltz knew that a successful propaganda effort, designed around illuminating the innocence of the Ten, could garner much needed public sympathy for their cause and force the government to take notice.

Foreshadowing what was to emerge two decades later with the Free Speech Movement, Maltz sought to rally progressive Americans around a call to uphold the merits of the Constitution. Maltz, who understood the "power of the people," proclaimed: "If on a given day in the United States, 50 million people walked all over the cities and towns in America saying 'free the Hollywood Ten,' or 'don't let them go to prison,' they would have a profound effect on the Supreme Court."[61] Unfortunately, due to the climate of the time and the Committee's success in concealing their insidious practices, the general public never received Maltz' message. Virtually muted during his 1947 hearing which served as a much larger stage, Maltz discovered, by the time he began his national tour in support of the Ten in late 1947, that most Americans had already condemned American Communism.

Despite the vigor he displayed in resisting the Committee, Maltz too felt the effects of the anti-Communist purge. As early as mid 1947 Maltz found work hard to come by which led to a loss of pride and a dwindling bank account.[62] Maltz' family struggled to come to grips with the blacklist's magnitude as well. Breaking the news to his son that his livelihood and status in the film industry was in jeopardy marked the lowest point for Maltz' as a blacklistee. "One problem that all of us with young children faced," he later remembered, "was the task of how to explain to them why we were in the trouble that we were in, why we were being written about in the newspapers and talked about on the radio, and this was not easy at all. At the time of the hearings, my son was ten."[63]

On November 26, 1947, Maltz and the Ten received another blow to their cause. A Screenwriters Guild meeting was held to allow members of The Producers Association to voice their concerns over the blacklist. Dore Schary, speaking for The Producers Association, proposed that the Guild accept the fate of the Ten in exchange for the impunity of its remaining members. "Give us these ten men," proposed Schary, "don't do anything about the fact that they have been blacklisted and we promise you that there will be no more blacklisting in the film industry."[64] This pitch stemmed from the same man who previously, in full support of both the Ten and the concept of political pluralism in America, had told the Committee: "I maintain a man's right to think politically as he chooses."[65]

Schary anchored his repudiation of the Ten in the rationale that he could not, given the anti-Communist atmosphere, afford to continue associating with "convicted" subversives. In addition, with the banks responsible for funding the studios united against Communism, Schary thought it necessary to isolate those within the industry still connected to the party. Without funding, movies could not be made. If Schary refused to cut the Ten loose, the banks would invest in less "controversial" mediums. To separate himself from the Ten, Schary remarked, "I felt the committee acted with absolute banality, the producers acted cowardly, but the Ten acted stupidly, they were trying by their hysterical acting to get the Committee to admit error."[66] Schary, however, failed to recognize the goal of the resistance. Making a spectacle out of the hearings provided a means by which the Ten could draw attention to the Committee's illegitimacy. In hindsight, this strategy may have hurt more than helped the Ten, but at the time, it appeared as the only option.

The Ten were arraigned in December of 1947. At the preliminary booking, conservative press agencies, namely the Hearst crew, had a field day with photographs and bail of one thousand dollars was assessed for each member. All entered a plea of not guilty and were duly charged with contempt. Maltz noted that at the time he did not experience fear, but rather pride in standing up for what he believed. Maltz remained determined to illustrate to the world that in principle America stood for freedom, but in practice freedom was clearly being compromised by tainted politics and unfounded threats.[67]

By late 1947, the loyalty oath program had begun to sink its teeth into the American psyche. The government laid off hundreds due to their refusal to sign oaths, and thousands more were targeted as potential threats to national security. It had become clear that American citizens had to either openly declare their loyalty by denouncing Communism or face the bitter consequence of being labeled a participant in a "red" conspiracy. Nevertheless, Maltz remained determined and traveled from Washington up to New York City in the spring of 1948 to give a speech at a "Stop Censorship" rally taking place at the Hotel Astor. At this gathering of progressives, Maltz issued a call for action. "It is urgent, that as artists working in different fields that we preserve for ourselves the right to work free of censorship, the right to our own ideas, the right to speak them or hold them in private, free of inquisition."[68] After delivering his speech, Maltz received a standing ovation from all those in attendance.[69]

As the Ten's case moved towards the Supreme Court for appeal, Maltz focused on gaining exoneration. Tension over the future of Berlin and the fate of China, however, had fueled the anti-Communist fire at home, diminishing the odds of a favorable outcome for the Ten. To further complicate the matter, Justices Rutledge and Murphy, the Court's two most left-leaning members, had recently passed away, leaving the court in the hands of predominantly conservative anti-Communists set on enforcing the citations. The Alger Hiss and the Klaus Fuchs convictions of 1950, based on the alleged connection between their ostensible rendering of relatively benign Atomic information to the Russians and the evolution of atomic power in the Soviet Union, also weakened the case of the Ten. The government's conviction of Hiss proved to many Americans that it had uncovered a Communist conspiracy, which bolstered the government's anti-Communist campaign.[70]

Hiss' conviction energized the anti-Communist crusade in America. "Red baiting" provided conservative America with both the means and the justification to fire an employee or silence a liberal voice. Countless numbers of progressive Americans (Communists and non-Communists alike) were not only put out of work, but were literally ostracized from mainstream American life based on their liberal convictions. "The readiness of so many politicians and employers to invoke the nation's security whenever they confronted the issue of Communism during the 1940's and 1950's makes it clear that *any* communist presence *anywhere* in American society could be seen as a threat," Ellen Schrecker observed, "Widely exaggerated though that perception was, it was plausible enough to convince important people in both the public and private sector to implement a wide ranging program of political repression.[71]

The Hollywood CP was only one of many agencies and organizations labeled subversive. Organized labor, civil rights groups, women's organizations, intellectuals, homosexuals, and many other innocent individuals were stigmatized as threats to democracy and the American way of life. In essence, the Committee attempted to purge the nation of all those that threatened the "status quo."

The government's domestic anti-Communist policies cultivated a repressive climate that made the Ten's appeal to the Supreme Court destined to fail. Consequently, in April of 1950, the Supreme Court rejected the Ten's appeal of their contempt citations and time in jail was imminent. Maltz, however, continued to tour America in his campaign to expose the Committee's "unconstitutionality." In a long diatribe delivered at a 1950 anti-HUAC rally, Maltz addressed both the Committee and the government that spawned it. The nation, in Maltz' eyes, had turned its back on its founding principles. Maltz, speaking passionately as was his custom, rebuked the Committee. "I abominate the manner in which our land is now being befouled by the men in charge of the machinery of government. I point to the evil actions of certain committees," screamed Maltz, "like the Un American Activities Committee, to certain individuals like J. Parnell Thomas, John E. Rankin, Attorney General Clark. But it would be blindness," Maltz continued, "to view such events as the work of a few individuals alone of a few reactionary committees of Congress. On the contrary, the time has come when it must be admitted that the work here is a total machinery of our men of government on a policy level and an executive level."[72]

The week before his incarceration, Maltz toured the nation's capitol. While in Washington, Maltz visited monuments and paid homage to the nation's democratic legacy at sites such as Mt. Vernon and the Lincoln Memorial. Maltz remembered the Mt. Vernon excursion as being "extremely moving" for he considered George Washington "the leading force of liberty in the world at his time."[73] Starring at the grand home of the nation's first president, Maltz found it perplexing that the HUAC campaign had originated in a city long regarded as an international bastion of liberty. It was at this time that the screenwriter stopped, took a good look around, and let the Virginia sun soak his face. He was a long way from Hollywood and his career was certainly at a crossroads. What did the future hold? What was next for America? Would he ever enjoy success in Hollywood again? At least his time in Washington allowed him a moment to celebrate liberty. It would be a while before he would feel that free again.

Ultimately, Albert Maltz remained true to his convictions. His willingness to stand up for what he believed in drove his crusade against the Committee. Along with his fellow dissidents, Maltz realized that the HUAC investigation of Hollywood was only a small piece of a nationwide purge of progressivism. Cognizant of this grim reality, Maltz hoped to use the visibility of Hollywood and the film industry's influence to rally America behind both the Ten and all those victimized by the HUAC purge.

Although his campaign proved "unsuccessful," the passion and energy that Maltz invested in combating HUAC reflected his desire to challenge injustice. The "activist" legacy that he and his fellow "Unfriendlies" engendered during the anti-HUAC crusade survived McCarthyism and inspired the next generation of progressives. Screenwriters and Young Communist League Veterans Michael Wilson and Paul Jarrico, who produced (along with Herbert Biberman) the socially progressive 1952 film *Salt of the Earth*, carried on the defiant legacy embodied by Maltz and the "Unfriendly" resistance and sent a message to the coming generation that repressive conservatism must be confronted. In exercising their liberal voice, they demonstrated to Cold War America that a citizen's right to express any and all ideas regardless of their design is a democratic staple that must not be suppressed. Jarrico and Wilson forfeited their personal and professional reputations along with their financial security to expose exploitation and signaled that the time for change had come. With their decision to produce *Salt of the Earth*, Jarrico and Wilson illustrated that HUAC's inquisition had not been completely successful in silencing the voice of the Hollywood Left. *Salt of the Earth* proved that there were ways to circumvent the blacklist and further evinced that Hollywood's progressives remained determined to combat intolerance and discrimination in America.

Salt of the Earth's "radical" message contributed to the activist tenor that came to dominate the late 1950's and 1960's. The movie, its message, and its filmmakers shared the same progressive views adopted by the New Left and the student movements of the 1950's and 1960's. "American film had simply never seen anything like it," note Paul Buhle and Dave Wagner, "*Salt of the Earth* did indeed achieve cult status on college campuses."[74] Clear links exist between Jarrico and Wilson's Old Left and the emergence of the student-oriented New Left that emerged later in the decade. According to Todd Gitlin, a 1960's activist and author of *The Sixties: Years of Hope, Days of Rage,* the radical movement was not an overnight sensation: "In the fifties, while the bulk of the middle class busied itself with PTA meetings and the *Saturday Evening Post,* there were, dotted around the country, enclaves where groups of adults carried on in opposition to prevailing values. It was in these enclaves of elders that unconventional wisdoms, moods, and mystiques were nurtured." [75] *Salt of the Earth*, by challenging the status quo, inspired those desiring change in America.

Paul Jarrcio, born Israel Shapiro, was one of a small number of Hollywood Communists outside of the Ten who shared the humanitarian crusade spearheaded by Maltz and other Hollywood "Unfriendlies." Jarrico, a moderate Communist, followed the Ten and stood firm against HUAC and its oppressive agenda. The son of Socialist parents, Jarrcio was trained in the art of political activism at a very young age and felt born to challenge the socio-economic inequalities prevalent in America. Looking back, Jarrico remembered, "the highest praise my mother could ever give to someone would be to call them a radical person."[76] Jarrico grew to embody his mother's activist spirit as he personified the adage that "actions speak louder than words."

His mother's words would echo in his mind throughout his screenwriting career as Jarrico pushed the progressive limits of film. His career in the industry, however, was often overshadowed by his Hollywood CP membership. Although responsible for several successful screenplays including *Men of Timberland* (1941) and *Rip Van Winkle* (1943), Jarrico, partly due to his progressive views, was not known, in the mid-1940's, as one of Hollywood's elite. He had made a name for himself, however, as one unafraid to challenge socio-political norms in his scripts. As Jarrico later told an interviewer, "I included a line in *Tom, Dick, and Harry* 'I don't believe in everyman for himself, I get lonesome' [cooperation was equated with Communism], it was a dangerous line but well worth it."[77]

In late 1943, Jarrico thought he had finally found the project that would take him into the upper echelon of Hollywood's screenwriting hierarchy. With *Song of Russia,* a film intended to highlight the amiable wartime relationship between the U.S. and the Soviet Union, Jarrico felt he had completed his best screenplay. Due to its highly controversial title and suspected "subversive" content (it "featured" Soviet collectivized agriculture), however, it failed to succeed on a broad scale. Nevertheless, the film, because of the 1947 HUAC testimony of friendly witness Ayn Rand, would become one of the most recognizable of the HUAC era. Rand, during her testimony, claimed the film to be subversive based on its inclusion of "[Russian] women smiling."[78] Rand, a Russian immigrant, remembered a very different Russia growing up, and strove to make it clear to the Committee that the Soviet Union was not a utopia. Many in Hollywood, however, did not interpret her claim that way and linked it with the unjust nature of the investigation.

The *Song of Russia,* although not a cinematic success, reflected the type of script that Jarrico enjoyed most. Although controversial, a sociocultural message wound its way through the screenplay. Jarrico, a dedicated progressive, took on projects that presented him with the chance to challenge conservativism and to celebrate his vision for a more just society. Commenting on a progressive script created to promote gender equality titled *Action in the Living Room,* Jarrico noted, "It was a comedy, which was also about women's equality, women's liberation, which was predictably not made." Jarrico's dream of making a socially progressive film centered on women's liberation did not end with *Action,* however, for he refused to relinquish that goal despite mounting HUAC pressure.

With anti-Communist fever heating up in the aftermath of the war, Jarrico's "radical" tastes eventually caught up with him. Based on his membership in the Hollywood CP and his status as a writer of several "subversive" works, namely *Song of Russia*, HUAC subpoenaed Jarrico in 1951. After Jarrico received the subpoena, a local newsman asked him if he would name names. Taking advantage of the spotlight, Jarrico proclaimed: "If I had to chose between crawling in the mud with [Friendly Witness] Larry Parks or going to jail like my courageous friends the Hollywood Ten, you can be sure I would chose the latter."[79] Jarrico made good on his claim by refusing to cooperate with the Committee. His decision to challenge HUAC and become an "Unfriendly" made him a victim of the blacklist. Still, he did not let the blacklist end his career. Before departing for Europe to write in France, Jarrico had one more picture in mind. Fortunately, his last film, *Salt of the Earth,* would also be his best.

Jarrico's dream of creating a film documenting the social and economic struggles of a New Mexico mining town emerged in the months leading up to his hearing. He had become so tied up with the 1951 HUAC investigation, however, that he could not find the time or the effort to put his vision to paper. After conducting a brief survey of available socially progressive screenwriters, his friend and fellow activist Michael Wilson emerged as the perfect candidate for the job.

Wilson, a swashbuckling intellectual known for his charismatic whit, was revered throughout Hollywood as one of the film community's brightest minds. Responsible for such acclaimed scripts as *A Place in the Sun, The Men in Her Life,* and *It's a Wonderful Life,* Wilson built his reputation on both his creative ingenuity and his desire to illuminate inequality. Wilson had taken a similar path to Jarrico's on his way to tinseltown and the connections between the two men would forge one of the most creative tandems in film.

Wilson, along with Jarrico, had grown up a member of the Young Communist League (YCL) and catered his work to suit his progressive inclinations. His youthful experiences inspired him as he rose to become an elite screenwriter. Wilson, who like Jarrico, considered himself an "activist," remembered the first time he tasted activist politics during a 1939 anti-Franco rally in Oakland. Looking back on the rally (an ominous sign of what was to come twenty years later regarding the violence that accompanied the student movement), Wilson recalled:

> It was a peaceful picket line and well organized, but while this was going on, a young campus Trotskyite appeared with an anticommunist placard which he waved, and because he was very vocal, the police started pushing him around, and I believe his placard accidentally touched the shoulder or the helmet of one of the cops, and they began to beat him unmercifully. He fell to the ground and three of them stood over him with billy clubs and beat him into insensibility by hitting him on top of the head. My comrades were appalled by this brutality and began to hurl insults at the cops and the police responded with tear gas and the calling of the paddy wagon; and a number of people were taken off to jail, but quickly released within hours.[80]

Wilson's experiences as a YCL member profoundly influenced his character and his career. Although from a wealthy family, he grew up wanting to challenge inequality and social repression in America. While at the University of California, Berkeley in late 1939, Wilson traveled to Mexico to assist villagers in a small rural town. His humanitarian venture motivated him to become a screenwriter and use the power of film to combat inequality. "It was about this time," Wilson later recalled, "that I got the idea of doing a series of short stories about minority workers, rural workers of the west and all of the various ethnic groups."[81] Little did Wilson know that his trip to Mexico would serve him invaluably when writing the script for *Salt of the Earth*.

By 1940, a veteran of the YCL, Wilson looked to film as an artistic medium through which to express his compassionate voice. After a few months in Hollywood, Wilson's career was fortuitously boosted upon being introduced to his "brother-in-law" (the husband of his wife's sister), Paul Jarrico. Jarrico's fiery demeanor and progressive tastes immediately impressed Wilson. "Paul Jarrico," Wilson afterward recollected, "pointed out to me the wisdom of screenwriting. He sold me on the basis that I could write what I wanted to write. I was flat broke and decided to at least give Hollywood a try."[82]

So began the relationship that would, ten years later, produce one of the most socially progressive films to date. Wilson provided the text and Jarrico, with the help of friend, confidant, and former member of the Hollywood Ten Herbert Biberman, served as the film's visionary and producer. Their combined ingenuity and drive made the film a reality. The trio created *Salt of the Earth* in the same spirit of free speech, civil rights, and progressivism that soon after spawned the evolution of Students for a Democratic Society and the Free Speech Movement in Berkeley. It represented a groundbreaking cinematic effort in the campaign for equality and its legacy is still revered today. "Salt of the Earth stands today as one of the most explicitly feminist cultural creations to come out of the predominantly antifeminist 1950's," historian Kate Weigand observes, "It shows that the Communist Party and its supporters did not ignore the personal and cultural aspects of women's oppression and that they actually took such concerns very seriously. The film was a direct reflection of Communists' efforts to develop their understandings of the relationships among class, gender, and race," continued Weigand, "and to politicize culture and personal life in the decade between 1946 and 1956. It revealed the impressive progress," maintained Weigand, "that Communists had made by the mid 1950's in their struggles to create cultural artifacts that empowered women, and to promote an alternative subculture that abandoned patriarchal customs and modeled egalitarian family life for all those exposed to it."[83]

Although *Salt of the Earth* is currently recognized by many as the classic progressive film of the "blacklist" period, it came very close to becoming a casualty of the "Red Scare" climate. Jarrico, Wilson, and Biberman faced incredible hostility from both Washington and the film industry as they attempted to produce the film. With the film's socially progressive theme, it was not surprising that it became a target of the conservative right. Schrecker noted that "The producers controlled the final project and they were not going to let anything "subversive" on to the screen."[84] Not long after starting work on *Salt of the Earth,* Jarrico discovered that film mogul Howard Hughes and Congressman and HUAC member Donald Jackson had assembled a right-wing coalition to halt the film. A Republican from California, Jackson became a thorn in the side of Jarrico and his production crew by linking the film with un-Americanism. Jackson claimed that the film was merely a front to conceal a Communist undercover operation intended to acquire nuclear information from nearby Los Alamos.[85] A proud conservative, Jackson expressed concern over the film's theme. Fearing the effects that a full-length progressive feature film might have on the psyche of the nation, Jackson set out to undermine the film's production. "Jackson repeated many false allegations about the film, including the assertion that it promoted race hatred and subverted national security," maintained historian James Lawrence, "moreover, he insisted that the picture exaggerated portrayals of police violence against the worker community. Jackson promised to 'do everything in his power to prevent the showing of this Communist made film in America.'"[86] Once again, the conservative right tried to block an attempt to challenge the status quo. Communism may have been at issue here, but the real concern for Jackson was the progressive content of the film. Women on strike and men in the kitchen painted a picture just too unorthodox for Jackson and his conservative cohorts.

Howard Hughes provided Jackson with the Hollywood muscle that he needed to cripple the film's production. Jarrico recalled that "Hughes told Jackson that he would stop us, that people like Jarrico and Biberman don't have the technical facilities to make the film, they can be stopped in the labs, they can be stopped in the cutting rooms and they can be stopped in the sound rooms, and he outlined a real blueprint to stop the film. But there was personal vindictiveness at the time. He was," Jarrico remembered, "posing as the All American anti-Communist opposing spies and saboteurs or whatever we were supposed to be."[87]

Knowing that Jarrico and his fellow producers were struggling with the economic consequences of the blacklist, Hughes, an eccentric who had experienced quite a bit of controversy himself over the "racy" (for the time) content of several of his films, realized that the most effective way to halt the production of the film was to handicap the filmmakers financially. By cutting off their resources, Hughes could avoid looking socially regressive while at the same time ensuring that *Salt of the Earth* never got off the ground. With syphilis-related paranoia fueling a fear of international "Stalinism," Hughes proved willing to play the "red" card if it meant undermining Jarrico and the *Salt of the Earth* effort. Additionally, Jackson represented a Washington insider who could "work" for the Texan on Capitol Hill. In this regard, Hughes was more than willing to assist the congressman in "jumpstarting" his career at the expense of the *Salt of the Earth* crew.

Jarrico, Biberman, Wilson, and Adrian Scott, who assisted with the writing, eventually got the film produced, but not without draining their own bank accounts in the process. All in all, they spent over two hundred and fifty thousand dollars of their own money to have the film made.[88] Thanks to the fact that the government barred the film's release in the United States (it was eventually released in a limited number of theatres in Canada and Europe), they only got a quarter of that money back, a verity acknowledged by Kate Weigand. "Despite the numerous obstacles encountered during processing and editing, Jarrico, Wilson, and Biberman refused to give up their fight and went deep into debt to complete *Salt of the Earth* in 1953."[89] Looking back in 1975, Jarrico recalled the film was "Recognized as a classic, but it never did make any money. Money would have allowed us to make other pictures so *Salt of the Earth* was our only picture, but we were very proud of it."[90]

Although prohibited from being released on a broad scale in American theatres, *Salt of the Earth* was still shown in a small number of liberal outposts. It was instantly acclaimed as a revolutionary achievement because of its challenge to conservative socio-cultural platforms and it received rave reviews in publications throughout the country. In a June 4, 1954 review of *Salt of the Earth,* Roy Ringer of the *L.A. Daily News* wrote: "America is a complex of racial minorities and their struggle for economic and social integration in our society is a significant aspect of our national life," recognized Ringer, "yet you can count on the fingers of one hand the plays or pictures which have chosen to deal with this suggestion. Which brings us to *Salt of the Earth*," continued Ringer, "and without passing political judgment on screenwriter Michael Wilson, director Herbert Biberman, or producer Paul Jarrico-all of whom have backgrounds of defiance before the Committee on Un-American Activities-I found their movie a deeply moving story and an artistic achievement of high order. A script that concerns itself with breaking down the barriers of racial prejudice, if there is propaganda in this picture," Ringer surmised, "it is not an alien one, but an assertion of principles no thoughtful American can reject.[91]

Despite being an economic failure, *Salt of the Earth* conveyed a message that could not be measured in dollars and cents. Jarrico, however, did not produce the film to generate a profit. In fact, Jarrico, Wilson, and Biberman, along with most of those who resisted HUAC, were not concerned with money. Had they been, they would have acquiesced to the demands of the Committee and retained their status in the industry. Willing to sacrifice material comfort for the sake of addressing a multitude of social inadequacies would become the mantra of various protest movements that emerged later in the decade. Although members of the next generation of "radicals" were still in grammar school at the time of *Salt of the Earth's* release, the spirit of both the film and its producers burned in those who fought injustice during the "age of protest." Dan Bessie, who worked on *Salt of the Earth* and whose brother in law is former counterculture guru and Palladium publicist Wes Wilson, has noted that the "New and Old Left drew from the same communal spirit, a spirit rooted in celebrating the common good."[92] New Left historian George R. Vickers, discussing the roots of the New Left, has observed "The *new* left can only be understood in relation to the left that preceded it. The New Left," Vickers asserted, "has often been described as a break with the Old Left, but it was a *response* to the Old Left. It was precisely because members of Old Left organizations often were active in efforts at dissent, and because they brought with them systematic and coherent analysis of how change should occur."[93]

Although its impact was somewhat lost amidst Cold War hysteria, *Salt of the Earth* reflected the Old Left resolve, manifest in Maltz, which refused to fold in the face of McCarthyism. In fact, the resilient spirit of the Old Left, seen through the Hollywood resistance, kept the activist flame lit just long enough for it to be refueled by the student movements of the late 1950's and early 1960's. As expressed by sixties radical Todd Gitlin: "Battered remnants of the Old Left carried their torches for some kind of social-ism, rejected the orthodoxies of the Cold War to one degree or another, and felt the national security state to be a menace rather than a guarantor of true blue liberties. Critical intellectuals," remarks Gitlin, "set the tone for a rebellion when rebels came up from the underground stream, looked around, and decided to make history."[94]

The Old Left's quest to oppose conservatism and engender equality had not been waged in vain. As seen by Gitlin, the legacy of those vilified by HUAC in the late 1940's and early 1950's did not evanesce into the mist of McCarthyism. On the contrary, the lingering spirit left behind by members of the moderate Hollywood CP contributed to the radicalism of the student movements of the late 1950's and early 1960's. Gitlin argues that, although the New Left was not Communist in orientation, their movement was undoubtedly influenced by those who championed progressivism ten years before. "The majority of the New Leftists were not the children of Com-munists or socialist parents, but sometime in adolescence were touched, influenced, fascinated, by children who were."[95] Many of the platforms adopted by the New Left were carved out of the progressive mold created by moderate Communists such as Healy, Trumbo, Jarrico, and Maltz. "The Old Left was there," recognized Free Speech Movement veteran David

Lance Goines, "things were discussed with old line Communists and we formed the core of political youth who were active in the early civil rights movement in the Bay Area."[96] Moderates in Hollywood advocated equality and set the liberal tone (especially in the West), as evidenced by *Salt of the Earth,* that would govern the intellectually driven student movement of the late 1950's, early 1960's. According to Kate Weigand, "Communists most public effort to demonstrate that individual men and women could free themselves from patriarchal assumptions and customs and transcend sexism and classism so pervasive in bourgeoisie culture was the making of the film *Salt of the Earth* in 1953. Made by the black listed progressive film makers Michael Wilson, Herbert Biberman, and Paul Jarrico, all of whom were deeply influenced by CP thinking about the politics of culture, *Salt of the Earth,*" contends Weigand, "showed how surpassing traditional gender roles had the potential to liberate an entire community.[97]

Embodying the same anti-conservative spirit synonymous with the Hollywood resistance, the student movements of the late 1950's and early 1960's extended the campaign against repression and kept alive Maltz' dream of a more just society. The legacy of the Ten lived as their refusal to capitulate in the face of congressional hostility contributed inspiration to a generation collectively engaged in a similar quest. The men and women who resisted the Committee in the 1930's, 1940's, and 1950's were not heroes in an idolatrous sense of the word. They were resolute progressives who possessed the acumen to see through the Committee's patriotic shroud into the heart of an ultraconservative organ. Those who challenged the integrity of HUAC perceived the bigger picture. Life, for these individuals, consisted of more than money, materials, and fame. Such comforts were viewed as temporary. The Committee, however, symbolized a potentially permanent shift in American political and social perception and, as seen through the evolution of McCarthyism, set the tone for one of the most suppressive eras in American history. These men and women recognized that the Committee had come to Hollywood looking for a spark and a failure on the part of Hollywood progressives to combat HUAC's efforts would have constituted a failure to live up to the social, cultural, and economic principles that they held so dear to their hearts. In the end, HUAC proved that those who resisted were indeed correct in their assumptions. Hollywood provided the Committee with the boost that it needed, catapulting HUAC into 1948, arguably its most successful year, and allowed Nixon, Thomas, and their conservative brethren to lay the groundwork for the coming of the McCarthy era.

Chapter Seven

The Red Raid in Retrospect: Reflections on HUAC's Hollywood Investigation and its Impact and the Evolution of McCarthyism

In June of 1950, members of the infamous Hollywood Ten headed off to various eastern United States prisons to begin serving out their one year contempt of Congress sentences. Their collective road to that point was riddled with controversy, blackmail, treachery, and deception. Ten men who had risked their careers for the sake of standing firm in their beliefs now faced a most uncertain future permanently stained by an ever tainted past. The contempt citations issued by HUAC chair J. Parnell Thomas in 1947, however, were not simply the product of in-court obstinacy on behalf of the Ten. The citations were the culmination of years of anticommunist build-up which began with the Palmer raids in 1920, picked up steam with the evolution of the Dies Committee in the 1930's, and climaxed with the Thomas Committee and its investigation of Hollywood in 1947. The citations can also be traced to the massive media campaign waged on behalf of the American Press throughout the "scare years."

Beginning in the late 1910's, the press picked up on the phenomenon that was slowly becoming the "Red Scare" and subsequently drove home the idea that revolution was at hand from within. Palmer captured head-lines throughout his campaign as "radicals" and "anarchists" were vilified in a media blitz that placed America on the verge of complete panic. Dies was also a master propagandist who used the media time and time again to demonize the left. His crusade to liquidate "subversion" garnered national attention as news outlets whipped the nation into a near national frenzy with a barrage of anticommunist articles, editorials, and cartoons. Although the production of anticommunist articles would slow during the second world war, as soon as the end became inevitable the pace of the rightist press picked up once again. Articles produced by *Life, Look, Reader's Digest,* and *The Saturday Evening Post* spoke of the imminent confrontation between communism and capitalism. The world would become an ideological battleground and a race for nuclear superiority would determine the balance of global power. HUAC and its post-war chair Thomas capitalized on growing anticommunist energy and used the momentum to thrust the revived Committee into the nation spotlight.

Needing a highly public "trial" to validate the legitimacy of his institution, Thomas steered the Committee west and placed Hollywood on trial in arguably the most important set of hearings in Committee history. Success in its action against the film industry solidified HUAC as the front line against domestic subversion. With strong federal backing and a firm public support, the Committee built on its "success" in Hollywood and forged ahead into 1948. The Committee's "Vintage Year," as recognized by Walter Goodman, included a series of "victories" against subversive foes which invariably contributed to the establishment of the repressive tenor that welcomed Wisconsin Senator Joseph McCarthy on to the national stage. Ultimately, it was the combination of the public creation of the "Red Menace," the national hysteria that it generated, and the insidious conduct of the Committee that not only landed the "Ten" in jail, but also paved the way for the creation of the Hollywood blacklist. Had the Ten been afforded a forum absent of paranoia and regulated in accordance with the constitution, their effort to combat the Committee would have undoubtedly been more fruitful. Had the Ten been successful in exposing HUAC as an oppressive organ, the course of "Red Scare" history would have been drastically altered. The issuance of the contempt citations, however, served as a victory for the Committee and placed the body in position to elevate the intensity of its campaign while operating in the contentious atmosphere synonymous with the McCarthy age.

For those that suggest that the Hollywood hearings remain insignificant in Committee history (and the history of McCarthyism for that matter), a quick look at 1948 will demonstrate otherwise. "1948 stands as the most celebrated year of the Committee on Un-American Activities," writes Walter Goodman, "a year of threat and counterthreat to which the Committee responded with enormous gusto."[1] It was a year made possible by the Committee's 1947 achievements, most notably, its pervasive purge of Hollywood. The Hollywood hearing also afforded the Committee an opportunity to "polish" its investigative tactics and strategies as the very public affair provided each Committee member with invaluable experience "under the lights." With Hollywood "on trial" in Washington, the Committee arguably forged its collective chemistry as each member grew into a particular role. Although the young Californian Richard Nixon undoubtedly emerged from the events of 1947 with the greatest fanfare, one cannot overlook the fact that the Committee as a whole grew in ways that invaluably served it throughout 1948. "A philosophy that held not only that communism was a conservative doctrine, not only a threat to the nation, but that every communist should be exposed in his community, routed from his job, and driven into exile," Goodman observed, "flowered under the klieg lights of 1947 and would be an inspiration for much of the Committee's later work."[2] The establishment of an investigative "paradigm" combined with Nixon's emergence and an enhanced collective ego allowed the Committee to raise the bar in 1948 and solidify itself as America's front line in the domestic war against the "Red Menace." As the nation continued to grow weary of Red subversion, HUAC played on media inspired public paranoia and used the "clout" garnered from the Hollywood affair to mount the backs of Thomas, Rankin, and Nixon and continue the escalation of arguably the most destructive internal investigation in American history.

How things may have been drastically different had those who attempted to dismantle the Committee in 1947, namely the Hollywood Ten, been successful. HUAC's muzzling of the Ten combined with escalating fear of the media inspired "Red Menace," however, prevented the "truth" from emerging from the trials. This truth being that the ultimate threat to democracy did not lie with those facing the investigative bench, but with those seated on it. Within the course of its dealings, the Committee unarguably circumvented the Constitution and trampled on the rights of those that it deemed un-American. Although there existed communists, such as William Foster and perhaps, John Reed, that stood as conceivable threats to "the American way of life," many of those targeted by the Committee in Hollywood were curious liberals who bought wholesale the concept of Lenninistic utopia and dreamed of a poverty free America. "Communists, especially those in Hollywood, were not familiar with the peril of "Stalinism," stated historian and former member of the Hollywood Writers Mobilization Group (a so called Communist front organization) Knox Mellon in a recent interview, "Communists in Hollywood in the 1930's and 1940's were leaders in the call for civil rights and visible proponents of racial and economic equality. Even those that had traveled to Russia were oblivious to the labor camp realities," observed Mellon, "these truths were cleverly hidden by the Soviets. [Bolshevik Russia] for most constituted a society where poverty and racism were practically non-existent, a society where education was available to all and people lived in general harmony."[3] The fact that the Committee was unable to differentiate between "radical" and revolutionary, moderate and doctrinaire, communism with a "small c" and Communism with a "capital C," "parlor Reds" and Stalinists, Marxists or "Trotskyites," exposed its fallibility. All those even remotely affiliated with the "left," such as having a tie to a "front group" like the "Hollywood Writers Mobilization" group or those who shared an ongoing friendship with a "convicted" Communist, were all in essence victims of the Committee's blanket strategy. Blind to the intricacies of the party and to the many extant "brands" of Communism in 1930's, 1940's and 1950's America, the Committee prosecuted all "Reds" as instruments of sedition linking members, "fellow travelers," and sympathizers alike to a dreaded Soviet conspiracy. "Communist subversion is the liveliest issue in Congress," declared John Rankin in October of 1946, "we are being undermined at home and insulted abroad. It is the duty of Congress to expose every subversive element and drive it from our shores."[4] The 1947 formation of the Hollywood "blacklist" marked the translation of Rankin's threats into action as its evolution secured HUAC's harrowing Hollywood legacy and crippled a once flourishing progressive community that, by January of 1948, faced complete fragmentation.

For those that cooperated and "named names," however, the Committee offered royal treatment. In the process, HUAC revealed its insidious nature by treating these men and women as welcome guests affording them the opportunity to speak at length and to purge their souls of "communist stain." "While investigator Robert Stripling, Chairman J. Parnell Thomas, and first term Congressmen Richard Nixon treated the "trained seals" with deference and respect and let them hurl gossip at anyone they cared to," recalled Dan Bessie in reference to Committee's impartiality on display during the 1947 Hollywood hearings, "the attitude shifted the moment John Howard Lawson took the stand. Lawson wanted to make a statement: Denied."[5] Not to say that these "trained seals" were not victims of the paranoia infused environment because they certainly were, but their actions came with grave consequences. Such was the case in Hollywood were "friendly" witnesses offered up names in return for impunity. Men such as Edward Dmytryk, Roy Huggins, and Elia Kazan have gone down in infamy as "stool pigeons" that squealed to the Committee in order to save their careers, and in some cases, their families. The case of screenwriter Roy Huggins offers insight into the power and magnitude of Hollywood's blacklist age.

An aspiring screenwriter-director with a career on the rise, Roy Huggins' life was arguably redefined the moment he glanced upon his HUAC subpoena in September of 1952. Responsible for a number of successful films including *The Fuller Brush Man* (1948) and *Good Humor Man* (1950), Huggins was just hitting his cinematic stride when his career came to abrupt halt upon receiving his Committee summons. A loving husband and father who undoubtedly understood full well the pervasiveness of the "blacklist," Huggins wrangled over whether or not to name names. In fact, he was quoted in a later interview as having "welcomed" the subpoena as a means in which to "criticize" the Committee.[6] The bright lights of the 1952 hearings quickly altered Huggins mindset, however, as he proceeded to offer up names in an effort to clear his own. "Afterward I regretted the decision," lamented a remorseful Huggins, "In retrospect, it is appalling to me that I cooperated in anyway. The truth is, I was ashamed of myself."[7] It was more than just the bright lights of the Committee room that swayed the screenwriter, however. Huggins was yet another victim of the atmosphere which surrounded the investigations. A circus show-like environment infused with deep seeded, media charged "Red Scare" paranoia, the electrified social milieu encompassing the HUAC trials coerced many into going against their instincts. Many, like Huggins, who, despite their "friendly" testimonies, still maintained the progressive proclivities that initially lured them left.

Huggins, like Rosenberg, Kazan, Jarrico, and so many others, became drawn to the CP in the mid 1930's based on its anti-Nazi platform. He was introduced to Marxism while a student at UCLA and became enamored with its egalitarian tenets. After initially joining the CP in 1940, Huggins quickly discovered that he "was a Marxist and not a communist" and quit "after attending 3 or 4 meetings."[8] He rejoined in 1943 and remained a committed member until 1947. A "lack of democracy" within the party, however, prompted Huggin's withdrawal from the organization in 1947.[9] Huggins had apparently become convinced that the Hollywood CP was an organ of the USSR and belonging to such an organization made it impossible, according to Huggins, "to be a loyal American."[10] His falling out with the party established Huggins as an ideal candidate for the HUAC inquisition. The committee preyed on former CP members who had presumably "rediscovered" their patriotism amidst "Red Scare" paranoia and stood anxious to absolve their resumes of Communist taint. Huggins, although less than enthusiastic about naming names, revealed the identities of several of his former Communist colleagues, including Albert Maltz, and was subsequently granted reprieve by the Committee.

Director Edward Dmytryk fell into the same category as Huggins as a quintessential HUAC witness. An original member of the Hollywood Ten, Dmytryk was known throughout Hollywood as one of the film industry's most talented directors. He was also a man who had been lured to the Hollywood CP by its altruistic orientation. "There was no word there of revolution, violence, or terrorism" Dmytryk asserted, "nothing but pious promises of reliance on the constitutional rights of citizens to create a perfect world."[11] Responsible for such highly acclaimed pictures as *Crossfire*,

Dmtryk arguably had the most to lose among the original Hollywood Ten. As a director, the black-market was not an option. He could not write in exile like Maltz and Trumbo and continue to make a living. Dmytryk was stuck and his only option if he wished to continue his trade was to take action to remove his name from the blacklist. This required naming names, something that he knew would prove devastating to those affected but a necessary "evil" if he wished to maintain his position in the industry.

The fact that Dmytryk's case could be considered "special" given his directorial status does not take away from the fact that his actions contributed to the perpetuation of both the blacklist and the HUAC investigation. Although many of those that he named had already been mentioned by prior "Friendly" witnesses, his cooperation provided the Committee with more ammunition in the so called battle against Hollywood Bolshevism. Certainly his career would have been all but lost had he not come forward, but there were many, including Maltz and Alvah Bessie, who traded a career for their integrity. One could argue that neither possessed the talent of Dmytryk or that Bessie and Maltz were writers and could therefore utilize the black-market as a means of mitigating the damage. The truth is, however, that neither of the two ever achieved the level of success that they had enjoyed prior to the blacklist. They basically exchanged their careers and lifestyles for the opportunity to expose HUAC as the oppressive institution that history has shown it to be. Dmytryk elevated his own welfare over that of his friends and confidants and returned to work with a clean bill of health from the Committee. Bessie and Maltz, on the other hand, served their one year contempt sentences and worked in relative obscurity until the blacklist was eventually "lifted" in the mid 1950's. Does this reality make Bessie and Maltz heroes and Dmytryk a goat? Absolutely not. What it illustrates is the gravity of the situation in Hollywood and the pressure that targeted men and women were under to make life altering decisions under the heat of the HUAC strobe lights. "I was on top of the world and confident in the future," recalled Dmytryk, "the way things were going I was going to be rich in a few years. The next day, I was handed a pink subpoena."[12]

Lost amidst the finger pointing and vitriol regarding who named and who didn't was the effect that the hearings had on relationships. Bessie, Dmtryk and Maltz had been friends, comrades, confidants, members of a burgeoning progressive community. A community comprised of individuals who may have admired certain tenets of what they thought to be Soviet Communism but who never, as cooperative witness David Raskin announced to the Committee in 1952, "put the interest of any other country before his own."[13] Nevertheless, HUAC, blind to the ultimate intentions the vast majority of those its targeted, pillaged indiscriminately destroying careers, friendships, and families along the way.

Extravagant threats such as that of an "internment camp" also served to motivate the testimonies of more than one "friendly witness." With the camps used to inter Japanese Americans during the Second World War very much operational, the FBI began to float rumors that a defiant attitude could lead to physical imprisonment.[14] Dorothy Healy, head of the Southern California branch of the American CP at the time of the Hollywood hearings, remembered sitting in a restaurant and being approached by a strange man in a tight suit. The FBI agent offered Healy an ultimatum. Name names or face internment. "Certain individuals were designated to be placed in concentration camps," observed Healy, "and I was on that list."[15] Friendly witness Roy Huggins found himself in a similar situation. After having learned of the "camp" option, Huggins began to contemplate the impact that internment would have on his wife and children. "So there I was," proclaimed Huggins, "faced with the possibility of being hustled into a concentration camp wile having several people completely dependant upon me."[16] A dedicated father, the decision was easy for Huggins at the time to come forward. His actions, however, perhaps unbeknownst to him at the time, cost others facing a similar predicament the opportunity to enjoy that same fatherly luxury he so desperately sought to preserve.

When looking at the larger picture, however, it is difficult to lay too much blame on Dmytryk, Kazan, Huggins and others "Friendlies" who empowered the Committee with names. The asphyxiating environment alone was enough to bring men and women to the brink of insanity. As Dalton Trumbo so eloquently observed in a 1970 speech to the Screenwriter's Guild, "it would do no good to search for villains or heroes or saints or devils because there were none; only victims."[17] With the "red scare" having morphed into a nationwide epidemic, those brought before the Committee had to have believed that anything was possible. The media coverage of the red hunt had become so perverse that it was virtually impossible to ignore the specter of red hysteria.

Articles, stories, features, films, and books all dedicated to the propagation of the "Red Menace" were seemingly ubiquitous in late 1940's America. The FBI's "100 Things You should Know about Communism in the U.S.A.," released in the aftermath of the 1947 Hollywood affair, reflected the tenor of the time. "For every member of the communist party," purported the FBI, "ten others are willing and able to do the party's work."[18] Movies began to propagate anticommunist themes as producers, against the wall in an ever competitive, television flooded entertainment market, catered to rising anticommunist tastes while indulging ultraconservative government officials. *I Married a Communist* (1949), *The Red Menace* (1949), *I Was a Communist for the FBI* (1951), and *Big Jim McLain* (1952), featuring the ever popular, ever conservative John Wayne, reflected a growing anticommunist trend in filmmaking.

Newspapers kept up the anticommunist barrage as anti-Red articles became daily features. On May 2, 1948, the *New York Times* released "What is a Communist and How Can You Spot Him," a virtual manual on how to effectively practice anticommunism in the United States. "A believer in Russian can take no shelter behind idealism, he is a believer in a police state of the most ruthless character," wrote historian and Columbia professor Allen Nevins, "he believes in a system that has killed millions, in imperialist aggression. His party doctrine," continued Nevins, "is Communist rule or general ruin. They concoct plots, infiltrate at all weak points, cripple every machine that they can touch and stand at any moment necessary to seize power by force. Unceasing vigilance is necessary," Nevins pronounced, "we cannot let our armed services, State Department personnel, or the agencies concerned with atomic energy be invaded who may become secret agents of a foreign power."[19]

Products of the passion charged post war environment, Nevins' words symbolized the intensification of the Red Scare and the mounting pressure on Americans to combat communism before it crippled capitalism. In this environment it was very difficult to go against the anticommunist grain. In Hollywood, men and women consumed with communist hysteria acted impetuously and made decisions that they would long regret. Cleary, more was at stake than simply money and materials. Lives and lifestyles, families and friends, careers and reputations were all threatened by the Un-American investigation. The blacklist era was a time, professed Albert Maltz in a 1975 interview, when "any position left of center was considered Red. Over night, at the drop of an issue, you could become red, even though you did not know Karl Marx from Groucho Marx."[20] Loss of one's job was in many cases the least of the concerns for Committee targets. Perhaps of greatest worry was the loss of one's reputation. Valued above all else in Hollywood, the tarnishing of one's reputation could mean the end of a career. In a city where status meant everything, anyone varnished red could simply forgo any thought of success in the industry. A career on the black-market under a pseudonym, as Trumbo did when he won an Oscar as "Robert Rich" with the *The Brave One* in 1957, or in "exile" abroad was about as good as one could expect. The HUAC query touched the lives of nearly all involved in Hollywood in the 1940's and early 1950's and its potency undoubtedly changed the face of the industry forever. It is in this light that the actions taken by those who named become somewhat understandable, yet remain, to many, unforgivable.

Given the incendiary climate and the suffocating pressure associated with the HUAC assault on Hollywood, the "blame" for the blacklist cannot be placed on the "Friendly" individuals many suggest stood responsible for it. Ultimately it was the Committee and its panel members that wrought grief and despair down upon American progressives during the scare years. It is Un-American Activities Committee that is to blame (acting in conjunction with the studio heads), not the men and women paraded before it. In the case of Hollywood, the Committee's collective myopia and power lust prevented it from seeing the folly of its investigation. Hollywood was not a bastion of militarism. Revolution was not brewing in tinseltown. As Knox Mellon remembers, "there was no talk of revolution in Hollywood, that is ridiculous. The Committee had an agenda, and that agenda included the persecution of those deemed a threat to the status quo. It began back in the 1930's," Mellon recalled, "with the elevation of Communism over fascism as the ultimate threat to national security and this sentiment only intensified in the years following the war [World War II]. HUAC acted on the assumption that if you joined the CP, you immediately swallowed whole revolutionary rhetoric. This was not the case," continued Mellon, "it was an intentional misread on behalf of HUAC because they wanted to crucify those guys [Hollywood CP members]."[21] In reality, it could be argued that the only thing truly brewing in "red circles" in and around the film industry was an altruistic attitude and a genuine compassion for the less fortunate and disenfranchised of the world. The moderate Hollywood Party, notes Mellon, was home to some of the most outspoken proponents of greater social and economic democracy in Southern California at the time. These men and women "sought to make Civil Rights more meaningful, to create opportunities for the disenfranchised, economically, politically, and socially speaking. Certainly there may have been a few hardliners," admitted Mellon, "but the majority of the party consisted of concerned intellectuals who were fascinated with the concept of a more equitable society."[22]

Yet in spite of the primarily benign nature of the Hollywood Communism, those affiliated with it were viewed as enemies of the state and persecuted as traitors. The Hollywood investigation not only established arguably the most recognizable feature of the "Red Scare" age in the "blacklist," it also injected the Committee with the "sense of purpose" that carried it into its banner year of 1948. The Hollywood hearings were also critical to the establishment of the repressive social tone commensurate with the "McCarthy age," an environmental framework pivotal to arguably the greatest American witch hunt, as Carey McWilliams has sagaciously observed, since Salem in the 1600's. Hollywood provided the Committee a stage upon which to demonstrate their value to the nation. It was also no coincidence that the stage just happened to be the most recognizable in the world. "During the last two weeks of October 1947, the Un-American Activities Committee staged the most flamboyant and widely publicized hearing in its history," remarked historian Robert K. Carr, "Not even the Hiss-Chambers hearings [part of HUAC's banner 1948] quite matched the sensations of the nine days in which the committee tried to track the foot-prints of Karl Marx in movie land."[23] Hollywood offered HUAC the per-fect opportunity. For the Committee, it was a match made in heaven. For those it targeted, however, Hollywood in the 1940's and 1950's resembled anything but paradise.

The "symbiotic" (or utilitarian) relationship shared between HUAC and Hollywood in the late 1940's is what arguably saved the Committee from extinction. There is little doubt that the Committee stood on shaky ground in the aftermath of the Second World War with both the Ameri-can public and members of Congress. There were many who doubted the legitimacy of both HUAC and its investigative aims. Although John Rankin was successful in reviving the organization, the Committee faced a strong contingent of cynics who undoubtedly sought its demise. Many, such as Democratic Representatives Emanuel Celler and Vito Marcantonio of New York, felt as though HUAC was no longer viable given its inactivity during the war years coupled with the war-time decrease of subversive activity on American soil. It had also come under fire for its failure to observe basic constitutional liberties within the course of its investigation. According to Marcantonio, it was the Committee itself that was "un-American."[24] By the end of the war "only a few people," wrote historian William F. Buckley Jr., "still believed in the mission of HUAC" as there "emerged a feeling that HUAC was doomed."[25] Rankin, however, thought otherwise. He, along with Thomas, a man once quoted as stating "going after Reds is going to make me," and their fellow conservatives realized that Hollywood, with its global appeal and star power, would provide the Committee with the publicity required to demonstrate its value.[26] In the final analysis, they were right. "The early hearings were heard nationally on the radio and [all] were reported nationally in the press," Griffin Fariello confirmed, "As in a play, the actors [HUAC] were never really talking to each other but for an audi-ence, and HUAC could confidently feel that its audience was not limited to guests physically present. The Committee performed for a nation, present and future."[27] Regardless of what others, such as Walter Goodman, have suggested regarding Hollywood's centrality to the Committee's mission, the film industry unquestionably offered HUAC the most unique opportunity of its career. The Un-American Activities Committee may not have uncovered any propaganda but its members vilified Hollywood as Red nonetheless. "We are exposing Communism in Hollywood" proclaimed Thomas following the 1947 hearings, "They are going to be exposed and they are going to be exposed for what they are."[28]

Although the liberal press worked to portray the Committee as undemocratic, mainstream America received Thomas' version of the story. Major publications, such as the *New York* and *Los Angeles Times,* routinely quoted the chair verbatim on both the effectiveness of his campaign and the salient threat presumably posed by Hollywood Reds. "The Committee's hearings of the past two weeks have clearly shown the need for this investigation," wrote Thomas in a statement published by the *New York Times,* "It is not necessary to emphasize the harm which the motion picture industry suffers from the presence within its ranks of known communists who do not have the best interests of the United States at heart. The industry," Thomas maintained, "should set about immediately to clean its own house and not wait for public opinion to force it to do so."[29] Luckily for Thomas, public opinion, thanks in part to Hollywood electricity, was firmly in his corner.

A close examination of both the national and congressional "mood" in the months following the trial reveals the ultimate impact of the Hollywood event. Mainstream Americans, in the latter half of 1947 and the early months if 1948, had begun to accept the gravity of the "red situation" brewing within America's borders and those on Capitol Hill would soon respond in turn. The Committee had silenced its challengers in Hollywood and contributed to the escalation of an intense anticommunist environment which only strengthened as concerns over Soviet aggression abroad grew. With HUAC having achieved "victory" in "the greatest hotbed of subversive activity in the United States," it had become clear that the Red Menace had merely hibernated during the war only to resurface with even greater vigor and ferocity.[30] Now, with Hollywood serving as a notch in the belt, the Committee looked to broaden the investigative effort. With its penchant for the sensational, there existed only one target with the "fantastic" value that Un-American Activities Committee craved: the Government.

Although a tall order, the Committee had ostensibly earned the so called right to expand its investigation following Hollywood to include the highest echelons of American society. Thomas had actually hinted at a potential "inside" investigation while probing the film community when he suggested that certain government "officials" had encouraged the production of pro-Soviet films. According to the *New York Times,* Thomas felt as though the Hollywood-Capitol Hill connection was reflective of a large "Soviet presence" within governmental ranks. "We have recorded testimony that even the White House exerted its influence on certain people in Hollywood to have certain pro-Russian motion pictures filmed," announced Thomas, "[clearly] the government wielded the iron fist to get the companies to put on certain Communist propaganda."[31] Although such "propaganda pieces" were made in the interest of generating support for the Allied cause, Thomas demonstrated a short memory in the heat of the "Cold War" and, like McCarthy in the 1950's, called for an all out assault on all instruments of subversion no matter where their location. Thomas was ready, the Committee was ready, and fortunately for them, so was Whittaker Chambers.

The Hiss case of 1948 stands arguably as HUAC's greatest "accomplishment." The case not only amplified fear of Red terror by introducing the phenomenon to millions of previously disinterested Americans, but it also marked a moment of paramount importance in American history. It was a case, according to historian Patrick Swan, which "played a major role in defining the post-World War II political battle lines between the emerging anticommunist conservative movement of the right and the nascent anti-anticommunist reactionaries on the left."[32] The emergence of Richard Nixon, highlighted by the infamous "pumpkin papers" crusade, signified a Republican thrust and a conservative shift in American social and political milieus. "Nixon's career began with Hiss and espionage," wrote historians Morton and Michael Levitt."[33] Nixon, according to historian Earl Latham, "made a national career out of the Hiss case."[34] GOP gains in the House and the Senate coupled with the rise of Nixon as a young, dynamic conservative leader served as a stern sign to the American left that the 1950's were sure to be a troubling time. According to Gallup polls, in the aftermath of the Hollywood hearings, popular opinion was overwhelmingly in HUAC's favor. Additionally, the polls revealed communist concern at incredible high levels with over 60 percent of Americans believing that the Communist Party should be outlawed in the United States.[35] Regarding the Committee, an early 1948 poll showed that over 60 percent of all college educated adults felt as though the Committee should continue with its investigation. The significance of this number lies in the fact that the 60 percent is clearly reflective of the massive propaganda campaign that had been and was currently being waged by the media. From newspapers to magazines to movies, publishers, editors, and producers recognized a growing anticommunist market audience and pandered to consumer fears.

It did not take long for Congress to acknowledge the burgeoning popular support for the un-American investigation. On March 9, 1948, Congress, by a vote of 337 to 37, "granted $200,000 to its Committee on Un-American activities. This," recognized William S. White of the *New York Times,* "was the largest sum ever singly authorized in the ten years of its life."[36] HUAC undoubtedly viewed this generous appropriation as validation for a job well done. It was also a mandate, a license to increase the intensity and scope of the investigation. With its member's popular appeal rising coupled with firm congressional backing, the possibilities seemed limitless for the conservative organ that once bordered on extinction. With the Hiss case, HUAC finally hit the "big time" as "the American people saw plain [what appeared to be] the bland face of treason."[37]

Somewhat lost in Hiss hysteria was the plight of the Hollywood Ten, their effort to reverse their convictions, and their subsequent journey(s) to various prisons. The *New York Times* ran brief pieces on the more high profile members of the Ten and their convictions but they were all but buried under HUAC press pieces and routine newspaper fodder. "Dalton Trumbo, a film writer, was convicted today of contempt of Congress by a jury of seven men and five women in Federal District Court," noted the *New York Times* on May 6, 1948.[38] Commenting on the significance of the conviction, assistant United States Attorney William Hitz declared the decision to send Trumbo to jail "an extremely important one."[39] The article did note, however, that Trumbo and his attorney were not extended the opportunity to cross examine the witnesses used in the case against him. Nevertheless, it is consistent with the mainstream position that Trumbo, along with Lawson, Maltz, and the rest of the "Unfriendly 10," were guilty as charged and deserving of their time behind bars.

The resistance had seemingly failed and HUAC, riding a wave of Hollywood charged momentum, set out to execute the ambitious 1948 agenda that arguably etched its place in Cold War history. Hollywood could have been the Committee's albatross. Had the Ten, along with their fellow "resistors," prevailed and turned popular support against HUAC, the entire course of the anticommunist "era" may have been dramatically altered. Instead, Hollywood served as a bridge linking pre-war anticommunist success with post-war anticommunist hysteria. As a result, HUAC drove forward in a blind charge that ultimately paved the way for the emergence of McCarthy and a legitimate epoch of un-Americanism.

Not long after Trumbo's May conviction, he and his fellow "Unfriendlies" disappeared into various prison cells across the east. Their physical evanescence, however, did not correspond with a total annihilation of their legacy. The resiliency shown by the Ten inspired a number of left wing Hollywood figures, including screenwriters Paul Jarrico, Michael Wilson, and Herbert Biberman, to continue the effort to expose the Committee as an arm of injustice.[40] As the investigation resumed under Georgia's John S.

Wood in 1950, hundreds of Hollywood figures appeared before HUAC with their careers and lifestyles on the line. Although most would crack under both internal and media driven external "red scare" pressure, there existed a few who carried on the legacy of the Ten and accepted a position on the infamous Hollywood blacklist. This collective effort served as inspiration to many across the country who, by the end of the second round of Hollywood hearings, had grown suspect of the Committee and its dealings.

One "radical" group in particular seemed to catch the combative spirit of the Ten as it searched for an identity in an ever hostile ultraconservative environment. A student "radical" organization at the University of California at Berkeley, operating under the acronym SLATE, had begun to resist extreme conservativism and press for a greater extension of Civil Rights in the late 1950's. This organization had communist with a "small c" underpinnings as many of its members were familiar with the Hollywood-HUAC clash. In fact, there were several members of SLATE, and later the FSM (Free Speech Movement) who were directly connected to the event either through a relative or close acquaintance.[41] Many of these individuals sought to use the knowledge gained from studying the Hollywood investigations to enhance the effectiveness of their organization. A 1960 anti-HUAC rally conducted in San Francisco in response (in part) to the Committee's subpoena of Douglas Watcher, an eighteen-year-old Berkeley campus "radical," arguably represented the fusion of Old Left resilience with New Left enthusiasm. Two progressive bodies stemming from differing generations but bonded by the same egalitarian ethos, Old Leftists and New leftists converged on San Francisco, radicalism's Rome, to join in a galvanized effort to expose ultraconservative insularity. "The San Francisco anti-HUAC demonstration really galvanized the Old and New Left in the West," remembered former SDS chapter head and director and producer of the acclaimed SDS documentary *Rebels With a Cause* Helen Garvy, "It had a huge impact on the forging of the two groups."[42] Recognized by rally participant Bob Gill, "The HUAC demonstrations on May 12, 13, and 14 were the unofficial opening of the sixties. Never sense the thirties," remembered Gill, "had so many and such a diverse group of radicals come together in one cause."[43] The rally led to the formation of The Bay Area Student Committee Against HUAC, (BASCAHUAC), an organization comprised of "American kids," recalled Gill, "who got together and asked each other just why things were the way they were and how they could do something about it."[44] Motivation for liberals in the late 1950's was not hard to come by and HUAC served, ironically, as a unifying force for student leftists as they rallied around a call to enact necessary change.

As SLATE eventually evolved into the FSM and as the FSM joined hands with Midwestern headquartered SDS (Students for a Democratic Society), the one constant galvanizing factor among all three organizations remained a dedicated spirit of resiliency in the face of unjust hostility. In the spirit of *Salt of the Earth,* a film written and produced by blacklistees Jarrico, Wilson, and Biberman, young men and women from across the country stood shoulder to shoulder and captured global attention in a crusade to engender "a better world." Had it not been for the anticommunist campaign, initiated by HUAC, the bond that held this incredible group together would have arguably been missing. "The 1960's movements could not elude the influence of progressive activism that preceded them," writes Historian Kate Weigand, "the Communist Party itself was not a significant political force in the 1960's, but important elements of its materialist analysis of race, class, and imperialism survived into the decade."[45] It was indeed the anticommunist purge in America that ignited the type of passion that led to a call for justice in all corners of America. It had become clear that the status quo was no longer sufficient and that the effort to preserve it need not only be challenged, but conquered. "The tonic for my inchoate lefty yearnings and unformed ideology came in my first semester in the spring of 1960," former FSM member Kate Coleman recalled, "when the House Un-American Activities Committee came to San Francisco. Zap! I came over to the 'dark side,' happily pitching myself under the aegis of student leftyism."[46] From the call for civil rights in the south, to the call for women's equality in the northeast, to the call for gay rights in the west, it was the HUAC campaign that served as the spark which ultimately lit the most ferocious social fire that the world had ever seen. The legacy of the Ten certainly lived on, and in fact, continues to inspire to this day.

The 1947 HUAC investigation of Hollywood was in fact one of the most significant events of the nascent Cold war period. It not only united the Committee and provided it with the energy that it used to create global headlines in 1948, it also inspired a zealous Wisconsin senator who happened to keep a watchful eye on the proceedings. The integral nature of the hearings is also seen in the fact that they marked a pivotal point in Committee history. The Ten posed a direct challenge to both the authority and constitutionality of HUAC and could have conceivably derailed the entire HUAC investigation. Instead, the Committee silenced the Hollywood resistance and gained a critical victory without having even accomplished its primary objectives. Feeding off of media inspired anticommunist paranoia, the Committee virtually had its way with the "Unfriendlies" in Hollywood and arguably established the repressive tenor that dominated the McCarthy age. The Hollywood hearings were not a peripheral event. They, in fact, were central to HUAC's existence and the "triumph" that the Committee enjoyed in investigating the film industry came with repercussions that extended far beyond the confines of "movie land." To suggest that the HUAC-Hollywood clash is of secondary importance within the scope of HUAC history (and to a larger degree, McCarthyism) is to commit an oversight of prodigious proportion. One would be hard pressed to convince Dan Bessie that the HUAC investigation was a failure. Same for the Maltz family, forced to watch Albert suffer with the realities of exile at the high point of his career. The Committee succeeded in Hollywood and its success shaped the evolution of the "domestic" cold war like few other events of the era. Its success, however, will forever be accompanied by an asterisk. If Cold War history has shown us anything, it has demonstrated that totalitarianism is impervious to totalitarian tactics. Tyranny is only vulnerable to its ultimate antithesis, democracy. It is for this very reason that HUAC won the battle versus Hollywood, but in the end, McCarthy lost the war against America.

Notes

NOTES TO CHAPTER ONE

1. Edmond Morris, *Dutch: A Memoir of Ronald Reagan* (New York: Random House, 1999), 130.
2. Ibid., 125.
3. Screenwriter Abraham Polansky refers to the Hollywood CP as a "social club" routinely in Paul Buhle and Dave Wagner, *Abraham Polansky: A Very Dangerous Citizen* (Berkeley: University of California Press, 2001).
4. Kai Bird and Martin J. Sherwin, *The American Prometheus: The Triumph and Tragedy of J. Robert Oppenheimer* (New York: Alfred A. Knopf, 2005), 500.
5. Ibid., 436.
6. Ibid., 495.
7. Ed Sikov, *Sunset Boulevard: The Life and Times of Billy Wilder* (New York: Hyperion, 1998), 131.
8. John Rankin as quoted in Cedric Belfrage, *The American Inquisition 1945–1960* (Indianapolis: The Bobbs-Merril Company, Inc., 1973), 52.
9. John Rankin as quoted in Robert K. Carr, *The House Committee on Un-American Activities: 1945–1950* (Ithaca: Cornell University Press, 1952), 56.
10. Walter Goodman refers to 1948 as a "vintage year" for the Committee as HUAC began work on "its great case," the investigation of Alger Hiss. See Walter Goodman, *The Committee: The Extraordinary Career of the House Committee on Un-American Activities* (New York: Farrar, Straus and Giroux, 1968), 244.
11. Victor Navasky, *Naming Names* (New York: Hill and Wang, 2003).
12. Although influential Ten member Dalton Trumbo and Ten veteran turned "friendly" witness Edward Dmytryk have argued that a united effort against the committee was not the order of the day, the majority of those who resisted the Committee in 1947 (John Howard Lawson, Ring Lardner Jr., Albert Maltz, and Alvah Bessie, being the most prominent) perceived HUAC to be an arm of repression and a threat to the nation's democratic

fabric. Their actions both during and after the hearings were waged not
only to gain personal and collective exoneration, but reflected a broader
effort to derail the Committee before it derailed democracy.

13. HUAC employed tactics designed to achieve its aims at the expense of the
"accused." The Committee's relationship with J. Edgar Hoover and the FBI
provided HUAC with surreptitiously ascertained information that it used
to vilify those condemned as Red. See Eric Bentley, *Thirty Years of Treason:
Excepts From Hearings Before The House Committee on Un-American
Activities 1938–1968* (New York: Thunder's Mouth Press, 2002), page 947
for further elaboration on this contention. Additionally, the Committee,
in most cases, prevented "defendants" from viewing evidence presented
against them, from cross examining witnesses whose testimony criminalized them, and from reading statements designed to exhibit their allegiance
to the principles of democracy. In this sense, the Committee's conduct can
not be seen as consistent with the American "code of conduct" as pre-
scribed in the Constitution. "McCarthyism got its power from the willingness of the men who ran the nation's main public and private institutions,"
posits Ellen Schrecker, "to condone serious violations of civil liberties in
order to eradicate what they believed was the far more serious threat of
communism." The "unjust proceedings" executed by the committee, main-
tains Schrecker (along with several prominent Cold War historians such
as Kenneth O'Reilly, Griffin Fariello, and Eric Bentley) created a scenario
where American political "power was used to repress a politically unpopu-
lar minority." See Ellen Schrecker, *Many are the Crimes: McCarthyism in
America* (Princeton: Princeton University Press, 1998), xiii, xx.

14. William F. Buckley Jr., *The Committee and Its Critics: A Calm Review of
the House Committee on Un-American Activities* (New York: G.P Putnam's
Sons, 1962), 103.

15. Karl Mundt as quoted in Walter Goodman, *The Committee,* 162.

16. Ayn Rand, "The Only Path to Tomorrow," *Reader's Digest* (January 1944),
88.

17. Demaree Bess, "Will Europe Go Communist After the War?" *Reader's
Digest* (March 1944), 25–28.

18. Many scholars refer to the Palmer raids of 1919–1920 as America's original "Red Scare."

19. Bentley, *Thirty Years of Treason,* 948.

20. Robert K. Carr, *The House Committee on Un-American Activities 1945–
1950* (Ithaca: Cornell University Press, 1952), 19.

21. This contention is discussed in greater detail later in the work.

22. Griffin Fariello, *Red Scare: Memories of the American Inquisition, An Oral
History* (New York: Avon Books, 1995), 255.

23. Oliver Carson, "The Communist Record in Hollywood," *The American
Mercury* (February 1948), 135–143.

24. Ibid., 135–143.

25. Dalton Trumbo as quoted in Bruce Cook, *Dalton Trumbo* (New York:
Charles Scribner's Sons, 1977), 309.

26. Cook, 310.
27. Nearly all of these individuals would suffer tremendous shock as the Stalin "revelations" regarding camps and executions came to light.
28. Ron Rosenbaum, "My Lunch With Alger" in Patrick A. Swan, *Alger Hiss, Whittacker Chambers, and the Great Schism in the American Soul* (Wilmington: ISI Books, 2003), 295.
29. "Communism with a Small C" is how Ellen Schrecker describes cultural or non-revolutionary communists in her work *Many Are The Crimes* (Princeton: Princeton University Press, 1998). "Parlor Reds" is a more common label but seen in Robert K. Murray *Red Scare: A Study in National Hysteria hhuu1919–1920* (New York: McGraw-Hill, 1955).
30. Bird and Sherwin, *The American Prometheus*, 132–133.
31. Schrecker, *Many are the Crimes*, xv.
32. Buckley, *The Committee and its Critics*, 104.
33. Goodman, *The Committee*, 162.
34. In reference to former Attorney General Mitchell A. Palmer, the chief architect of the nation's original "red raid" of 1919–1920.
35. "The Hollywood Ten" included screenwriters Alvah Bessie, Herbert Biberman, Lester Cole, Ring Lardner Jr., John Howard Lawson, Albert Maltz, Samuel Ornitz, Robert Adrian Scott, Dalton Trumbo, and director Edward Dmytryk.
36. Todd Gitlin, *The Sixties: Years of Hope, Days of Rage* (New York: Bantam Books, 1993).
37. For further discussion on "Red Diaper Babies" and their involvement in the radical movement(s) of the 1960's, see Judith Kaplan and Linn Shapiro, *Red Diapers: Growing Up in the Communist Left* (Urbana: University of Illinois Press, 1998).
38. W.J. Rorabaugh as quoted in Waldo Martin, "Holding One Another," in Robert Cohen and Reginald E. Zelnick, *The Free Speech Movement: Reflections on Berkeley in the 1960's* (Berkeley: University of California Press, 2002), 89.
39. The loyalty oaths refer to the mandatory oaths required of all University of California employees as a means of demonstrating their aversion to Communism in 1949 and the early 1950's. There existed a significant minority of Berkeley professors who refused to swear the oaths. Their actions precipitated widespread unrest among Berkeley administrators, "loyal" faculty members, and conservative forces in government (both state and federal) alike.
40. Gerald Horne, *Class Struggle in Hollywood 1930–1950: Moguls, Mobsters, Stars, Reds, and Trade Unionists* (Austin: University of Texas Press, 2001).
41. Irving Howe and Lewis Coser, *The American Communist Party: A Critical History* (New York: Frederick A. Pareger, 1962).

NOTES TO CHAPTER TWO

1. Robert K. Murray, *Red Scare: A Study in National Hysteria 1919–1920* (New York: McGraw-Hill, 1955).
2. Robert Service, *Lenin: A Biography* (Harvard: Belknap Press, 2000), 5.

3. Philip S. Foner, *The Bolshevik Revolution: Its Impact on American Radicals, Liberals, and Labor* (New York: International Publishers, 1967), 20.
4. Ibid., 28.
5. Theodore Roosevelt as quoted in Julian F. Jaffe, *Crusade Against Radicalism: New York During the Red Scare 1914–1924* (Port Washington: Kennikat Press, 1972), 49.
6. Theodore Draper, *The Roots of American Communism* (New York: Viking Press, 1957), 175.
7. Foner, *The Bolshevik Revolution*, 34.
8. Stanley Coben, "A Study in Nativism: The American Red Scare of 1919–20," *Political Science Quarterly Vol. 79*, (1964): 53.
9. Frederick Lewis Allen, *Only Yesterday: An Informal History of the 1920's* (New York: John Wiley and Sons, 1959), 44.
10. It should also be noted that this nation was also built at the expense of this land's Native Peoples, viewed as mere "obstacles" in the path of country's evolution by many who shaped early America.
11. Coben, "A Study in Nativism," 54.
12. Benjamin Gitlow as quoted in Irving Howe and Lewis Coser, *The American Communist Party: A Critical History* (New York: Frederick A. Praeger, 1962), 91.
13. Woodrow Wilson as quoted in Arthur S. Link, *Woodrow Wilson and A Revolutionary World, 1913–1921* (Chapel Hill: University of North Carolina Press), 73.
14. Link, 87.
15. David S. Fogelsong, *America's Secret War Against Bolshevism: U.S. Intervention in the Russian Civil War 1917–1920* (Chapel Hill: The University of North Carolina Press, 1995), 287.
16. Ibid., 5.
17. Ibid., 5.
18. Howe and Coser, *The American Communist Party*, 93.
19. This perception, however, proved to be rather erroneous. Lenin, in actuality, was somewhat of an elitist who possessed a deep distaste for the peasant communities. A child of privilege, Lenin viewed the rural Russian as the source of the nation's "backwardness" and engineered several nationwide purges of the Russian peasantry. Campaigns of this nature would only intensify under Lenin's infamous successor.
20. Draper, *The Roots of American Communism*, 119.
21. Ibid., 119.
22. Ibid., 136.
23. Howe and Coser, *The American Communist Party*, 45.
24. Ibid., 34.
25. Nathan Glazer, *The Social Basis of American Communism* (New York: Harcourt, Brace, and World Inc., 1961), 38.
26. Draper, *The Roots of American Communism*, 194.
27. The New York police ambushed the rally with brutal abandon. Hundreds were injured and dozens wound up in jail. It was merely a sign of things to come as the red scare began to intensify in late 1919.

28. Draper, *The Roots of American Communism*, 194.
29. Theodore Draper, *American Communism and Soviet Russia*, (New York: Viking Press, 1960), 21.
30. Ibid., 21.
31. "Red" as in communist scare, not as in anarchist as seen with the Haymarket Square incident.
32. Howe and Coser, *The American Communist Party*, 93.
33. Percy Jones as quoted in Modris Eksteins, *Rites of Spring: The Great War and the Birth of the Modern Age* (Boston: Houghton Mifflin: 1989), 214.
34. Louis Mairet as quoted in Eksteins, 153.
35. Murray, *Red Scare*, 4.
36. Ibid., 4.
37. Ibid., 6.
38. Jaffe, *Crusade Against Radicalism*, 4.
39. Murray, *Red Scare*, 9.
40. Jack London in Alex Kershaw, *Jack London: A Life* (New York: St. Martin's Griffin, 1997), 159.
41. Murray, *Red Scare*, 106.
42. John Reed as quoted in Draper, *The Roots of American Communism*, 135.
43. Murray, *Red Scare*, 112.
44. Reed as quoted in Draper, *The Roots of American Communism*, 136.
45. Draper, *The Roots of American Communism*, 139.
46. Murray, *Red Scare*, 67.
47. Boris Reinstein as quoted in Foglesong, *America's Secret War Against Bolshevism*, 283.
48. Albert Johnson as quoted in Murray, *Red Scare*, 64.
49. V.I. Lenin as quoted in Foglesong, *America's Secret War Against Bolshevism*, 283.
50. Murray, 59.
51. Staff, "Reds Directing General Strike," *The Los Angeles Times*, 8 February 1919, 1.
52. "Reds Directing General Strike," 1.
53. "Reds Directing General Strike," 1.
54. "Reds Directing General Strike," 2.
55. Staff, "The Red Issue at Seattle," *The Los Angeles Times*, 12 February 1919, 114.
56. Murray, *Red Scare*, 61.
57. "The Red Issue at Seattle," 114.
58. "The Red Issue at Seattle," 114.
59. Murray, *Red Scare*, 65.
60. "Los Angeles Invaded," *The Los Angeles Times*, 17 August 1919, 114.
61. "Los Angeles Invaded," 114.
62. Murray, *Red Scare*, 68.
63. As quoted in Murray, *Red Scare*, 79.
64. "Palmer and Family Safe," *New York Times*, 3 June 1919, 1.
65. "Palmer and Family Safe," 1.

66. "Palmer and Family Safe," 3.
67. "Palmer Rejects Petitions for Debs," *The New York Times*, 8 April 1919, 8.
68. "Palmer and Family Safe," 2.
69. "Palmer and Family Safe," 3.
70. Reed as quoted in Murray, *Red Scare*, 80.
71. V.I. Lenin as quoted in Glazer, *The Social Basis of American Communism*, 44.
72. Clayton R. Lusk headed up the New York State Legislature's Joint Legislative Committee Against Seditious Activities. His crusade against New York's radical left during the spring and summer of 1919 brought the "peril" of socialism to light for millions across America and arguably sewed the seeds for the Palmer raids, the defining development of the 1919–1924 "Red Scare." For more insight, see Jaffe, *Crusade Against Radicalism*, 119–142.
73. Eugene Lyons, *The Red Decade: The Stalinist Penetration of America* (New York: Bobs-Merrill Company, 1941), 32.
74. Murray, *Red Scare*, 31.
75. Ibid., 23.
76. Ibid., 25.
77. Ibid., 25.
78. IWW constitution as quoted in Jaffe, *Crusade Against Radicalism*, 25.
79. Murray, *Red Scare*, 30.
80. Namely IWW organizer Frank H. Little of Butte, Montana (see Murray, 30).
81. Jaffe, *Crusade Against Radicalism*, 122.
82. Lusk Committee Report as quoted in Kovel, 18.
83. Jaffe, *Crusade Against Radicalism*, 124.
84. Ibid., 125.
85. "Raids on Reds Up-State," *The New York Times*, 31 December 1919, 19.
86. "Raids on Reds Up-State," 19.
87. Jaffe, *Crusade Against Radicalism*, 139.
88. Ibid., 139.
89. Joel Kovel, *Red Hunting in the Promised Land: Anticommunism and the Making of America* (New York: Basic Books, 1994), 19.
90. The Overman Committee refers to the judiciary subcommittee led by Senator Lee S. Overman designed to expose subversive activity (primarily of German origin) during the war. American Bolshevism became a priority for the committee in the months prior to the 1919 Red Scare.
91. Mitchell A. Palmer as quoted in Jaffe, 175.
92. Murray, *Red Scare*, 53.
93. Jaffe, *Crusade Against Radicalism*, 179.
94. J. Edgar Hoover as quoted Kovel, *Red Hunting in the Promised Land*, 19.
95. Hoover in Kovel, 19.
96. Jaffe, *Crusade Against Radicalism*, 194.
97. Draper, *The Roots of American Communism*, 202.
98. Lyons, *The Red Decade*, 32.
99. "Bolshevism's Champion," *The Los Angeles Times*, 28 January 1919, II4.

100. "Bolshevism's Champion," II4.
101. "Bolshevism's Champion," II4.
102. "Bolshevism's Champion," II4.
103. "Flynn Prepares Big Haul of Reds," *The New York Times,* 19 June 1919, 13.
104. "Flynn Prepares Big Haul of Reds," 14.
105. "Flynn Prepares Big Haul of Reds," 14.
106. Harris and Ewing, "Unpreparedness In the War Against Radicalism," *The New York Times,* 23 November 1919, XX1.
107. "Unpreparedness In The War Against Radicalism," XX1.
108. "Unpreparedness In The War Against Radicalism," XX1.
109. "Unpreparedness In The War Against Radicalism," XX3.
110. "Ark With 300 Reds Sails Early Today for Unnamed Port," *New York Times,* 21 December, 1919.
111. "Palmer Promises More Soviet Arks," *New York Times,* 20 February, 1920, E1.
112. "Palmer Promises More Soviet Arks," E1.
113. "Palmer Promises More Soviet Arks, E1.
114. "Palmer Wants a Law to Punish Disloyal," *New York Times,* 28 February, 1920, 2.
115. "Palmer Wants a Law to Punish Disloyal," 2.
116. Murray, *Red Scare,* 212.
117. Ibid., 219.
118. Lyons, 33.
119. Howe and Coser, *The American Communist Party,* 52.
120. James G. Ryan, *Earl Browder: The Failure of American Communism* (Tuscaloosa: University of Alabama Press, 1997), 24.
121. Allen, 47.
122. "Gompers Takes Up Bolshevism Fight," *New York Times,* 8 January 1919, 3.
123. "Gompers Takes Up Bolshevism Fight," 3.
124. F. Scott Fitzgerald as quoted in Allen, *Only Yesterday,* 69.
125. Ibid., 69.
126. Howe and Coser, *The American Communist Party,* 152.
127. Ibid., 151.
128. Ibid., 160.
129. Ruthenberg as quoted in Draper, *American Communism and Soviet Russia,* 162.
130. Lovestone as quoted in Howe and Coser, *The American Communist Party,* 164.
131. Kovel, *Red Hunting in the Promise Land,* 165.
132. Howe and Coser, *The American Communist Party,* 176.
133. Kenneth Lloyd Billingsley, *Hollywood Party: How Communism Seduced the American Film Industry in the 1930's and 1940's* (Rocklin: Forum, 1998), 45.
134. Howe and Coser, *The American Communist Party,* 199–200.
135. Lyons, *The Red Decade,* 130.

136. Howe and Coser, *The American Communist Party*, 192.
137. William E. Leuchtenburg, *Franklin D. Roosevelt and the New Deal* (New York: Harper and Row, 1963), 282.
138. Leuchtenburg in reference to the years 1930–1935, 282.
139. Idid., 282.
140. Howe and Coser, *The American Communist Party*, 364.

NOTES TO CHAPTER THREE

1. Walter Goodman, *The Committee: The Extraordinary Career of the House Committee on Un-American Activities* (New York: Foster, Straus, and Giroux, 1968), 3.
2. Hamilton Fish as quoted in Kenneth O'Reilly, *Hoover and the Un-Americans: The FBI, HUAC, and the Red Menace* (Philadelphia: Temple University Press, 1983), 15.
3. Hamilton Fish as quoted in August Raymond Ogden, *The Dies Committee: A Study of the Special House Committee for the Investigation of Un-American Activities, 1938–1944* (Westport: Greenwood Press, 1984), 22.
4. Ogden, *The Dies Committee*, 23.
5. Goodman, *The Committee*, 9.
6. O'Reilly, *Hoover and the Un-Americans*, 16.
7. Ogden, *The Dies Committee*, 25.
8. William Gellermann, *Martin Dies* (New York: The John Day Company, 1944), 143.
9. I am specifically referring to the majority of early 20th century white Southerners here, by no means all white Southerners. Although most of the Southern white population believed in a racial hierarchy, there existed a significant minority who refused to accept such a standard. Having spent a good portion of my life in the South, I can confidently assert that by some accounts, the kinship between blacks and whites is actually stronger in the South than it is in other regions of the nation. Years of living side by side has forged a bond between the communities that many unfamiliar with the South find hard to comprehend. Nevertheless, never before in Southern History had the racial divide been as salient as it was during the Jim Crow years. Martin Dies and John Rankin were products of this age and embodied the sectarian mentality that arguably defined the South for nearly one-hundred years following the "Compromise of 1877." For more on this subject, see C. Vann Woodward, *The Strange Career of Jim Crow* (Oxford: Oxford University Press, 2002).
10. Ted Morgan, *Reds: McCarthyism in America* (New York: Random House, 2004.), 184.
11. Martin Dies as quoted in Ted Morgan, *Reds*, 184.
12. Morgan, *Reds*, 185.
13. Martin Dies as quoted in Gellermann, *Martin Dies*, 32.
14. Gellermann, *Martin Dies*, 31.
15. Dies as quoted in Gellerman, *Martin Dies*, 34.

16. Martin Dies, *The Trojan Horse in America* (New York: Dodd Mead, and Company, 1940), 235.
17. O'Reilly, *Hoover and the Un-Americans,* 16.
18. Goodman, *The Committee,* 10.
19. Ibid., 10.
20. Charles Higham, *American Swastika* (New York: Doubleday and Co., 1985), 5.
21. Ibid., 5.
22. Ibid., 7.
23. Leland V. Bell, *In Hitler's Shadow: The Anatomy of American Nazism* (Port Washington: Kennikat Press, 1973), 21.
24. Goodman, *The Committee,* 35.
25. Ogden, *The Dies Committee,* 31.
26. Higham, *American Swastika,* 9.
27. O'Reilly, *Hoover and the Un-Americans,* 40.
28. Ogden, *The Dies Committee,* 43.
29. Dies, *The Trojan Horse in America,* 236.
30. O'Reilly, *Hoover and the Un-Americans,* 40.
31. Bell, *In Hitler's Shadow,* 68.
32. Dickstein's frustration with the lack of antifascist enthusiasm shown by his colleagues manifested itself in the form of his 1937 decision to serve the USSR as a Soviet Agent. It had become clear to the congressman that the United States was not committed to confronting fascist aggression either overseas or at home. Given the Soviet Union's support of the Loyalists in Spain, it was evident to Dickstein that Soviet Russia stood as the world's leading opponent of fascist totalitarianism. A Jew who was well aware of Hitler's socially Darwinian policy, Dickstein viewed his decision to provide information on US antiCommunist policy as a contribution to the larger antifascist cause. It was a decision that he certainly came to regret and one that has, to a large degree, come to define his legacy.
33. Dies, *The Trojan Horse in America,* 247.
34. Martin Dies, "The Immigration Crisis," *Saturday Evening Post* (April 25, 1935), 27.
35. Ibid., 27.
36. Ibid., 105.
37. Dr. George H. Gallup, *The Gallup Poll: Public Opinion, 1935–1971, vol. I, 1935–1948* (New York: Random House, 1972), 144.
38. Ibid., 199.
39. Ibid., 195.
40. Morgan, *Reds,* 302.
41. "The New Deal Is Held Communist Tool: Thomas of Dies Committee Says Reds Have Gained Most in Roosevelt Regime," *New York Times* (October 15, 1938).
42. Ibid.
43. Ibid.

44. Joel Kovel, *Red Hunting In The Promised Land: Anticommunism and the Making of America* (New York: Basic Books, 1994), 130.
45. According to the Audit Bureau of Circulation, September 27, 1947.
46. *Los Angeles Times,* August , 1940.
47. John Leech as quoted in *The Los Angeles Times* (August 7, 1940).
48. Ibid.
49. O'Reilly, *Hoover and the Un-Americans,* 80.
50. Ibid., 76.
51. Goodman, *The Committee,* 113.
52. See Gallup Poll taken on 1/7/49, which showed that 41 percent of the people who had heard of the Committee believed it should continue versus 11 percent that felt it should be abolished. Notably, 63 percent of those with a college education felt it should continue. *Gallup: Vol I,* 787.
53. According to the Audit Bureau of Circulations, 1947.
54. Antifascist articles such as S.K Padover's "Unser America" (January) and "Nazi Scapegoat Number 2" (February) were contained in the 1939 issue.
55. Douglass Reed, "Nazi Number Two," *Reader's Digest* (November 1939), 53.
56. Reed, "Nazi Number Two, 53.
57. Stuart Chase, "The Common Sense of American Neutrality," *Reader's Digest,* (November 1939), 18.
58. Ibid., 18.
59. Ogden, *The Dies Committee,* 213.
60. Dies, *Trojan Horse in America,* 237.
61. David Caute, *The Great Fear: The Anti-Communist Purge Under Truman and Eisenhower* (New York: Simon and Schuster, 1978), 349.
62. Stanley High, "Rehearsal for Revolution," *Reader's Digest* (June 1941), 89.
63. Ibid., 89.
64. Ibid., 89.
65. Ibid., 89.
66. Stanley High, "We Are Already Invaded," *Reader's Digest* (July 1941), 122.
67. Ibid., 122.
68. Ibid., 122.
69. Ibid., 126.
70. Samuel Dickstein as quoted in Ogden, *The Dies Committee,* 233.
71. It should be known that Krebs, a leading German Communist, was forced to "convert" to fascism in order to escape execution in Germany. Having left the country a certified fascist, he was picked up by the Soviets and understandably treated as a member of the Third Reich, despite his previous Communist affiliation.
72. Jan Valtin, "Academy of High Treason," *Reader's Digest* (August 1941), 52.
73. Ibid., 53.
74. Ibid., 55–56.
75. See Gallup, *The Gallup Poll, Vol. I,* 285.

76. Max Eastman, "Stalin's American Power," *Reader's Digest* (December 1941), 39.
77. Editors note included in Eastman's "Stalin's American Power," 39.
78. Irving Howe and Lewis Coser, *The American Communist Party* (New York: Frederick A. Praeger, Inc., 1962), 298.
79. Eastman, "Stalin's American Power." 47.
80. Ibid., 48.
81. Coser and Howe, *The American Communist Party,* 161.
82. Ibid., 386.
83. Ogden, *The Dies Committee,* 252.
84. Goodman, *The Committee,* 120.
85. Ibid., 125.
86. Martin Dies as quoted in Gellerman, *Martin Dies,* 127.
87. Martin Dies as quoted in Gellerman, *Martin Dies,* 127.
88. Goodman, *The Committee,* 127.
89. Adolph Sabath as quoted in Gellerman, *Martin Dies,* 238.
90. Gellerman, 257.
91. Morgan, 220.
92. Alexander Barmine, "The New Communist Conspiracy," *Reader's Digest* (October, 1944), 27.
93. Ibid., 27–28.
94. Ibid., 28.
95. Ibid., 33.
96. Robert K. Carr, *The House Committee on Un-American Activities: 1945–1950* (Ithaca: Cornell University Press, 1952), 20.
97. Ibid., 21.
98. Rankin as quoted in Goodman, *The Committee,* 172.
99. Cedric Belfrage, *The American Inquisition: 1945–1960* (New York: The Bobs-Merrill Company, Inc., 1973), 62.
100. Goodman, *The Committee,* 174.
101. The ADA was an organization developed to challenge the growth of the "Red Menace" in all facets of American life, particularly in politics. It vehemently opposed the campaign of progressive Henry Wallace for president in 1948 labeling the party and its candidate Communist tainted.
102. Arthur M. Schlesinger, *The Politics of Upheaval: Volume III of the Age of Roosevelt* (Cambridge: The Riverside Press, 1960), 189, 193.
103. Steven M. Gillon, *The American Paradox: A History of the United States Since 1945* (Boston: Houghton Mifflin Company, 2003), 50.
104. Navasky, *Naming Names,* 47.
105. Arthur M. Schlesinger as quoted in Ellen Schrecker, *Many Are the Crimes: McCarthyism in America* (Princeton, Princeton University Press, 1998), 151.
106. Arthur M. Schlesinger, "The U.S. Communist Party," *Life Magazine* (April 29, 1946), 84.
107. Ibid., 84.
108. Ibid., 84, 90.
109. Ibid., 88.

110. John Foster Dulles, "Thoughts on Foreign Policy and What To Do About It," *Life* (June 10, 1946), 119.
111. Ibid., 119.
112. "U.S. Communists New Line: Open Drive For More Power," *United States News* (March 22, 1946), 13.
113. Ibid., 13.
114. Ibid., 13.
115. Gallup, *The Gallup Poll, Vol I.,* 587.
116. O'Reilly, *Hoover and the Un-Americans,* 76.
117. Sally Belfrage, *Un-American Activities* (New York: Harper Collins, 1994), 98.
118. Ibid., 61.
119. O'Reilly, *Hoover and the Un-Americans,* 81.
120. J. Edgar Hoover, "Red Fascism in the United States Today," *The American Magazine* (February 1947), 24.
121. Ibid., 24.
122. Ibid., 25.
123. Ibid., 90.
124. Ibid.," 90.
125. Ibid., 90.
126. Thomas M. Johnson, "The Red Spy Net," *Reader's Digest* (June, 1947), 59.
127. Ibid., 59.
128. See *Time Magazine* (4 April, 1946), 95.
129. Johnson, "The Red Spy Net," 59.
130. Ibid., 60.
131. Ibid., 61.
132. Gallup, *The Gallup Poll, Vol. I,* 639.
133. Other anti-Communist articles ran by *Reader's Digest* in 1947 included "I Didn't Want My Children to Grow Up in Soviet Russia " by Nina I Alexeiv (June), "The Soviet Spies" by Richard Hirsch (May), and "The Truth About Soviet Russia's 14,000,000 Slaves" by Max Eastman (April).
134. Leo Churne, "How to Spot a Communist," *Look Magazine* (3 March 1947), 21.
135. By 1950, the Party possessed less than 40,000 members and associates in a nation of over 200 million people-see Howe and Coser, 478.
136. Churne, "How to Spot a Communist," 21.
137. Ibid., 23.
138. Ibid., 22.
139. Ibid., 24.
140. Ibid., 24.
141. Ibid., 25.
142. Dan Bessie, *Rare Birds: An American Family* (Lexington: University of Kentucky Press, 2001), 223.
143. "Hunting Hollywood's Red's," *Los Angeles Times,* (October 21, 1947).
144. "79 In Hollywood Found Subversive Inquiry Head Says," *Los Angeles Times* (October 23, 1947).

145. "Un-American Committee Puts on Big Show," *New York Times* (October 26, 1947).
146. Sidney Olsen, "The Movie Hearings," *Life* (November 24, 1947), 138.
147. Ibid., 139.
148. Dalton Trumbo to Mr. W.F.K., 2 December, 1947, in Helen Manfull, *Additional Dialogue: Letters of Dalton Trumbo1942–1962* (New York: M. Evans and Company, 1970), 60.
149. Gerald Horne, *Class Struggle in Hollywood 1930–1950: Moguls, Mobsters, Stars, Reds, and Trade Unionists* (Austin: University of Texas Press, 2001), 72.
150. Olsen, "The Movie Hearings," 145.
151. Ibid., 145.
152. Ibid., 145.
153. "Kill or Cure," *Time Magazine* (November 10, 1947), 26.
154. Albert Maltz, "Letter to the editors of the *Saturday Evening Post,*" *The Saturday Evening Post* (May 28, 1951).
155. James A. Wechsler, "How To Rid The Government of Communists," *The American Mercury* (November 1947), 438.
156. Ibid., 438.
157. Ibid., 442.
158. Ibid., 442.
159. Dorothy Thompson, Does CommunismThreaten Christianity?," *Look* (January 20, 1948), 40–41.
160. Ibid., 42.
161. Ibid., 42.
162. Ibid., 42.
163. John Adams as quoted in Gordon S. Wood, *The Radicalism of the American Revolution* (New York: Vintage Books, 1991), 330.
164. Thomas Jefferson as quoted in Wood, *The Radicalism of the American Revolution,* 330.
165. Ibid, 330.
166. Frederic Nelson, "Is America Immune to the Communist Plague?," *The Saturday Evening Post* (April 24, 1948) 15.
167. Ibid., 15.
168. Ibid., 15.
169. Oliver Carson, "The Communist Record in Hollywood," *The American Mercury* (February 1948), 135.
170. "Kill or Cure," 26.
171. Ibid., 135.
172. John Gallup, *The Gallup Poll, Vol. II,* 787.
173. "Dupes and Fellow Travelers Dress Up Communist Fronts," *Life* (April 4, 1949), 42–43.
174. "Up The Red Flags," *Life* (June 6, 1949).
175. Craig Thompson, "Here's Where Our Young Commies Are Trained," *The Saturday Evening Post* (3 March, 1949), 39.
176. Thompson, "Here's Where Our Young Commies Are Trained," 150.
177. Victor Navasky, "Naming Names (New York: Hill and Wang, 2003), 23.

178. John Gallup, *The Gallup Poll, Vol. II,* November 1, 1949, 873.

NOTES TO CHAPTER FOUR

1. John Parnell Thomas was indicted on charges of conspiracy to defraud the government and convicted of salary fraud in 1950. He served 9 months in a Danbury, Connecticut prison as a result. Ironically, Thomas shared the prison with two familiar inmates—Lester Cole and Ring Lardner Jr., both members of the Hollywood Ten.
2. Gerald Horne, *Class Struggle in Hollywood 1930–1950: Moguls, Mobsters, Stars, Reds, and Trade Unionists* (Austin: University of Texas Press, 2001), 27.
3. See Melvyn P. Leffler, *The Specter of Communism: The United States and the Origins of the Cold War* (New York: Hill and Wang, 1994), 97–112.
4. Elaine Tyler May, *Homeward Bound: American Families in the Cold War Era* (New York: Basic Books, 1999), xviii.
5. The Southern California regional Party was headed by moderate Communist Dorothy Healy, a progressively patriotic American featured in this work.
6. United States Congress, House Committee on Un-American Activities, *Communist Infiltration of the Hollywood Motion-Picture Industry,* Hearings, Eighty-Second Congress, First Session, Part 3, 25 May, 1951.
7. Ibid.
8. As quoted in Victor Navasky, *Naming Names* (New York: Viking Press, 1980), 405.
9. Gerda Lerner *Fireweed: A Political Autobiography* (Philadelphia: Temple University Press, 2002), 255.
10. Oral Interview with Dan Bessie by author (March 23, 2004). Hereafter cited as Bessie Interview.
11. United States Congress, House Committee on Un-American Activities, *Communist Infiltration of the Motion Picture Industry,* Hearings Eighty-Second Congress, 1951, Part 1, 21 March, 88. Hereafter cited as *The Motion Picture Hearings.*
12. *The Motion Picture Hearings,* 1951, Part 1, 21 March.
13. Nancy Lynne Schwartz, *The Hollywood Writer's Wars* (New York, Alfred K. Knopf, 1982), 86.
14. Kate Weigand, *Red Feminism: American Communism and the Making of Women's Liberation* (Baltimore: Johns Hokins University Press, 2001), 46.
15. Susan Lynn "Gender and Progressive Politics" in Joanne Myerowitz *Not June Clever* (Philadelphia: Temple University Press, 1994), 105–06.
16. Butler as quoted in Horne, *Class Struggle in Hollywood,* 76.
17. Other progressive women's groups included The National Women's Party (NWP), The American Association of University Women, The League of Women Voters, The National Council of Jewish Women, The National Council of Negro Women, The Women's International League for Peace

and Freedom, The Women's Christian Association, and the National Association for the Advancement of Colored People (NAACP).

18. Ellen Schrecker, *Many are the Crimes* (Princeton: Princeton University Press, 1998), 387.
19. Horne, *Class Struggle in Hollywood,* 66.
20. Dorothy Healy, *Tradition's Chains Have Bound Us.* Interview by Joel Gardner, 1982. Oral History Department, California State University, Long Beach., 47.
21. Ibid., 50
22. Ibid., 50.
23. Ibid., 96.
24. Betty Friedan as quoted in Elaine Tyler May, *Homeward Bound* (New York: Perseus Books, 1999), 191.
25. Schrecker, *Many are the Crimes,* 387.
26. Weigand, *Red Feminism,* 3.
27. Contributions from Healy came in the form of her service as head of the Southern California branch of of the Communist Party where, as previously illustrated, she advocated gender equality. Polansky and Jarrico gave women dominant roles in their scripts. Polansky cast a female Protagonist in his work *I can Get it for You Wholesale* and Jarrico followed suit in *Salt of the Earth.*
28. May, *Homeward Bound,* 61.
29. Ibid., 85.
30. Weigand, *Red Feminism,* 47.
31. Ibid., 63.
32. Bessie Interview, March 23, 2004.
33. Maltz, Albert. "The Citizen Writer in Retrospect: Oral History Transcript." Interview by Joel Gardner, Oral History Program, University of California, Los Angeles (1975, 1976, 1978, 1979), 311.
34. Ibid.,313.
35. Manifest not only in the statement above, but also in the literature produced by student groups such as SLATE, the Du Bois Club, the Free Speech Movement, and eventually Students for a Democratic Society that emerged in the late 1950's and early 1960's and served as cultivators of gender and racial equality.
36. Bessie Interview, March 23, 2004.
37. Kevin Starr, *Embattled Dreams: California in War and Peace, 1940–1950* (Oxford: Oxford University Press, 2002), 290.
38. Schrecker, *Many are the Crimes,* 317.
39. Maltz, "The Citizen Writer in Retrospect," 749.
40. Paul Jarrico, "Hollywood Blacklist Oral History Transcript," interview by Larry Ceplair, Oral History Program, University of California, Los Angeles, (1991), 120.
41. Bessie Interview, March 23, 2004.
42. Buhle and Wagner, *Radical Hollywood: The Untold Story Behind America's Favorite Movies,* (New York: The New Press, 2002), 202.
43. Horne, *Class Struggle in Hollywood,* x.

44. Jarrico, "Hollywood Blacklist Oral History Transcript," 112.
45. Horne, *Class Struggle in Hollywood*, 71.
46. David Raskin as quoted in Navasky, *Naming Names*, 252.
47. Horne, *Class Struggle in Hollywood*, 8–9.
48. Kaplin, Mike. *Daily Variety*, New York, New York. (September 17, 1951) 1:1.
49. California Legislature, *Fourth Report: Un-American Activities in California, 1948: Communist Front Organizations* (Sacramento: California Senate, 1948), 50.
50. Horne, *Class Struggle in Hollywood*, 128.
51. Champlin, Charles. *The Los Angeles Times-Calendar Section* (October 18, 1985), 2.
52. Ibid., 2.
53. The Committee cited Adrian Scott's film *Crossfire* (1947) as propaganda, a work that was designed not only to to combat anti-Semitism, but to advocate female independence. Polansky's *I Can Get it for you Wholesale* (1949) was also considered tainted by the Committee. The script was built around a female protagonist.
54. Jarrico, "A Hollywood Blacklist Oral History Transcript," 120.
55. *Motion Picture Hearings*, 1951, Part 1, 21 March.
56. *Motion Picture Hearings*, 1951, Part 1, 21 March.
57. Healy, *Traditions*, 289.
58. Schrecker, *Many are the Crimes*, 318.
59. McWilliams, Carey. "With Whom is the Alliance Allied?" in Harold J. Salemson's *Thought Control in the U.S.A: The Film, The Actor, No. 5.* Los Angeles: Adeline Printing Co., 1947. 306.
60. See Dalton Trumbo, *Time of the Toad: A study of Inquisition in America (New York, Harper and Row, 1972).*
61. McWilliams, "With Whom is the Alliance Allied?" 312.
62. Bessie Interview, March 23, 2004.
63. Horne, *Class Struggle in Hollywood*, 76.
64. Griffin Fariello, *Red Scare: Memories of the Inquisition, An Oral History* (New York: Avon Books, 1995), 470.
65. Schrecker, *Many are the Crimes*, 331.
66. Horne, *Class Struggle in Hollywood*, 79.
67. United States Congress, House Committee on Un-American Activities, *Communist Infiltration Of Hollywood Motion Picture Industry*, Hearings, Eighty-Second Congress, 1951, Part 2, 25 April.
68. Ibid.
69. U.S. Congress, House Committee on Un-American Activities, *Communist Infiltration of Hollywood Motion Picture Industry*, Hearings, Eighty-Second Congress, 1951, Part 3, 25 June.
70. *Communist Infiltration of Hollywood Motion Picture Industry*, Hearings, 1951, Part 3, 25 June.
71. U.S. Congress, House Committee on Un-American Activities, *Communist Infiltration of Hollywood Motion Picture Industry*, Hearings, Eighty-Second Congress, 1952, Part 9, 29 September.

72. Kaplin, Mike. "Dramatic Buchman's Story, Jackson's Surprise Exit, Turnburg, Mark Last Day." Staff Writer. *The Daily Variety* (September 26, 1951), 1.
73. To avoid this in the twenty-first century, corporations move their operations out of the United States.

NOTES TO CHAPTER FIVE

1. Robert Service, *Lenin: A Biography* (Cambridge: Belknap Press, 2000), 484, 486.
2. Robert K. Murray, *Red Scare: A Study in National Hysteria 1919–1920* (New York: McGraw Hill, 1955), 53.
3. United States Congress, Special Committee on Un-American Activities, *Investigation of Un-American Activities and Propaganda,* Report, 76th Congress, 1st Session, 1939, 3 January.
4. Ibid.
5. Ibid.
6. United States Congress, House Committee on Un-American Activities, *Communist Infiltration of Hollywood Motion Picture Industry-Part I,* Hearings, 82nd Congress, 1st Session, 1951, 13 April.
7. Ibid.
8. United States Congress, House Committee on Un-American Activities, *Communist Infiltration of Hollywood Motion Picture Industry-Part 7,* Hearings, 82nd Congress, 2nd Session, 1952, 10 April.
9. Walter Goodman, *The Committee: The Extraordinary Career of the House Committee on Un-American Activities* (New York: Farrar, Strauss, and Giroux, 1964), 60.
10. Ibid. 60.
11. James G. Ryan, *Earl Browder: The Failure of American Communism* (Tuscaloosa: The University of Alabama Press, 1997), 172.
12. Earl Browder as quoted in Ryan, 173.
13. August Raymond Ogden, *The Dies Committee: A Study of the Special House Committee for the Investigation of Un-American Activities 1938–1944* (Westport: Greenwood Press, 1945), 134.
14. United States Congress, House Committee on Un-American Activities, *Investigation of Un-American Propaganda Activities in the United States,* Hearings, Seventy-Sixth Congress, 1939, Part 9, 29 September.
15. Ibid.
16. Ibid.
17. Ogden, *The Dies Committee,* 143.
18. *Un-American Propaganda Activities in the United States Hearings,* 1939, Part 9, 29 September.
19. Ibid.
20. Ibid.
21. Ibid.
22. Ibid.
23. Ibid.

24. John Cogley, *Report on Blacklisting: I Movies,* (New York: The Fund for the Republic, 1956), 27.
25. U.S. Congress, House Committee on Un-American Activities, *Communist Infiltration of Hollywood Motion Picture Industry-Part 9,* Hearings, Eighty-Second Congress, 1952, 29 September.
26. Goodman, 68.
27. William E. Leuchtenburg, *Fransklin D. Roosevelt and the New Deal 1932– 1940* (New York: Harper and Row, 1963), 126.
28. Ogden, *The Dies Committee,* 63.
29. Dr. George H. Gallup, *The Gallup Poll: Public Opinion 1935–1971, Vol. I 1935–1948* (New York: Random House, 1972), 195.
30. Eugene Lyons, *The Red Decade: The Stalinist Penetration of America* (New York: The Bobbs-Merrill Company, 1941), 129.
31. Kenneth Lloyd Billingsly, *Hollywood Party: How Communism Seduced the American Film Industry in the 1930's and 1940's* (New York: Forum, 1998), 46.
32. *Communist Infiltration of Hollywood Motion Picture Industry Hearings,* 1952, 10 April.
33. *Communist Infiltration of Hollywood Motion Picture Industry Hearings,* 1952, 29 September.
34. J. Parnell Thomas as quoted in Goodman, *The Committee,* 45.
35. Ryan, *Earl Browder,* 221.
36. Mark Sullivan, "Uproot the Seeds of Totalitarianism," *Reader's Digest* (October 1939), 5.
37. Ibid., 6.
38. Ibid., 6.
39. "125 Students Seized Picketing a Movie," *New York Times,* 5 October 1935, 8.
40. Irving Howe and Lewis Coser, *The American Communist Party: A Critical History* (New York: Frederick A. Praeger, 19570, 91.
41. Ibid., 91.
42. Andre Sennwald, "On Anatomy of Americanism," *New York Times* (October 6, 1935), 159.
43. Ibid., 159.
44. Sennwald, "On Anatomy of Americanism," 159.
45. Michael J. Strada and Harold R. Trooper, *Friend or Foe? Russians in American Film and Foreign Policy 1933–1991* (Lanham: The Scarecrow Press, 1997), 24.
46. Ibid., 19.
47. Frank S. Nugent, "It Happens: One in a Blue Moon," *New York Times* (February 16, 1936), x5.
48. Ibid., x5.
49. Strada and Trooper, *Friend or Foe?,* 19.
50. Ogden, *The Dies Committee,* 36.
51. Strada and Troper, *Friend or Foe?,* 18.

52. Edwin Schallert, *"Tovarich* Sparkling Screen Fare at Warners," *Los Angeles Times* (January 1, 1938), A7.
53. David Shipman, *The Great Movie Stars: The Golden Years* (New York: Hill and Wang, 1988), 483.
54. Frank S. Nugent, "The Screen in Review: Jacques Deval's Light Comedy "Tovarich" is Shown at the Music Hall," *New York Times* (31 December, 1937), 9.
55. Frank S. Nugent, "The Screen: Action-Crammed Melodrama is "Spawn of the North" at Paramount," *New York Times* (8 September, 1938), 27.
56. Ibid., 27.
57. Billy Wilder as quoted in Sam Staggs, *Close-Up on Sunset Boulevard: Billy Wilder, Norma Desmond, and the Hollywood Dream* (New York: St. Martin's, 2002), 5.
58. Ibid., 5.
59. Lincoln Barnett, "The Happiest Couple in Hollywood," *Life Magazine* (21 December, 1944), 112.
60. Staggs, *Close-Up on Sunset Boulevard,* 5.
61. Ibid., 5.
62. Richard Armstrong, *Billy Wilder: American Film Realist* (Jefferson: McFarland and Company Inc., 2000), 52.
63. Scott Eyman, *Ernst Lubitsch: Laughter in Paradise* (New York: Simon and Schuster, 1993), 265.
64. Ibid., 266.
65. Ibid., 267.
66. Nora Henry, *Ethics and Social Criticism in the Hollywood Films of Eric Von Stoheim, Ernst Lubitsch, and Billy Wilder* (Westport: Praeger, 2001), 85.
67. Edvard Radzinsky, *Stalin* (New York: Anchor Books, 1996), 229.
68. Eyman, *Ernst Lubitsch,* 244.
69. Ibid., 244.
70. J.E.P Dunn as quoted in Eyman, *Ernst Lubitsch,* 238.
71. Strada and Troper, *Friend or Foe?,* 16.
72. Charles Brackett, Billy Wilder, and Walter Reisch, *Ninotchka: a Screenplay* (New York: Viking Books, 1972), 24.
73. Ibid., 25.
74. Ibid., 31.
75. Ibid., 91.
76. Edwin Shallert, "Lubitsch and Garbo Victorious," *Los Angeles Times* (October 7, 1939), A7.
77. Ibid., A7.
78. Ibid., A7.
79. Staff, "The New Pictures: Ninotchka," *Time Magazine* (November 6, 1939), 76.
80. Frank S. Nugent, "The Screen in Review: Ninotchka, an Impious Soviet Satire Directed by Lubitsch opens at the Music Hall," *New York Times* (November 10, 1939), 31.

81. Strada and Troper, *Friend or Foe?*, 32.
82. Ibid., 31.
83. Bosley Crowther, "The Screen in Review: Comrade X and 'Chad Hanna' Christmas Entries at the Capitol and Roxy," *New York* Times (December 26, 1940), 23.
84. Ibid., 23.
85. "Clark Gable Goes Hunting," *Los Angeles Times* (December 9, 1940), A13.
86. "Attendance Spurt for Holliday Weekend, 462,000 Seeing Pictures in Six Houses," *New York Times* (December 31, 1940), 18.
87. Wilder, in fact, is infamously connected to the "Ten" based on his brash quote "of the ten, only two had any talent." See Victor Navasky, *Naming Names* (New York: Hill and Wang, 2003), 80.

NOTES TO CHAPTER SIX

1. United States Congress, House Committee on Un-American Activities, *Hearings Regarding The Communist Infiltration Of The Motion Picture Industry Activities In The United States,* 80th Congress, First Session, 20 October, 1947.
2. Most of the names provided by Warner during his testimony had already been revealed to Thomas during his May 1947 executive session in Hollywood.
3. *Hearings Regarding The Communist Infiltration Of The Motion Picture Industry Activities In The United States*, 20 October, 1947.
4. Meyer as quoted in Kahn, *Hollywood on Trial* (New York: Boni and Gaer, 1948), 29.
5. *Hearings Regarding The Communist Infiltration Of The Motion Picture Industry Activities In The United States*, 20 October, 1947.
6. Menjou as quoted in Kahn, *Hollywood on Trial,* 48.
7. *Hearings Regarding The Communist Infiltration Of The Motion Picture Industry Activities In The United States*, 20 October, 1947.
8. Robert Vaughn, *Only Victims* (New York: G.P. Putnam's Sons, 1972), 108.
9. United States Congress, House Committee on Un-American Activities, *Hearings Regarding The Communist Infiltration Of The Motion Picture Industry Activities In The United States,* 80th Congress, First Session, 23 October, 1947.
10. As coined by Victor Navasky in *Naming Names* (New York: Hill and Wang, 2003), 314.
11. McDowell as quoted in Kahn, *Hollywood on Trial,* 52.
12. Ellen Schrecker, *The Age of McCarthyism: A Brief History with Documents* (Boston: Bedford/St. Martins: 1994), 24.
13. United States Congress, Committee on Un American Activities, *Annual Report of the Committee on Un American Activities For the Year 1952* (Washington D.C.: US House of Representatives, 1952), 40.

14. Dalton Trumbo, *Time of the Toad* (New York: Harper and Row, 1972), 11.
15. Griffin Fariello, *Red Scare: Memories of the American Inquisition, An Oral History* (New York: Avon Books, 1995), 469, 471.
16. United States Congress, House Committee on Un-American Activities, *Hearings Regarding The Communist Infiltration Of The Motion Picture Industry Activities In The United States,* 80th Congress, First Session, 28 October, 1947.
17. *Hearings Regarding The Communist Infiltration Of The Motion Picture Industry Activities In The United States,* 28 October, 1947.
18. Kevin Starr, *Embattled Dreams: California in War and Peace* (Oxford: Oxford University Press, 2002), 316.
19. *Hearings Regarding The Communist Infiltration Of The Motion Picture Industry Activities In The United States,* 28 October, 1947.
20. See both Trumbo and Kahn or simply examine the hearing documents: U.S. Congress, House Committee on Un-American Activities, *Hearings Regarding The Communist Infiltration Of The Motion Picture Industry Activities In The United States,* 80th Congress, First Session, 20–30 October, 1947.
21. See Dalton Trumbo, *Time of the Toad.*
22. Thomas as quoted in Kahn, *Hollywood on Trial,* 66.
23. United States Congress, House Committee on Un-American Activities, *Hearings Regarding The Communist Infiltration Of The Motion Picture Industry Activities In The United States,* 80th Congress, First Session, 27 October, 1947.
24. Ibid.
25. Trumbo as quoted in Kahn, *Hollywood on Trial,* 84.
26. See Victor Navasky *Naming Names* chapter 7 "Elia Kazan and the Case for Silence."
27. *Hearings Regarding The Communist Infiltration Of The Motion Picture Industry Activities In The United States,* 28 October, 1947.
28. Ibid.
29. Trumbo, *Time of Toad,* 6.
30. Trumbo's infamous "victims" speech was delivered in 1970 following his acceptance of the Laurel Award as presented by the Hollywood Screenwriters Guild. See Bruce Cook, *Dalton Trumbo* (New York: Charles Scribner and Sons, 1977), 310.
31. *Hearings Regarding The Communist Infiltration Of The Motion Picture Industry Activities In The United States,* 27 October, 1947.
32. *Hearings Regarding The Communist Infiltration Of The Motion Picture Industry Activities In The United States,* 28 October, 1947.
33. Albert Maltz, "The Citizen Writer in Retrospect: Oral History Transcript," interview by Joel Gardner, Oral History Program, University of California, Los Angeles (1975, 1976, 1978, 1979), 739.
34. "Yes or No" to the standard Committee question regarding ones' membership in the Communist Party of the United States.

35. As quoted in Dan Bessie, *Rare Birds: An American Family* (Lexington: University of Kentucky Press, 2001.

36. *Hearings Regarding The Communist Infiltration Of The Motion Picture Industry Activities In The United States,* 28 October, 1947.

37. Trumbo, *Time of Toad,* 62.

38. *Hearings Regarding The Communist Infiltration Of The Motion Picture Industry Activities In The United States,* 28 October, 1947.

39. Ibid.

40. Ibid.

41. Screenwriters such as Trumbo, who effectively broke the blacklist with his work on both *Spartacus* and *Exodus* in 1960, and Abraham Polansky, who has worked on contemporary films such as *Force of Evil,* stand as examples of men whose careers were not lost to the blacklist.

42. Maltz, "The Citizen Writer in Retrospect," 324.

43. As in the Frenchman Jaques Duclos who penned the infamous "Duclos" letter chastising American Party head Earl Browder for assuming a patriotic "soft-line" position during the Second World War.

44. Maltz as quoted in Navasky, *Naming Names,* 288.

45. In reference to Communist Political Association head Earl Browder who steered the party in a patriotic direction during World War II. Many progressives were attracted to this "moderate" position and the party grew as a result. Following Browder's ouster, however, party appeal began to decline rapidly.

46. Jack Salzman, *Albert Maltz* (Boston: Twayne Publishers, 1978), 94.

47. Carey McWilliams, *Witch Hunt* (Boston: Little, Brown and Company, 1950), 7.

48. Ibid., 16.

49. Fariello, *Red Scare,* 37.

50. Maltz, "The Citizen Writer in Retrospect," 609.

51. Ibid., 609.

52. Schrecker, *The Age of McCarthyism,* 23.

53. Maltz, "The Citizen Writer in Retrospect," 613.

54. Ibid., 682.

55. Edvard Radzinsky, *Stalin* (New York: Anchor Books, 1997), 271.

56. Evidence of this is seen in the production of anticommunist films such as *Behind the Iron Curtain* (1948), *Guilty of Treason* (1949), *I Married a Communist* (1949), and *Big Jim McLain* (1952) among others.

57. Maltz, "The Citizen Writer in Retrospect," 313.

58. Schrecker, *The Age of McCarthyism,* 38.

59. Letter from Maltz to Margolis, 18 August, 1976, Dorothy Healy Collection, Special Collections Library, California State University, Long Beach.

60. Letter from Maltz to Margolis, 18 August, 1976, Dorothy Healy Collection, Special Collections Library, California State University, Long Beach.

61. Maltz, "The Citizen Writer in Retrospect," 700.

62. Ibid., 692.

63. Ibid., 693.

64. Schary as quoted in Maltz, "The Citizen Writer in Retrospect," 706.

65. Schary as quoted in Kahn, *Hollywood on Trial,* 183.
66. Schary as quoted in Navasky, *Naming Names,* 84.
67. Maltz, "The Citizen Writer in Retrospect," 870.
68. Ibid., 717.
69. See Maltz papers, Special Collection Research Center, University of California, Los Angeles.
70. Maltz notes that he was fully aware at the time this interview was conducted that Nixon's supposed discovery of incriminatory microfilm regarding Hiss and his association with the Soviet Union was a complete farce and served as an example of the despicable manner in which the government surreptitiously conducted its campaign against American Communism.
71. Ellen Schrecker, *Many Are the Crimes* (Princeton: Princeton University Press, 1998), 190.
72. Maltz, "The Citizen Writer in Retrospect," 761.
73. Ibid., 763.
74. Paul Buhle and Dave Wagner, *Hide in Plain Sight: The Hollywood Blacklistees in Film and Television, 1950–2002* (New York: Palgrave Macmillan, 2003), 136.
75. Todd Gitlin, *The Sixties: Years of Hope, Days of Rage* (New York: Bantam Books, 1993), 28.
76. Paul Jarrico, "Hollywood Blacklist Oral History Transcript," interview by Larry Ceplair, Oral History Program, University of California, Los Angeles, (1991), 20.
77. Paul Jarrico, "A Hollywood Red: An Oral History" interviewed by Anne A, Morris, California State University, Long Beach, 1982., 44.
78. Fariello, *Red Scare,* 261.
79. Jarrico, "Hollywood Blacklist Oral History Transcript," 97.
80. Michael Wilson, "I am the Sum of My Actions," interview by Joel Gardner, Oral History Program, University of California, Los Angeles (1975), 86.
81. Ibid., 93.
82. Ibid., 106.
83. Kate Weigand, *Red Feminism* (Baltimore: Johns Hopkins University Press, 2001), 134.
84. Schrecker, *Many are the Crimes,* 317.
85. Ibid., 332.
86. James J. Lawrence, *The Suppression of Salt of the Earth* (Albuquerque: University of New Mexico Press, 1999), 82.
87. Paul Jarrico, "A Hollywood Red: An Oral History."
88. Ibid.
89. Weigand, *Red Feminism,* 133.
90. Jarrico, "Hollywood Blacklist Oral History Transcript," 135.
91. Ringer, Roy, "Salt of the Earth Review," *L.A. Daily News.* June 4, 1954.
92. Oral Interview of Dan Bessie by author (March 23, 2004).
93. George R. Vickers, *The Formation of the New Left* (Lexington: Lexington Books, 1975), 29.
94. Gitlin, *The Sixties,* 28.
95. Ibid., 67.

96. David Lance Goines, *The Free Speech Movement: Coming of Age in the 1960's* (Berkeley: Ten Speed Press, 1993), 87.
97. Weigand, *Red Feminism*,131.

NOTES TO CHAPTER SEVEN

1. Walter Goodman, *The Committee: The Extraordinary Career of the House Committee on Un-American Activities* (New York: Farrar, Straus, and Giroux, 1968), 226.
2. Goodman, 225.
3. Oral History Interview with Knox Mellon conducted by author, Riverside, California, (September 7, 2005). Hereafter cited as Mellon interview.
4. John Rankin as quoted in C.P Trussel, "Eisler Subpoena Ordered in House," *New York Times*, 22 October, 1946, 18.
5. Dan Bessie, *Rare Birds: An American Family* (Lexington: The University Press of Kentucky, 2001), 223.
6. Victor S. Navasky, *Naming Names* (New York: Hill and Wang, 2003), 258.
7. Huggins as quoted in Navasky, 262.
8. United States Congress, House Committee on Un-American Activities, *Communist Infiltration of Hollywood Motion Picture Industry-Part 9*, Hearings, 82nd Congress, Second Session, 29 September, 1952.
9. Ibid.
10. Ibid.
11. Edward Dmytryk, *Odd Man Out: A Memoir of the Hollywood Ten* (Carbondale: Southern Illinois University Press, 1996, 8.
12. Edward Dmytryk, *A Memoir of the Hollywood Ten* (Carbondale: Southern Illinois University Press, 1996), 2.
13. United States Congress, House Committee on Un-American Activities, *Communist Infiltration of Hollywood Motion Picture Industry-Part 5*, Hearings, 82nd Congress, First Session, 20 September, 1951.
14. Title II of the Internal Security Act legalized the use of concentration camps in times of national emergency, invasion, or insurrection.
15. Dorothy Healy as quoted in Griffin Fariello, *Red Scare: Memories of the American Inquisition, an Oral History* (New York: W.W. Norton and Co., 1995), 224.
16. Roy Huggins as quoted in Victor Navasky, *Naming Names*, 260.
17. Dalton Trumbo as quoted in Navasky, *Naming Names*, 387.
18. "100 Things to Know About Reds," *New York Times*, (18 June, 1948), 7.
19. Allen Nevins, "What is a Communist? How Can You Spot Him?" *New York Times*, 2 May, 1948, 141.
20. Albert Maltz, "The Citizen Writer in Retrospect: Oral History Transcript," interview by Joel Gardner, Oral History Program, University of California, Los Angeles (1975, 1976, 1978, 1979), 616.
21. Mellon interview (September 2005).
22. Ibid.

23. Robert K. Carr, *The House Committee on Un-American Activities: 1945–1950*, (Ithaca: Cornell University Press, 1952), 55.
24. William S. White, "House Un-American Inquiry Gets $200,000 to Spur Work," *New York Times* (March 10, 1948), 12.
25. William F. Buckley Jr., *The Committee and its Critics: A Calm Review of the House Committee on Un-American Activities* (New York: G.P. Putnam and Sons, 1962), 103–104.
26. J. Parnell Thomas as quoted in Cedric Belfrage, *The American Inquisition, 1945–1960* (Indianapolis: The Bobbs-Merrill Company, Inc.), 65.
27. Griffin Fariello, *Thirty Years of Treason: Excerpts From Hearings Before The House Committee on Un-American Activities 1938–1968* (New York: Thunder's Mouth Press/Nation Books, 2002), xxx.
28. "Film Inquiry Only Begun," *New York Times* (November 5, 1947), 29.
29. J. Parnell Thomas, "Statement by Thomas," *New York Times* (October 31, 1947), 3.
30. John Rankin as quoted in Carr, *The House Committee*, 56.
31. Gladwin Hall, "Says Government Aided Film Reds," *New York Times* (May 17, 1947), 8.
32. Patrick A. Swan, *Alger Hiss, Whittaker Chambers, and the Schism in the American Soul* (Wilmington: ISI Books, 2003), xxii.
33. Morton Levitt and Michael Levitt, *A Tissue of Lies: Nixon vs. Hiss* (New York: McGraw Hill and Co., 1979), xix.
34. Earl Latham, *The Communist Controversy in Washington: From the New Deal to McCarthy* (Cambridge: Harvard University Press, 1966), 185.
35. Dr. George H. Gallup, *The Gallup Poll: Public Opinion, 1935–1971, vol. I, 1935–1948* (New York: Random House, 1972), 690.
36. William S. White, "House Un-American Inquiry Gets $200,000 to Spur Work," 1.
37. Buckley Jr., 143.
38. "Trumbo Convicted of Congress Contempt, Film Writer Faces Jail in Communist Case," *New York Times* (May 6, 1948), 18.
39. William Hitz as quoted in "Trumbo Convicted of Congress Contempt, Film Writer Faces Jail in Communist Case," 18.
40. It should also be noted that their defiance also turned several Hollywood figures, including many once associated with the "Committee for the First Amendment," against the Ten. More than a few Hollywood liberals viewed Lawson and Trumbo's "antics" in Washington as evidence of their un-Americanism and made the decision to part ways with convicted "seditionists." Edward Dmytryk, in fact, cited Lawson's behavior as one of the prime motivating factors in his decision to come forth and name names during the second wave of Hollywood-HUAC hearings.
41. Future Berkeley FSM leader Bettina Aptheker, for example, was the daughter of Columbia professor and noted Communist Herbert Aptheker, a champion of civil rights in the Northeast.
42. Oral Interview of Helen Garvy with the author, (April 7, 2004).

43. Bob Gill as quoted in David Lance Goines, *The Free Speech Movement: Coming of Age in the 1960's* (Berkeley: Ten Speed Press, 1993), 72.

44. Bob Gill as quoted in Goines, 72.

45. Kate Weigand, *Red Feminism: American Communism and the Making of Women's Liberation* (Baltimore: The Johns Hopkins University Press, 2001), 141.

46. Kate Coleman as quoted in Richard Cohen and Reginald Zelnik, *The Free Speech Movement: Reflections on Berkeley in the 1960's,* (Berkeley: University of California Press, 2002), 186.

Bibliography

Government Publications:

California Legislature. *Report Joint Fact Finding Committee on Un-American Activities in California*. Sacramento: California Senate, 1943.

California Legislature. *Report Joint Fact Finding Committee on Un-American Activities in California*. Sacramento: California Senate, 1945.

California Legislature. *Third Report of the Senate Fact-Finding Committee On Un-American Activities*. Sacramento: California Senate, 1947.

California Legislature. *Fourth Report of the Senate Fact-Finding Committee On Un-American Activities: Communist Front Organizations*. Sacramento: California Senate, 1948.

California Legislature. *Fifth Report of the Senate Fact-Finding Committee On Un-American Activities*. Sacramento: California Senate, 1950.

California Legislature. *Sixth Report of the Senate Fact-Finding Committee On Un-American Activities*. Sacramento: California Senate, 1951.

California Legislature. *Report Joint Fact Finding Committee on Un-American Activities in California*. Sacramento: California Senate, 1953.

U.S. Congress. Special Committee on Un-American Activities. *Investigation of Un-American Propaganda Activities In The United States*. Hearings, Seventy-Sixth Congress, First Session, Volume 5, 18, 22, 23, 24, 31, May, 1, June 1939.

U.S. Congress. Special Committee on Un-American Activities. *Investigation of Un-American Propaganda Activities In The United States*. Hearings, Seventy-Sixth Congress, First Session, Volume 6, 16, 17, 18, 21, 22, 23, 24, 28, and 29, August 1939.

U.S. Congress. Special Committee on Un-American Activities. *Investigation of Un-American Propaganda Activities In The United States*. Hearings, Seventy-Sixth Congress, First Session, Volume 9, 28, 29, 30 September, 5, 6, 7, 8, 9, 11, 13, 14 October 1939.

U.S. Congress. Special Committee on Un-American Activities. *Investigation of Un-American Propoganda Activities In The United States*. Report, Seventy-Fifth Congress, First Session, 3 January, 1939.

U.S. Congress. *Special Report On Subversive Activities Aimed At Destroying Our Representative Form Of Government*. Report, Seventy-Seventh Congress, Second Session, 1942.

U.S. Congress, House Committee on Un-American Activities, *Hearings Regarding The Communist Infiltration Of The Motion Picture Industry Activities In The United States*. 80th Congress, First Session, 20 October, 1947

U.S. Congress, House Committee on Un-American Activities, *Hearings Regarding The Communist Infiltration Of The Motion Picture Industry Activities In The United States*. 80th Congress, First Session, 23 October, 1947.

U.S. Congress, House Committee on Un-American Activities, *Hearings Regarding The Communist Infiltration Of The Motion Picture Industry Activities In The United States*. 80th Congress, First Session, 27 October, 1947

U.S. Congress, House Committee on Un-American Activities, *Hearings Regarding The Communist Infiltration Of The Motion Picture Industry Activities In The United States*. 80th Congress, First Session, 28 October, 1947

U.S. Congress, House Committee on Un-American Activities, *Communist Infiltration Of Hollywood Motion Picture Industry*. Hearings, Eighty-Second Congress, First Session, Part 1, 8 and 21 March, 10, 11, 12, and 13 April, 1951.

U.S. Congress, House Committee on Un-American Activities, *Communist Infiltration Of Hollywood Motion Picture Industry*. Hearings, Eighty-Second Congress, First Session, Part 2, 17, 23, 24, 25 April and 16, 17, and 18 May, 1951.

U.S. Congress, House Committee on Un-American Activities, *Communist Infiltration Of Hollywood Motion Picture Industry*. Hearings, Eighty-Second Congress, First Session, Part 3, 22, 23, 24, 25 May and 25, and 26 June, 1951.

U.S. Congress, House Committee on Un-American Activities, *Communist Infiltration Of Hollywood Motion Picture Industry*. Hearings, Eighty-Second Congress, First Session, Part 4, 17, 18, 19 September, 1951.

U.S. Congress, House Committee on Un-American Activities, *Communist Infiltration Of Hollywood Motion Picture Industry*. Hearings, Eighty-Second Congress, First Session, Part 5, 20, 21, 24, and 25 September, 1951.

U.S. Congress, House Committee on Un-American Activities, *Communist Infiltration Of Hollywood Motion Picture Industry*. Hearings, Eighty-Second Congress, First Session, Part 6, 10 May, 10, 11, and 12 September, 1951.

U.S. Congress. House Committee on Un-American Activities. *Annual Report of the Committee On Un-American Activities:1951*. Washington: U.S. House of Representatives, February 17, 1951.

U.S. Congress, House Committee on Un-American Activities, *Communist Infiltration Of Hollywood Motion Picture Industry*. Hearings, Eighty-Second Congress, Second Session, Part 7, 24 and 28 January, 5 February, 20 March, and 10 and 30 April, 1952.

U.S. Congress, House Committee on Un-American Activities, *Communist Infiltration Of Hollywood Motion Picture Industry*. Hearings, Eighty-Second Congress, Second Session, Part 8, 19, 20, and 21 May, 1952.

U.S. Congress, House Committee on Un-American Activities, *Communist Infiltration Of Hollywood Motion Picture Industry*. Hearings, Eighty-Second Congress, Second Session, Part 9, 19 August and 29 September 1952.

U.S. Congress, House Committee on Un-American Activities, *Communist Infiltration Of Hollywood Motion Picture Industry.* Hearings, Eighty-Second Congress, Second Session, Part 10, 12 and 13 November, 1952.
Books:
Baer, William. *Elia Kazan: Interviews.* Jackson: University of Mississippi Press, 2000.
Belfrage, Cedric. *The American Inquisition: 1945–1960.* New York: The Bobs-Merrill Company, Inc., 1973.
Bell, Leland B., *In Hitler's Shadow: The Anatomy of American Nazism.* Port Washington: Kennikat Press, 1973.
Bentley, Eric. *Are You Now or Have You Ever Been: The Investigation of Show Business by the Un-American Activities Committee, 1957–1958.* New York: Harper and Row, 1972.
"———." *Thirty Years if Treason: Excerpts From Hearings Before The House Committee On Un-American Activities, 1938–1968.* New York: Thunder Mouth Press/Nation Books, 2002.
Bessie, Alvah. *Inquisition in Eden.* New York: Macmillan, 1965.
Bessie, Dan. *Rare Birds: An American Family.* Lexington: University of Kentucky Press, 2001.
Biberman, Herbert. *Salt of the Earth.* Boston: Beacon Press, 1965.
Billinglsey, Lloyd. *The Hollywood Party: How Communism Seduced the American Film Industry in the 1930's and 1940's.* Rockland: Forum, 1998.
Kai Bird and Martin J. Sherwin. *The American Prometheus: The Triumph and Tragedy of J. Robert Oppenheimer.* New York: Alfred A. Knopf, 2005.
Buckley, William F. Jr. *The Committee and Its Critics: A Calm Review of the House Committee on Un-American Activities.* New York: G.P Putnam's Sons, 1962.
Buhle, Paul and McGilligan, Patrick. *Tender Comrades.* New York: St. Martin's Press, 1997.
"———." *A Very Dangerous Citizen: Abraham Lincoln Polansky and the Hollywood Left.* Berkeley: University of California Press, 2001.
"———." *Hide in Plain Sight: The Hollywood Blacklisteed in Film and Television, 1950–2002.* New York: Palgrave Macmillan, 2003.
"———." *Radical Hollywood: The Untold Story Behind America's Favorite Movies.* New York: The New Press, 2002.
Caute, David. *The Great Fear: The Anti-Communist Purge Under Truman and Eisenhower.* New York: Simon and Schuster, 1978.
Carr, Robert K. *The House Committee on Un-American Activities: 1945–1950.* Ithaca: Cornell University Press, 1952.
Carr, Steven. *Hollywood and Anti-Semitism: A Cultural History up to World War II.* Cambridge: Cambridge University Press, 2001.
Cohen, Robert and Zelnik, Reginald. *The Free Speech Movement: Reflections in Berkeley in the 1960's.* Berkeley: University of California Press, 2002.
Combs, James. *American Political Movies: An Annotated Filmography of Featured Films.* New York: Garland Publishing, 1990.
Communist Party of the United States. *Resolution on Youth, 18th Convention, CPUSA.* (CPUSA: 1967).

Chang, Nancy. *Silencing Political Dissent: How Post September 11 Anti-Terrorism Measures Threaten Our Civil Liberties.* New York: Seven Stories Press, 2002.

Cogley, John. *Report on Blacklisting: Movies.* New York: The Fund for the Republic Inc., 1956.

Cook, Bruce. *Dalton Trumbo.* New York: Charles Scribner and Sons., 1977.

Dick, Bernard F. *Radical Innocence.* Lexington: University of Kentucky Press, 1989.

Dies, Martin. *The Trojan Horse in America.* New York: Dodd, Mead & Company, 1940.

Dmytryk, Edward. *A Memoir of the Hollywood Ten.* Carbondale, Southern Illinois University Press, 1996.

Draper, Theodore. *The Roots of American Communism.* New York: Viking Press, 1957.

"———." *American Communism and Soviet Russia.* New York: Viking Press, 1960.

Eksteins, Modris. *Rites of Spring: The Great War and the Birth of the Modern Age.* Boston: Houghton Mifflin: 1989.

Eyman, Scott. *Ernst Lubitsch: Laughter in Paradise.* New York: Simon and Schuster, 1993.

Fariello, Griffin. *Red Scare, Memories of The American Inquisition: An Oral History.* New York: Avon Books, 1995.

Foner, Philip S. *The Bolshevik Revolution: Its Impact on American Radicals, Liberals, and Labor.* New York: International Publishers, 1967.

Fogelsong, David S. *America's Secret War Against Bolshevism: U.S. Intervention in the Russian Civil War 1917–1920.* Chapel Hill: The University of North Carolina Press, 1995.

Gellerman, William. *Martin Dies.* New York: The John Day Company, 1944.

Gitlin, Todd. *The Sixties: Years of Hope, Days of Rage.* New York: Bantam Books, 1993.

Glazer, Nathan. *The Social Basis of American Communism.* New York: Harcourt, Brace, and World Inc., 1961.

Goins, David Lance. *The Free Speech Movement: Coming of Age in the 1960's.* Berkeley: Ten Speed Press, 1993.

Goodman, Walter. *The Committee: The Extraordinary Career of The House Committee on Un-American Activities.* New York: Farrar, Straus and Giroux, 1968.

Griffith, Robert and Baker, Paula. *Major Problems in American History Since 1945.* Boston: Houghton Mifflin, 2001.

Griffith, Robert and Theoharis, Athan. *The Specter: Original Essays on the Cold War and the Origins of McCarthyism.* New York: New Viewpoints, 1947.

Harris, Leon. *Upton Sinclair: American Radical.* New York: Thomas Y. Crowell Company, 1975.

Healy, Dorothy and Isserman, Maurice. *Dorothy Healy Remembers.* Oxford: Oxford University Press, 1990.

Henry, Nora. *Ethics and Social Criticism in the Hollywood Films of Erich von Stroheim, Ernst Lubitsch, and Billy Wilder.* Westport: Praeger, 2001.

Higham, Charles. *American Swastika*. New York: Doubleday and Company, 1985.

Hobsbawm, Eric. *The Age of Extremes: A History of the World, 1914–1991*. New York: Vintage Books, 1994.

Horne, Gerald. *Black and Red: W.E.B. Du Bois and the Afro-American Response to the Cold War, 1944–1963*. Albany: State University of New York Press, 1986.

"————." *Class Struggle in Hollywood 1930–1950: Moguls, Mobsters, Stars, Reds, and Trade Unionists*. Austin: University of Texas Press, 2001.

Howe, Irving and Coser, Lewis. *The American Communist Party: A Critical History* New York: Frederick A. Pareger, 1962.

Jaffe, Julian. *Crusade Against Radicalism: New York During the Red Scare, 1914–1924*. Port Washington: Kennikat Press, 1972.

Kahn, Gordon. *Hollywood on Trial*. New York: Boni and Gaer, 1948.

Kaplan, Judy and Shapiro, Lynne. *Red Diapers: Growing up in the Communist Left*. Chicago: University of Illinois Press, 1998.

Kazan, Elia. *Elia Kazan: A Life*. New York: Alfred A. Knopf, 1988.

Kershaw, Alex. *Jack London: A Life*. New York: St. Martin's Griffin, 1997.

Kovel, Joel. *Red Hunting in the Promise Land: Anticommunism and the Making of America*. New York: Basic Books, 1994.

Lardner, Ring Jr. *The Lardners: My Family Remembered*. New York: Harper and Row, 1976.

Lawson, John Howard. *Film in the Battle of Ideas*. New York: Masses and Mainstream, 1953.

Lerner, Gerda. *Fireweed: A Political Autobiography*. Philadelphia: Temple University Press, 2002.

Leffler, Melvyn P. *The Specter of Communism: The United States and the Origins of the Cold War*. New York: Hill and Wang, 1994.

Lorence, James J. *The Suppression of Salt of the Earth*. Albuquerque: University of New Mexico Press, 1999.

Manfull, Helen. *Letters of Dalton Trumbo 1942–1962*. New York: M. Evans and Co., 1970.

May, Elaine Tyler. *Homeward Bound: American Families in the Cold War Era*. New York: Basic Books, 1998.

McCarthy, Joe. *McCarthyism: The Fight for America*. New York: The Devin-Adair Company, 1952.

McWilliams, Carey. *Witch Hunt: The Reprisal of Heresy*. Boston: Little Brown, 1950.

Meyerowitz, Joanne. *Not June Clever: Women and Gender in Postwar America, 1945–1960*. Philadelphia: Temple University Press, 1994.

Morris, Edmund. *Dutch: A Memoir of Ronald Reagan*. New York: Random House, 1999.

Murray, Robert K. *Red Scare: A Study in National Hysteria 1919–1920*. Minneapolis: University of Minnesota, 1955.

Neve, Brian. *Film and Politics In America: A Social Tradition*. London: Routledge Books, 1992.

Ogden, August Raymond. *The Dies Committee: A Study of the Special House Committee for the Investigation of Un-American Activities 1938–44*. Westport: Greenwood Press, 1984.

O'Reilly, Kenneth. *Hoover And The Un-Americans: The FBI, HUAC, And The Red Menace.* Philadelphia: Temple University Press, 1983.

Pardun, Robert. *Prairie Radical: A Journey Through The Sixties.* Los Gatos: Shire Press, 2001.

Phillips, Gene D. *Exiles in Hollywood: Major European Film Directors in America.* Bethlehem: Lehigh University Press, 1998.

Navasky, Victor. *Naming Names.* New York: Viking Press, 1980.

Radzinsky, Edvard. *Stalin.* New York: Anchor Books, 1997.

Roszak, Theodore. *The Making of a Counter Culture.* Garden City: Anchor Books, 1969.

Ryan, James G. *Earl Browder: The Failure of American Communism.* Tuscaloosa: The University of Alabama Press, 1997.

Salemson, Harold J. *Thought Control in the U.S.A., No. 5: The Film, The Actor.* Los Angeles: Adeline Printing Co., 1947.

Jack Salzman, *Albert Maltz.* Boston: Twayne Publishers, 1978.

Schrecker, Ellen. *The Age of McCarthyism: A Brief History with Documents.* Boston: Bedford/St. Martin's, 1994.

"———." *Many are the Crimes: McCarthyism in America.* Princeton: Princeton University Press, 1998.

"———." *No Ivory Tower: McCarthyism and the Universities.* New York: Oxford University Press, 1996.

Shills, Edward A. *The Torment of Secrecy.* New York: The Free Press, 1956.

Ed Sikov, *Sunset Boulevard: The Life and Times of Billy Wilder.* New York: Hyperion, 1998.

Schwartz, Nancy Lynne, completed by Schwartz, Sheila. *The Hollywood Writer's War.* New York: Alfred A. Knopf, 1982.

Staggs, Sam. *Close-up on Sunset Boulevard: Billy Wilder, Norma Desmond and the Dark Hollywood Dream.* New York: St. Martin's Press, 2002.

Starr, Kevin. *Embattled Dreams: California in War and Peace 1940–1950.* Oxford: Oxford University Press, 2002.

Steinberg, Peter L. *The Great Red Menace: United States Prosecution of American Communists 1947–1952.* Westport: Greenwood Press, 1984.

Swan, Patrick A., *Alger Hiss, Whittacker Chambers, and the Schism in the American Soul.* Wilmington, ISI Books, 2003.

Tenney, Jack B. *Red Fascism; Boring From Within by the Subversive Forces of Communism.* Los Angeles: Federal Printing Co., 1947.

Trumbo, Dalton. *The Time of the Toad.* New York: Harper and Row, 1972.

Vickers, George R. *The Formation of the New Left.* Lexington: Lexington Books, 1975.

Vaughan, Robert. *Only Victims: A Study of Show Business Blacklisting.* New York: Putnam, 1972

Weigand, Kate. *Red Feminism: American Communism and the Making of Women's Liberation.* Baltimore: Johns Hopkins University Press, 2001.

Zinn, Howard. *A Peoples History of the United States: 1492-Present.* New York: Harper Collins, 1999.

Articles:

Baer, Donald. "Leftists in the Wilderness." *U.S. News and World Report*, March 19, 1990.

Barmine, Andrew. "The New Communist Conspiracy." *Reader's Digest*, October 1944, 27–33.

Bernstein, Richard. "Long Bitter Debate From the 50's: Views of Kazan and his Critics." *The New York Times*, May 3, 1988.

Bess, Demaree. "Will Europe Go Communist After the War?" *Reader's Digest*, March 1944, 25–28.

Bosley, Crowther. "Review: Salt of the Earth." *New York Times*, March 15, 1954.

Carson, Oliver. "The Communist Record in Hollywood." *The American Mercury*, February 1948, 135–142.

Cameron, Kate. "Salt of the Earth." *New York Daily News*, March 15, 1954.

Champlin, Charles. "Ring Lardner Jr. and the Hollywood Ten." *The Los Angeles Times-Calendar Section*, October 18, 1997.

Chase, Stewart. "The Common Sense of American Neutrality," *Reader's Digest*, November 1939, 16–20.

Churn, Leo. "How to Spot a Communist." *Look Magazine*, March 3, 1947, 21–25.

Commons, Michael Lamport and Solomon, Hadley Anne. "The Beginnings of the Free Speech Movement within Slate" [online] (accessed 4 November 2003) available from http://www.fsm-a.org/stacks/vets/fsmvets_CommonsFSMI.ht

Crowther, Bosley. "The Screen in Review: Comrade X and 'Chad Hanna' Christmas Entries at the Roxy." *New York Times*, December 26, 1940, 23.

D'Emilio, John. "The Homosexual Menace: The Politics of Sexuality in Cold War America" in Kathy Reiss and Christina Simmons, ed. *Passion and Power: Sexuality in History*. Philadelphia: Temple University Press, 1989. 226–240.

Dulles, John Foster. "Thoughts on Foreign Policy and What to do About It Part II." *Life Magazine*, June 10, 1946, 119- 130.

"Dupes and Fellow Travelers Dress Up Communist Fronts." *Life Magazine*, April 4, 1949, 42–43.

Eastman, Max. "Stalin's American Power," *Reader's Digest*, December 1941, 39–48.

Falber, Reuben. "Communist Factory Worker-The Key to Peace." *World News and Views*, May 10, 1951.

Harrison, Eric. "Director Edward Dmytryk Dies; Testified in Blacklist Era." *Los Angeles Times*, July 3, 1999.

High, Stanley. "Rehersal for Revolution," *Reader's Digest*, June 1941, 89–93.

"———." "We Are Already Invaded," *Reader's Digest*, July 1941, 122–126.

Hoover, J. Edgar. "Red Fascism in the United States Today." *The American Magazine*, February 1947, 24–25, 87–90.

Horowitz, Daniel. "Rethinking Betty Friedan and *The Feminine Mystique*: Labor Union Radicalism and Feminism in Cold War America." *American Quarterly*, Vol. 48, No. 1. 1996: 1–31.

"Hunting Hollywood's Red's." *Los Angeles Times*, October 21, 1947, 1.

"79 In Hollywood Found Subversive Inquiry Head Says." *Los Angeles Times*, October 23, 1947, 1.

Johnson, Thomas M. "The Red Spy Net." *Reader's Digest.* (June 1947), 59–63.
Kaplin, Mike. "Dramatic Buchman's Story, Jackson's Surprise Exit, Turnburg, Mark Last Day." *The Daily Variety*, September 26, 1951.
"———." "Red Probe Hits New Low." *Daily Variety*, September 17, 1951.
"———." "Hollywood A Fat Cow for Commie Fund-Milking, Red Probers Told." *Daily Variety*, September 18, 1951.
"———." "Ex-Red Writer Confesses." *Daily Variety.* September 19, 1951.
Kazan, Elia. "A Statement." *The Daily Variety*, April 14, 1952.
"Kill or Cure." *Time Magazine,* November 10, 1947, 26.
Lardner Jr., Ring. "Impenitent Perspective." *Los Angeles Times*, October 18, 1997.
Lowe, Florence S. "Anne Revere, Sam Moore Up Next for Grilling; Red Probers Take off Today." *The Daily Variety,* April 16, 1951.
Lowe, Herman A. "Collins Brands Score Of Filmsters Commies." *The Daily Variety,* April 13, 1951.
"———." "Buchman Ducks $64 Question." *The Daily Variety*, April 18, 1951.
"———." "Dmytryk Names over 25 Reds." *The Daily Variety*, April 26, 1951.
"———." "Tuttle Brands 39 As Commies." *The Daily Variety,* May 25, 1951.
Maltz, Albert. "Letter to the Saturday Evening Post." *The Saturday Evening Post,* May 28, 1951.
Michaelson, Judith. "The Blacklist Legacy." *Los Angeles Times,* October 18, 1997.
Nugent, Frank S. "The Screen in Review: Jacques Deval's Light Comedy "Tovarich" is Shown at the Music Hall." *New York Times,* December 31, 1937, 9.
"———." "The Screen: Action Crammed Melodrama Is "Spawn of the North" at Paramount." *New York Times,* September 8, 1938, 27.
"———." "The Screen in Review: "Ninotchka," an Impious Soviet Satire Directed by Lubitsch Opens at the Music Hall." *New York Times,* November 10, 1939, 31.
Nelson, Frederic. "Is America Immune to the Communist Plague?" *The Saturday Evening Post.* April 24, 1948, 15.
Olsen, Sidney. "The Movie Hearings." *Life Magazine,* November 24, 1947, 137, 141–148.
Rand, Ayn. "The Only Path to Tomorrow." *Reader's Digest,* January 1944, 88–90.
Reed, Douglass, "Nazi Number II," *Reader's Digest,* November, 1939, 52–55.
Rosenthall, Felix. "The Loyalty Oath Controversy, 1949–1951," [online] (Accessed 22 January 2003) available at: http://sunsite.berkeley.edu/uchistory/archives_exhibits/loyaltyoath/felix_rosenthal.htm
Schallert, Edwin. "Lubitsch and Garbo Victorious." *Los Angeles Times*, October 7, 1939, 76.
Schlesinger, Arthur M. "The U.S. Communist Party." *Life Magazine.* April 29, 1946, 84–90.
Smith, Robert L. "Jackson's Own Word's Show Liberties Periled." *Daily News,* March 20, 1953.
Sullivan, Mark. "Uproot the Seeds of Totalitarianism." *Reader's Digest,* October, 1939, 5–6.
Thompson, Craig. "Here's Where Our Young Commies Are Trained." *The Saturday Evening Post,* March 3, 1949, 39, 147–150.

Thompson, Dorothy. "Does Communism Threaten Christianity?" *Look Magazine,* January 20, 1948, 40–43.

Tuchman, Mitch. "UCLA's Red Tapes Make History." *Los Angeles Times,* September 28, 1993.

"Un-American Committee Puts on Big Show." *New York Times,* October 26, 1947.

University of California, Berkeley Faculty. "On Violence in Berkeley." *Los Angeles Times,* June 3, 1969.

"Up The Red Flags." *Life Magazine,* June 6, 1949, 38.

"U.S. Communists New Line: Open Drive For More Power." *United States News,* March 22, 1946, 13–14.

Valtin, Jan. "Academy of High Treason." *Reader's Digest,* August 1941, 52–56.

Wechsler, James A., "How To Rid The Government of Communists." *The American Mercury,* November 1947, 438–443.

White, Jefferey. "The Student Revolt at Berkeley" [online] (accessed 10 Novemer 2003); available from www.fsm-a.org/stacks/spartacist_analy.htm

Interviews/Oral Histories/Papers:

Aguilar, Elena. *Memories of a Party: Oral Histories of Ex-Members of the American Communist Party.* Oral History Department, California State University, Long Beach, 1992.

Bessie, Dan. *Oral History Interview.* Interview by John Gladchuk, March 23, 2004.

Healy, Dorothy. *Tradition's Chains Have Bound Us.* Interview by Joel Gardner, 1982.Oral History Department, California State University, Long Beach. Dorothy Healy Collection, Special Collections Library, California State University, Long Beach.

Garvy, Helen. *Oral History Interview.* Interview by John Gladchuk, April 7, 2004.

Jarrico, Paul. *Hollywood Blacklist Oral History Transcript.* Interview by Larry Ceplair, Oral History Program, University of California, Los Angeles, (1991).

Jarrico, Paul. *A Hollywood Red.* Interview by Anne A. Morris, Oral History Program, California State University-Long Beach, (1982).

Mellon, Knox. *Oral History Interview.* Interview by John Gladchuk, September 7, 2005.

Maltz, Albert. *The Citizen Writer in Retrospect: Oral History Transcript.* Interview by Joel Gardner, Oral History Program, University of California, Los Angeles (1975, 1976, 1978, 1979.

Albert Maltz Papers, Special Collections Research Center, University of California, Los Angeles.

Michael Wilson, *I am the Sum of my Actions.* Interview by Joel Gardner, Oral History Program, University of California, Los Angeles (1975), 72.

Dalton Trumbo Papers, Special Collections Research Center, University of California, Los Angeles.

Index